Analysis and Evalua
of Health Care Syst

Analysis and Evaluation of Health Care Systems

An Integrated Approach to Managerial Decision Making

by

Thomas T. H. Wan, Ph.D.
Department of Health Administration
Medical College of Virginia
Virginia Commonwealth University
Richmond, Virginia

HEALTH
PROFESSIONS
PRESS

Baltimore • London • Toronto • Sydney

Health Professions Press, Inc.
P.O. Box 10624
Baltimore, MD 21285-0624

Typeset by Brushwood Graphics, Inc., Baltimore, Maryland.
Manufactured in the United States of America by The Maple Press Company,
Binghamton, New York.

Library of Congress Cataloging-in-Publication Data

Wan, Thomas T. H.
   Analysis and evaluation of health care systems : an integrated approach to managerial
decision making / Thomas T. H. Wan.
      p.   cm.
   Includes bibliographical references and index.
   ISBN 1-878812-23-8
   1. Health services administration—Statistical methods.   2. Health services
administration—Research—Methodology.   I. Title.
RA394.W36   1995
362.1'068–dc20   95-5138
                                                                       CIP

British Library Cataloguing-in-Publication data are available from the British Library.

Contents

About the Author

Thomas T. H. Wan is Professor and Chair of the Department of Health Administration, Medical College of Virginia, Virginia Commonwealth University, Richmond, Virginia. He holds the Arthur Graham Glasgow Chair at the University. Professor Wan received a Bachelor of Arts in Sociology from Tunghai University, Taiwan; a Master of Arts and a doctorate in Sociology from the University of Georgia; and a Master of Health Sciences from the Johns Hopkins University School of Hygiene and Public Health, where he was also a National Institutes of Health postdoctoral fellow.

His over 20 years in academia encompass faculty positions at Cornell University; the University of Maryland, Baltimore County; and his current position at Virginia Commonwealth University, where he has been teaching since 1981.

As a leader in the field of medical sociology, Professor Wan has served in many capacities, including Director of the Williamson Institute for Health Studies at Virginia Commonwealth University; as the Associate Editor of the journal *Research on Aging*; as a member of the Editorial Board of the *Journal of Gerontology*; as a member of the Executive Committee for the Association for Social Scientists in Health; as a member of the Governing Council, Medical Care Section, American Public Health Association; as a Founding Member of the Asian American Caucus of the American Public Health Association; as a member of the Research Agenda Committee, National Institute on Drug Abuse; a Senior Research Fellow of the National Center for Health Services Research; as a member of the Study Section on Aging and Human Development II, National Institute on Aging; and as a National Institutes of Health–Housing and Urban Development Health Grant Review Consultant. Currently, he serves as a member of the National Committee on Vital and Health Statistics of the Centers for Disease Control and Prevention.

Dr. Wan is a highly productive scholar who has contributed numerous publications to the scientific literature, including articles for the *Journal of the American Geriatrics Society, Health Services Management Research, Journal of Health and Social Behavior, Community Mental Health Journal, Health Services Research, Medical Care, Journal of the American Medical Association*, and the *American Journal of Public Health*, and four books in the field of aging and health.

His research interests are centered in managerial epidemiology, long-term care, health services evaluation, and clinical outcome studies.

Foreword

As the health care environment becomes more volatile, providers are beginning to assume more of the risk in the payor and delivery processes. This entrepreneurial partnering demands that the decision grid and executive behavior not only be supported by but also be backed by analytical principles and tools that will allow credible validation of the work process and volume trends. The net result is the basic requirement of managers and executives to have support resources in place for studying, evaluating, and improving their system's operations.

As a corollary to this volatility, the process of health care delivery, its financing, and its market share retention will become more visibly competitive among individuals who manage, deliver, perform, and pay for the distribution of benefit streams of a covered population. The assumption of risk by providers will demand that more comprehensive, reliable, and predictable indicators be in place to project and track trends. Providing this continuum of qualitative, accessible, and affordable care for the consumer will require a research-based, data-driven effort.

Yesterday's agenda was a permissive one, which allowed health care providers and payors to rely on assumptions, not necessarily corroborated by substantial, related data and analytical models, in formulating strategic or operative plans for their organizations. However, to achieve a viable, affordable, and accessible health delivery system combined with actuarial soundness, performance, and risk, it is critical that managers and executives follow basic analytical principles in studying the system's current position and in planning for future commitments.

Such principles and analytical models will become the cornerstone upon which sound judgments and sensible economic forecasting will be built in the organizational environment that lies ahead. The analytical tools presented in this book will provide the strategic information needed by executives and managers for data analysis in health care delivery and payor systems. Further, this book will assist them in validating the data within a logical, accepted structure. These analyses will promote the opportunity to evaluate proper system performance, process, and credible outcome management.

The evaluations contained within will prove vital in decision making and in maintaining growth in volume and improvement in quality in an organization as it competes in today's market and that of the future. This text is technical, resourceful, supportive, and understandable for related levels of management and for support executives who will support the essentials that need to be in place, practiced, and predicted for the regimes of management which will exist or will be created within the structures of health delivery and payor organizations.

Paul A. Gross
Professor and Executive-in-Residence
Medical College of Virginia
Virginia Commonwealth University

Preface

In conducting managerial studies, the investigator must select appropriate analytical frameworks and research methods to deal with the study problem. Depending on the nature of the study problem, the form of research design, and the type of data available to an investigator, a variety of statistical analyses can be performed in order to draw appropriate inferences from the observed facts or phenomena. The use of statistical designs and analyses may serve the following purposes: 1) to provide descriptive or classificatory profiles of health care concepts in determining the structural or theoretical domains of a series of measures, 2) to illustrate the associations among several related variables with a cross-sectional survey design, 3) to trace past events retrospectively and determine the likelihood of their being considered causative agents for explaining managerial problems, 4) to identify prospectively a single factor or multiple factors as possible causal factors of the study problem, 5) to predict or forecast the future trend of health care demand for a specific type of service, and 6) to assess and evaluate the independent and interaction effects of interventions on health care outcomes or on performance of health care organizations.

Ten chapters illustrate the above-listed purposes in this book. Chapter 1 presents a comprehensive overview of the health systems approach to health care management problems. Chapter 2 illustrates scientific procedures in identifying and framing research inquiries for managerial studies. Chapter 3 discusses the issues in measurement and quantification of variables in the area of health services research.

Two chapters cover analytical designs that can help explore the relationships among multiple variables. Chapter 4 presents an example of performing a cross-sectional analysis of survey data. In this chapter hypothesis testing and inferential statistics are presented and the concepts of sampling are explained. Chapter 5 introduces time-span or longitudinal study designs, including retrospective and prospective studies.

Chapter 6 offers managerial applications of epidemiology in health services management and research. Chapter 7 gives a step-by-step procedure for making a yearly forecast and an intermediate forecast of hospital bed need in a community general hospital. Regression and analysis of variance are introduced in this chapter.

A useful evaluation of health care programs or managerial interventions must be conducted while recognizing a number of essential contingencies, such as the content and context of the program being assessed, the conceptual approach for the evaluation, the feasibility of data collection, the design or methodology, and the analytical training and skills of the evaluator. Chapters 8 and 9 present the principles and methods for conducting evaluation research. Chapter 8 explains evaluation concepts, principles, and approaches, and Chapter 9 introduces a variety of experimental evaluation designs and analyses.

   The assessment of organizational performance is an essential part of managerial studies. Multiple indicators can be used to determine the level of performance of a health organization such as a community hospital. For example, because of better management or more efficient use of resources to optimize organizational performance, certain hospitals or service agencies would perform well on measures of quality. Other hospitals or organizations would perform relatively poorly if they do not effectively manage and efficiently use resources. Chapter 10 analyzes how organizational factors may influence patient care outcomes and other performance indicators.

   Health services researchers recognize the power of an integrated approach to managerial problems employing epidemiology, social science methodology, and systems analysis. This book is an attempt to bring together in one volume a variety of quantitative methods and evaluation research designs and to provide useful information to graduate students in health services administration and public health. The book articulates the current issues in organizational performance and assessment. It has minimized the use of complex statistical language to the point where students of health care management and administration with an interest in assessing health care outcomes should feel comfortable with the format of illustration and analysis.

Acknowledgments

The ideas in this book might not have been formulated without the students who shared their insights and desires to learn quantitative methods and analyses. This book is dedicated to all those who have tried or will try to make health services research methods easy for students. Appreciation must be expressed to my associates — April Swineford, Lewis Isner, Emmy Miller, Ph.D., and MeriBeth Herzberg Stegall, Ph.D. — for their assistance in preparing this book, and to Dorothy Silvers for her editorial assistance. Finally, I want to thank my wife, Sylvia Wan, and sons, George and William, for their patience and endless support during the journey in completing this book.

Analysis and Evaluation
of Health Care Systems

1

Introduction to Health Care Management Study

Science is nothing but
trained and organized common sense.

T. H. Huxley, *The Method of Zadig*

The goals of health care management—to provide rational health care delivery systems, ensure equal access to health care, and reduce costs—require planning and management of health care services in a systematic and organized way. Planning health care services requires, for example, precise information about a population's health care needs; managing health care services requires effective strategies to identify appropriate objectives and then to ensure the objectives are met.

A manager who strives to plan and manage health care systems effectively has available a variety of theoretical frameworks, assessment approaches, and evaluation methods. The application of these strategies should be based on an understanding of how health care systems form part of the larger social system and should be guided by the principles of scientific inquiry.

KEY COMPONENTS OF A HEALTH CARE SERVICES SYSTEM

A *system* is a set of resources that are organized to perform designated functions in order to achieve desired results. The *resources* may include personnel, materials, facilities, and information. In the study of patient care, Howland and McDowell (1964) state that a system is an organization comprising man and machine components to be engaged in coordinated, goal-directed activity, linked by information channels, and influenced by an external environment.

Competitive advantage in the 1990s relies on an organization's ability to behave as a subsystem of an overall integrated system of health care and to work with all other subsystems to achieve the goal of quality patient care (Shortell, 1990). The integrated health care system includes the institutions and providers giving care, the relationships between them, and the various responsibilities of each (Shortell, Morrison, & Friedman, 1990; Zelman, 1994). This integrated system as a whole, in delivering quality services, must respond to the health care needs of its community. The dominance of various subsystems within the whole therefore will depend on local culture, circumstances, environment, and need. To assess how well the integrated system's goal of achieving the optimal health status of the community is being met, Year 2000 goals should be utilized. Year 2000 goals present strategies for improving the health of Americans in the decade preceding the year 2000. Healthy People 2000 has three main goals: increasing

1

Americans' healthy span of life, decreasing health disparities among Americans, and achieving access to preventive services for all Americans. If an integrated system is striving to meet these goals, the system is attempting to achieve the optimal health status of the community (National Center for Health Statistics, 1993).

Thus, in both the study of health care delivery systems and their organization and management, a systems approach examines resources, goals, and sources of information. Another critical factor is the environment, where services are provided.

For research and for evaluation, four components of a health care delivery system are important: 1) the environment, 2) the availability of resources and access to them, 3) the design of health care organizations or facilities, and 4) measurement of health care outcomes and provider performance (see Figure 1.1). Each of these dimensions, which will be discussed briefly in this chapter, embodies key issues for a systems approach to research and evaluation, and so will be examined from a number of perspectives throughout this book.

A key component of a health care system is the **environment**. The environment of a system may be defined as the specific surroundings—physical, technological, cultural, political, and social—in which an organization exists. It is useful to distinguish between two broad types of organizational environments, the technical environment and the institutional environment. The *technical environment* concerns the production of a product or service that is exchanged in a market, with rewards for effective and efficient performance. The *institutional environment* consists of the rules and requirements that individual organizations must observe in order to receive legitimacy and support (Scott, 1987). Both aspects of the environment are important in health services research and evaluation.

Several levels of the environment can be specified, using macro theory as the foundation (Begun & Lippincott, 1993; Knox, 1979; Silver, 1972; Wan & Broida, 1983); this specification process reflects both the technical task and the institutional aspects of the environment (Shortell et al., 1990). The first step in specifying the environment is to delineate the community characteristics—that is, the socioeconomic, demographic, health status, and environmental conditions that shape the demand for health services, as well as the community's health care resources and manpower needs. These environmental characteristics are also referred to as *contextual variables*.

Of particular importance in this analysis of environmental characteristics is the identification of a community's poverty level. Indeed, the poverty level has been shown to be inversely

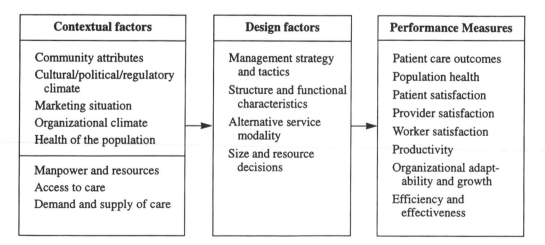

Contextual factors	Design factors	Performance Measures
Community attributes Cultural/political/regulatory climate Marketing situation Organizational climate Health of the population	Management strategy and tactics Structure and functional characteristics Alternative service modality Size and resource decisions	Patient care outcomes Population health Patient satisfaction Provider satisfaction Worker satisfaction Productivity Organizational adaptability and growth Efficiency and effectiveness
Manpower and resources Access to care Demand and supply of care		

Figure 1.1.   Components of a health care system.

related to the distribution in health services of both manpower and resources. Also important is another established relationship, that the higher the educational attainment in the community, the better is its level of health. Other characteristics that may be meaningful in analysis of the environment are rurality, population density, and proximity to a large metropolitan area. These contextual variables directly affect an area's supply of and demand for health services (Reinhardt, 1975).

The second component of a health care system is the **availability** of health care resources and community **access** to care. This dimension also may be considered a part of the context or environment. The management perspective also requires information about past and future **demand** for health services. This information emerges through the study of:

1. Actual use of hospital care and other ambulatory services
2. Factors affecting variation in the use of such services
3. The required level of care, both short and long term
4. Cost-effective alternatives in delivering modern health care services
5. The perceptions of those representing groups involved in health care: providers, managers, payors, and consumers of health care services

This information serves managers and policy makers as the basis for responsible and professional decisions about health care. Later chapters of this book discuss methods for obtaining such information.

Collection of information about the environment of a health care delivery system may be viewed from the perspective of *health planning*—that is, the application of scientific methods to organizations in order to achieve a set of goals by preferable means (Hyman, 1975; Spiegel & Hyman, 1991). An investigation based on this framework will focus on four areas. The first two areas concern the supply of and demand for health services. First, analysis identifies the market structure of a community's health care delivery systems, such as hospitals, community health agencies, ambulatory care centers, managed care organizations, and extended care facilities. Second, the market share of various patient populations held by each agency is determined. The two other areas to be investigated according to the health planning perspective concern the availability of health care services and access to care; these areas are assessment of community health care needs and establishing objective criteria to rank goals and objectives of health care delivery. To assess the health care needs of the community, epidemiological methods are used. To determine priorities for the delivery of health care services, the aspects to be examined include barriers within organizations and among health care providers, resource distribution, and how health care services are coordinated. Valuable information may emerge from examining the structural and functional features of the health care organization, as well as its policy and political aspects.

The third component of a health care service delivery system is the **design** of health care organizations and facilities. Any analysis of health care services should address explicitly the multiple contingencies within organizations that can facilitate or impede their effectiveness. Organizational design includes the forms and structures of management, the internal and external pressures for organizational performance.

In considering organizational design, the systems perspective is used. For example, a management study of the feasibility of establishing an ambulatory surgery program in a hospital will include decisions about size, technology, location, and resource allocation. In addition, the study must consider the two dimensions of health care delivery systems discussed previously—environment, and resource availability and access. Decisions about the health care needs of the community and the priorities of the health care organization, as well as other environmental variables, will be critical in planning, establishing, and managing the proposed ambulatory care facility.

The final component of a health care service delivery system is **measurement** of health care outcomes, patient satisfaction, provider productivity, organizational adaptability and growth, and other tangible indicators of organizational **performance**. These tangible indicators must be identified and quantified precisely to evaluate health care delivery systems (Aday, Begley, Laison, & Slater, 1993). Indicators may be specified for the patient, the provider, the health care organization, or the community, and whether they are at a micro or macro level (see Table 1.1). Furthermore, comparative research on health care outcomes can be done at the national level (Anderson, Alonso, Kohn, & Black, 1994; Schieber, Poullier, & Greenwald, 1993).

Evaluation and research in health care delivery systems depends on measuring indicators accurately to answer questions about the appropriateness, effectiveness, and success of organizations and programs. Some such questions, which are representative rather than exhaustive, include:

What normative standards can or should be used to define the success or failure of a particular program?

What particular aspects of health care organizations are responsible for variations in organizational performance?

How can valid measures of patient care outcomes be constructed that will be sensitive to clinical issues while also detecting the effects of organizational change?

Which factors affect the effectiveness or efficiency of a health care program in a particular community?

Difficulties arise with attempts to specify and measure indicators of the concepts identified in these important questions. However, a systems approach is a very useful framework for examining the relationship between contextual environmental variables, organizational design, and performance measures. The next step is to employ the principles of scientific inquiry to analyze each of the variables we have identified in that framework.

PRINCIPLES AND PRACTICE OF SCIENTIFIC INQUIRY

Sound management studies use scientific inquiry, a systematic thought process that begins with the collection of observable facts and then analyzes these to arrive at adequate explanations of

Table 1.1.   Tangible indicators of organizational performance

Indicator studied	Micro (personal) level	Macro (collective) level
Subject	Individual	Community
Institutions	Specific health facilities	Community social and health services
Providers	Physicians and others	Health department
Administrators	Administration of health institutions	Government
Health concern	Individual's health	Population health
Information system	Information held by doctors (symptoms)	Information held by health department (epidemiological)
Intervention mode	Treatment	Policy
Implementation	Regimen	Programming
Aggregation	Diagnostic care region (obstetrics, surgery, etc.)	Geographic care region
Service given	Care element(s)	Programs

the phenomenon or problem under study. Thus, health care service managers must avail themselves of clear factual information on which to base decisions. Both objective, quantifiable data and information about less tangible, qualitative aspects of the situation are essential.

Uses of Scientific Inquiry

Scientific inquiry is used in all forms of problem solving, specifically to support and verify or reject preconceived concepts and propositions about situations. At the lowest level, scientific inquiry helps to *describe* a phenomenon and the facts that surround it. At the next level, by identifying causal relationships, scientific inquiry helps to *explain* the phenomenon. *Predicting* future events, from historical trends of a phenomenon, is another use of scientific inquiry. At the highest level, scientific inquiry can provide the necessary information to *control*, *modify*, and *design solutions* to problems presented by a phenomenon.

Characteristics of Scientific Inquiry

The process of scientific inquiry has four characteristics: observability, verifiability, tractability, and manipulability. Each of these characteristics has a precise meaning for the process of scientific inquiry. Although all four elements typically are found in scientific investigation, they need not all be present in every case.

Observability is central to the empirical approach to the natural world: observations of sensory data that can be confirmed. Facts or data must be observable, through either an objective or a subjective procedure. For example, health status may be identified through clinical assessment and by laboratory results, which are objective measures of health. However, subjective measures such as surveys also provide observable (i.e., *empirical*) data about health status.

Verifiability is the second characteristic of scientific inquiry, and it is closely related to the first, observability. A phenomenon is considered verifiable when its existence or pattern is detected by repeated observations, verified by diverse observers. An example is the historical trend of hospital data that are used to estimate or forecast the use patterns of health service units. Forecasts of the demand for care would be useless unless based on a large amount of sequential, time series data.

A third characteristic of scientific inquiry is the **tractability** of the data; useful data must be tractable (i.e., accessible). This term indicates the degree to which observed facts and data are both accessible and controllable. From a medical perspective, for example, a tractable disease is one that has traceable etiology and is treatable.

The final characteristic of scientific inquiry is **manipulability**, or the degree to which experiments can be performed on the observed subjects. For example, human behavior is considered manipulable.

CONSTRUCTION OF THEORY IN SCIENTIFIC INQUIRY

The ultimate goal of scientific inquiry is to generate a set of hypotheses, which repeated observations then test and either confirm or reject. To derive, test, and confirm theory is a goal that requires the explication of concepts in a theoretical framework as well as adherence to the process of scientific inquiry. Although in health services evaluation and research an existing theoretical framework may prove useful, there are also instances in which unique aspects of health care delivery and health care organizations have not yet been given theoretical formulations. In constructing new theories, there are two basic approaches: induction and deduction.

The **inductive approach** to theory construction starts by observing specific facts and then formulating general principles based on them (Figure 1.2). For example, a professor of health administration was asked by the chief executive officer (CEO) of a health care system to study

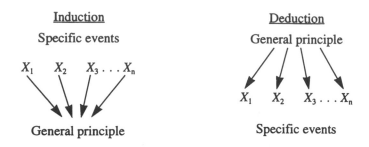

Figure 1.2. Induction and deduction. It should be noted that the deductive and inductive methods frequently are used together and very often are found to be inseparable in the conduct of scientific inquiry. Figure 1.3 summarizes the integrated approach to formulating a theory.

the overall performance of employees. Empirical data were collected by observing several groups of employees. Then conclusions were drawn as to which aspects of the work situation were associated with greater job satisfaction and higher productivity. The specific observations, when analyzed in terms of Herzberg's (1966) Motivation Theory, suggested that work incentives that enhance self-esteem and quality of life improve both job satisfaction and productivity. This type of generalization, based on specific facts, is called *logical induction*.

The **deductive approach** starts with general principles and derives specific expectations (Figure 1.2). The theory or framework provides the starting point from which specific hypotheses are proposed; these are tested empirically. In the previous example, the consultant might choose among hypotheses first, before observing the employees. If the theoretical framework chosen concerned the effects of negative feedback in a health care delivery system, for example, one hypothesis might be that negative sanctions increase productivity because they provide accurate feedback to the employee about performance. Observations that employees who performed unsatisfactorily got shorter coffee breaks, were more likely to be laid off, and were less likely to receive merit salary increases might be considered to support this hypothesis; then other data to correlate these strategies with productivity would have to be gathered, to either support or reject the hypothesis. In this way, a general principle or hypothesis about the effects of feedback on a system could have been tested with specific observations.

Often the deductive and inductive approaches are used together, and in fact in scientific inquiry they may be inseparable. In actuality, observations of specific events may lead to an inductive conclusion and generalization about a phenomenon. From this generalization, concepts and propositions may be formed and organized into an abstract theoretical structure. Then, using this theoretical structure, specific hypotheses can be proposed and tested by empirical data. This circular relationship of induction and deduction is represented in Figure 1.3.

Let us illustrate construction of a theory by using both inductive and deductive processes. Cost containment for hospitals is a pressing issue for which existing organizational theory does not offer much guidance. The first step in constructing a theory about this issue is **observation** of two specific situations: 1) sharing of resources between hospitals varies greatly, from constant exchange among some hospitals to almost none for others; and 2) those hospitals that frequently share resources seem to have lower annual deficits than those hospitals that do not.

These interesting observations about the financial effects of sharing hospital resources might be simple happenstance. In order to postulate the relationship between these observations, they must be defined and measured accurately. Thus, the next step in the theory development cycle is **measurement** of the two variables, resource sharing and annual deficit.

After the variables (resource sharing and annual deficit) have been defined and measured, the necessary data about these variables are collected. Then **data analysis** is done to identify any

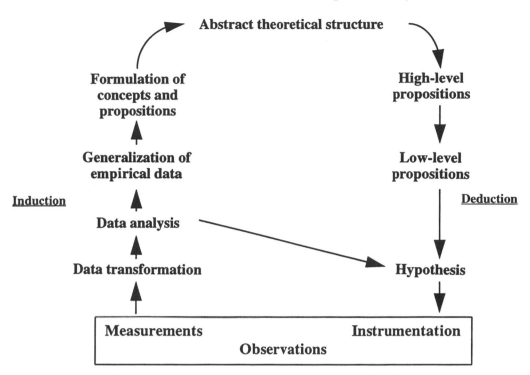

Figure 1.3. Integrated approach to theory formulation.

association or correlation, as well as the magnitude of each relationship, between these two variables; furthermore, the effect that a change in one variable may have on the other variable can be examined using predictive analytical techniques. In this step, any relationship between the two variables is defined and described.

This example began with a focus on specific data about an observed phenomenon. Now, after the data analysis step, **generalization**s can be made. These generalizations are tentative explanations about the relationship between the two variables, which might include:

1. More frequent exchange of resources leads to a better financial status
2. Exchange of resources varies directly with the hospital's need for cooperation
3. Exchange of resources is more frequent if a particular hospital has been positively affected by an established relationship with other hospitals
4. Financial performance varies directly with the degree to which resource exchanges have had positive results

These generalizations represent relationships between the concepts of resource sharing and financial performance, as defined within a health care organization.

From such generalizations, founded in observation and empirical data analysis, it is then possible to move into a deductive mode. In this phase of the theory construction, **propositions** can be formed. Propositions, or statements about the relationships between concepts, are an important part of the theoretical framework because they can be tested as hypotheses. Two propositions that could be derived here by deductive processes are:

1. More frequent exchange and establishment of joint programs (e.g., shared services) among hospitals leads to lower annual deficits, and a higher rate of innovative modes of service.

2. Integrated health delivery systems have better financial performance because their design supports and encourages highly developed programs for exchange of resources or shared services.

These theoretical propositions, describing possible relationships between two concepts, constitute hypotheses that can be tested. That returns us to the point of making observations about relationships in the real world, completing the circle of observation → deduction → concept formulation → hypothesis testing → observation.

Many people believe that theory is too abstract or vague to be useful in the real world. This is an unfortunate perception, because the purpose of theory is indeed to make it possible to explain the real world around us. Only such explanation and understanding enable us to predict and thus control events, or at least to try. In the complex, rapidly changing world of health care and health care organizations, many confusing and contradictory phenomena are yet to be defined, explained, and predicted. Integrating evaluation and research methods into health care management practices not only contributes to theory development, it also helps to accomplish the goals of successful administration of health care services.

THEORETICAL FOUNDATIONS FOR SCIENTIFIC INQUIRY IN HEALTH CARE MANAGEMENT

An important characteristic of scientific inquiry, as we have seen, is that a researcher formulates underlying assumptions that contribute to the process. These assumptions and propositions are stated explicitly by the theoretical framework a researcher uses as the foundation of the scientific process. The theoretical framework specifies the essential concepts and defines their relationships. The scope and significance of the theory also are described.

Management studies use a number of theoretical frameworks: theories of systems, of organizations, of leadership, of change, and of information. A brief review of those theoretical frameworks is presented here. The interested reader is referred to the wealth of literature on these topics, of which a representative selection is cited in the following text.

Systems Theory

A general systems theory was described by von Bertalanffy (1950, 1956) and has been used as a consistent operational model to study systems at all levels, from the single cell to complex social systems such as health care delivery systems. General systems theory distinguishes between *closed systems*, which are separated from their environment, and *open systems*, in which inputs and outputs move between the system and its environment.

The essential concepts of general systems theory are input, output, throughput, feedback, and environment. *Input* means the resources the system uses. *Throughput* refers to the processes and technology the system uses to transform inputs into *outputs*. *Feedback* is the information the system receives and uses to regulate itself; feedback may be positive, stimulating the system to continue its operation, or negative, prompting modification of the system.

The concept of *dynamic equilibrium* is also part of general systems theory. Dynamic equilibrium is a steady state of input–throughput–output–feedback (i.e., relatively consistent behavior over time). A major objective of any system is to achieve and then maintain this state, also referred to as *homeostasis*. Some variability can be tolerated, however, so long as the overall character and functioning of the system is maintained.

Organizational Theories

A number of theories employing the concepts of general systems theories, but specific to organizations, have been proposed. Organizations have been viewed as closed systems that demonstrate rational behavior, designed to achieve predetermined ends and uninfluenced by the perturbations and opportunities in the wider environment. This theory has been criticized because it does not recognize the impact of personal relationships and informal structure on the performance of the organization. The rational bureaucracy described by Weber (1947), in which employees' roles are based on technical qualifications and rules govern behavior, is a familiar example of the rational, closed-system approach to organizational behavior.

Organizations also have been examined as open systems, wherein the organization's interaction with its environment, as well as personal relationships, affects organizational behavior and performance. Open systems are viewed as either rational or natural models. In the rational open-system view, the organization is seen as open to the environment but limited by the cognitive limitations of individual decision makers (March & Simon, 1958). However, because the natural open-system view of organizations suggests that their structure is based on the requirements, or contingencies, of the environment, that approach has been named *strategic contingency theory* (Lawrence & Lorsch, 1967; Thompson, 1967).

Combining the rational and natural system approaches has been proposed in the *population ecology model* of organizations, relating the work of Darwin in biology to social systems. This model looks primarily at populations of organizations, rather than individual organizations, and it attempts to explain why some types of organizations survive and flourish while other types languish and die. The central tenet of this model is that environments select organizations for survival on the basis of fit between their organizational forms and the environment's characteristics; favored variations of organizational forms survive and reproduce similar organizations, while those organizational forms with a poor "fit" with their environment perish (Aldrich & Pfeffer, 1976; Hannan & Freeman, 1977; Scott, 1992).

A number of principles from open systems theorists describe the organization as a truly social system. These principles can be summarized as:

1. Organizations are social systems with interdependent parts. Change in one part of the organization inevitably influences other parts of the organization (Tausky, 1970).
2. There are two functions of an organization: a) creating the product or service, and b) distributing satisfaction among its members/employees.
3. The evaluation of organizational goals is multifaceted. It will vary depending on the perspective of the evaluator, which may be an individual, the organization, or society as a whole (Scott, 1992).
4. Every individual in an organization views any occurrence which lowers his status as unjust, making every event in the organization a basis for invidious comparisons. As a result, no person's behavior in the work place should be considered to be motivated strictly by economic or rational considerations. Values, beliefs, and emotions are inextricably involved in the behavior of members of an organization (Tausky, 1976).
5. Every organization has a formal and an informal structure. Rules, policies, regulations, and organizational charts represent the formal structure of the organization. Informal groups, spontaneous associations, and personal relationships between members constitute the informal structure of the organization. These groups and relationships act as carriers of the values, beliefs, norms, and culture of the organization, and they exert a great deal of influence on the organization (Scott, 1992).

These conclusions represent important assumptions about the behavior of the individuals in organizations and about the underlying social and psychological dynamics of organizational behavior.

Traditional management theory, which focused on the responsibilities of the manager to plan, coordinate, and control activities of the organization, was based on the assumption of rational behavior. As this approach has been challenged by research on organizational performance and behavior, using the assumptions just listed, new areas of management theory have emerged. These include leadership and motivation theories, change theory, and information processing theory.

Leadership and Motivation Theories

Leadership may be defined as interpersonal influence by which the efforts of a group are directed, through communication, toward a specified goal or goals in a given situation (McFarland, Leonard, & Morris, 1984, p. 69). Initial work in this area concerned the personality traits of recognized leaders; however, more recent trends have focused on the variables in the leadership process, the relationship of the leader and the group, and situational aspects of leadership. Theories about organizational behavior and performance now also include the perception that the motivation of the employee plays an important role. McGregor's (1960) Theory X and Theory Y, Situational Leadership Theory (Hersey & Blanchard, 1982), the Motivation Theory of Herzberg (1966), and Theory Z (Ouchi, 1981) are reviewed briefly here as classic examples of theory in this area.

The approach to leadership presented by McGregor (1960) is based on the leader's underlying beliefs about human nature. These beliefs fall into two major categories, resulting in two kinds of leaders. Theory X leaders believe that employees are generally unresponsive and lazy, and need constant supervision; Theory Y managers, in contrast, believe that employees are hardworking and responsible and need support and encouragement. It is not surprising that leaders with such different convictions about their employees demonstrate highly divergent leadership styles. Theory X leaders tend to be directive and authoritarian, while Theory Y leaders are more laissez-faire (McGregor, 1960).

Leadership may be considered to include five variables: the leader, the followers (employees), the situation, the process of communication, and the goals. Situational leadership theory concludes that no single style or type of leader behavior is effective in all situations; furthermore, certain types of leadership behavior are more effective in certain situations than others, so an effective leader attempts to match the type of leadership to the requirements of the situation. Leadership behavior is composed of two dimensions, task behaviors and relationship behaviors. These can be combined into four styles of leadership, which may be more or less effective depending on the variables in the situation (Hersey & Blanchard, 1982). The four styles have been described as: high-task/low-relationship, or telling; high-task/high-relationship, or selling; high-relationship/low-task, or participating; and low-task/low-relationship, or delegating (McFarland et al., 1984).

While the beliefs of the leader and the requirements of the situation can provide some useful insights into leadership, an interaction approach stresses the interaction of the individual within aspects of the job. Certainly the quality of leadership and supervision of the employee is crucial; furthermore, decisions made by the organization's leaders control many aspects of a job. The Motivation Theory of Herzberg (1966) identifies two distinctly different sets of factors that influence job satisfaction and productivity. Motivating, or satisfying, factors include achievement, recognition, the work itself, responsibility, advancement, and growth. Hygiene, or dissatisfying, factors are the quality of supervision, troubled interpersonal relationships with supervisors or co-workers, working conditions, salary, and job security. Interestingly, the motivating factors are those that enhance self-concept and self-esteem, while the hygiene factors are those that deal with the employee's need to avoid unpleasantness. According to this theory, a successful leader addresses both motivation and hygiene factors.

In somewhat of a departure from these leadership and motivation theories, Theory Z is concerned with the entire organization, although the quality and characteristics of relationships between leaders and employees form a critical element. The term *Theory Z* was proposed by Ouchi (1981) to describe the style of management used by successful Japanese businesses. The Theory Z organization has certain characteristics: a clearly stated philosophy that is consistent with actual management practice, matrix organizational structures, formal planning techniques such as management by objectives, and decision making that incorporates consensus through the use of quality circles. The *quality circle* is a gathering of employees to participate in decisions without regard to rank. This process is purposefully slow, so that fact gathering, opinion seeking, and the development of relationships can contribute to a true consensus decision. The Theory Z approach is designed specifically to manage people through cooperation, coordination, trust, subtlety, and productivity.

Although the use of organizational, leadership, and motivation theories can guide health services evaluation and research, health care organizations do differ from other types of organizations in a number of ways, which should be kept in mind. Two important differences are the complexity and diversity inherent in the daily work of caring for patients, and the variety and high ratio of health care providers needed to render these services. In addition, the outcomes of health care services are unpredictable, in that patients with the same condition may demonstrate a wide range of responses to the same treatment, for reasons sometimes impossible to determine. When these factors are combined with the health care consumer's concern for quality, increasing governmental regulation, and the common recognition of health care as a right, it becomes apparent that a theoretical framework must incorporate the unique aspects of health care organizations if evaluation and research are to be useful.

Total Quality Management Theory   Lately, the health care industry has given increasing attention to the practice of total quality management (TQM). Adoption of TQM has typically, as in manufacturing, been a response to overseas competition in an increasingly global marketplace. However, because the U.S. health care industry enjoys a comfortable dominance as a result of the absence of foreign competition, health care managers should view TQM as an industry-wide method of reducing waste and increasing efficiency. On a firm-by-firm, or micro scale, the principles of TQM are useful for increasing organizational strength through delivery of higher quality services at less cost (thereby providing greater value to patients).

It is important, however, to recognize that these techniques represent a dramatic change from the way in which health care organizations usually operate (Bader, 1992; Melum & Sinioris, 1992; Spath, 1989). TQM can succeed only if *all* members of the organization shift their paradigms for professional behavior to accommodate a totally different philosophy. TQM transforms corporate culture radically, from conventional standards of top-down management and individual achievement toward environments that emphasize teamwork, continuous learning, and prevention to improve faulty processes *before* they become problems.

Change Theory

Change is ever present, and significant. It may arise for individuals or for organizations. For individuals in the health care organization or for the organization itself, the need for change may be identified from problems with input–throughput–output processes, from fluctuations in the environment, from recognition of new goals or modifications of existing goals, and from perceived needs for growth.

Because change means doing something different or giving up something familiar, it invariably evokes strong feelings. To counter this, the concept of planned and deliberate change has evolved. Planned change is a deliberate and collaborative effort to use scientific knowledge to improve the operations of the human system, whether it is a self-system or a cultural system (Lippit, Watson, & Westley, 1958).

Four kinds of change have been identified: changes in knowledge, changes in attitudes, changes in behavior, and organizational change (Hersey & Blanchard, 1982). The first three kinds concern the individual; organizational change is accomplished when the number of individuals who have changed their behavior is enough to make the new behavior part of the organization's systems and culture.

Determining the type of change is an important step in any change project. Another aspect is the process of change. Three phases of the change process have been identified: unfreezing, moving or changing, and refreezing (Lewin, 1947). The *unfreezing* phase prepares individuals and systems in the organization for change. Careful planning, including specific objectives and evaluation criteria as well as strategies, is an important part of the unfreezing phase. The second phase of the change process is the actual *movement* from the existing set of conditions to the new condition or behavior. The success of this phase depends greatly on the success of the unfreezing phase, and on a plan for change that reflects the realities and has specific strategies for dealing with them. The last phase of change is *refreezing*: Successful change has occurred when the new conditions or behaviors are firmly fixed within individual behavior and organizational culture; deliberate refreezing is essential to accomplish this.

In planned, deliberate change, guidance of the change project comes from a change agent. Seven functions of the change agent have been identified: developing a need for change, establishing a relationship with the target population, identifying the problem that the change will correct, determining alternative courses of action for the target population, translating the desire to change into action, stabilizing the change, and terminating the change relationship with the target population (Rogers, 1962). An effective change agent must show proficiency in communication and interpersonal relationships, as well as other appropriate skills.

Unplanned or improperly managed change causes problems for individuals and for organizations. The use of change theory and concepts of planned change can be extremely helpful in planning, managing, and evaluating change. Yet, confronted with rapid and dramatic fluctuations in the health care environment, advances in technology, and issues of resource availability, health care organizations must change, albeit carefully and with clearly specified goals. Assessing the need for change and evaluating the effectiveness of change projects are major roles for health services evaluation and research.

Information Processing Theory

Much of what goes on in organizations is processing information and making decisions (Galbraith, 1977, p. 24). The concept of information processing refers to the sequence of cognitive processes used in particular problem-solving tasks and explanations of these processes in terms of psychological concepts and principles. One aspect of the study of information processing is the identification of cognitive strategies by which humans adapt to our limited capabilities for processing information (Newell & Simon, 1972). Organizations use a number of strategies to coordinate and control the way information is processed and decisions are made so that individual decisions match the goals of the organization. "An organization is, after all, a collection of people, and what the organization does is done by people" (Simon, 1957, p. 4). In a discussion of communication and coordination in organizations, March and Simon (1958), for example, suggested that organizations try to reduce the amounts of information handled and make communication more efficient, by converting large amounts of information and many alternative choices into "simplified models that capture the main features of a problem without capturing all its complexities" (p. 169). Mechanisms for decreasing the amount of information handled include technical languages and vocabularies, classification schemes, uncertainty absorption, and placing boundaries on rationality. Technical vocabularies and classification schemes increase the efficiency of communication by making it possible to communicate large amounts of information in relatively few symbols (March & Simon, 1958, pp. 162–164). *Uncertainty absorption* refers to drawing inferences from a body of evidence, but communicating only the inferences and not the evidence itself; this mechanism severely limits the recipient's ability to judge the accuracy of the information (March & Simon, 1958, pp. 164–166).

The concept of *bounded rationality* describes another important mechanism for handling information and making decisions. Because the number of possible alternatives in any situation is too vast for consideration, individual choice takes place within a set of "givens." These givens are the selected premises on which choices then are based. This leads to the phenomenon of *satisficing*, a situation in which alternatives are grossly simplified and the first acceptable, rather than the optimal, alternative is selected (Simon, 1957).

Another aspect of information processing is decision making. *Decision making* may be defined as the act or result of deciding. The traditional description of the decision-making activities of rational humans (March & Simon, 1958) was based on the existence of a set of alternatives and their consequences; the decision was made by selecting the alternative that leads to the preferred set of consequences. The difficulties in this model lie in the assumptions that all the alternatives and their consequences are known, and that rational humans have the ability to rank all of these consequences from most preferred to least preferred. However, the limitations of human cognition make the traditional assumptions about rational humans inaccurate. Rather, human beings are "intentionally rational," and, lacking a complete knowledge of alternatives and consequences, as well as the ability to obtain such knowledge, alternatives are grossly simplified and the first acceptable one is selected as the decision choice (March & Simon, 1958, pp. 137–138).

Information processing and decision making go on at all levels of the organization but with important differences depending on the level. Three levels within organizations as identified by Thompson (1967) are the technical core, the managerial level, and the institutional level. The technical core is concerned with the organization's central work processes, "the nature of the technical task, such as the raw materials which must be processed and the kinds of cooperation of different people required to get the job done efficiently" (Thompson, 1967, p. 10). A central concern of the organization is to protect the technical core from overwhelming uncertainties or contingencies in the environment (Thompson, 1967, p. 146).

The next level of the organization, the managerial, mediates between the technical level and those who use its products; procures the resources needed for the technical function; and administrates the technical core through key decisions about the scale of operations, purchasing, and employment. These managerial functions are viewed by Thompson as "servicing" the functional core (1967, pp. 10–11). The managerial level also has the challenging role of "translator" between the institution's long-range concerns and the technical level's short-term concern with certainty (Thompson, 1967, p. 150).

The highest level of the organization deals with its interactions within the wider social system in which it exists. This institutional level, which deals with elements of the environment over which the organization has no formal control, focuses on the overall articulation of the organization and agencies of the community (Thompson, 1967, pp. 11–12).

A framework based on information processing and decision making provides fruitful possibilities for research in health care services and the evaluation of health care delivery. Many critical health care issues, such as documentation of services, clinical and administrative decision making, classification of patients and patient conditions, and computerization, are actually issues of information processing. The theoretical foundations of information processing and decision making thus have much to contribute to research and evaluation.

HEALTH SYSTEMS ANALYSIS

Although health care organizations have many forms—hospitals, community health agencies, extended care facilities, and health maintenance organizations, to name but a few—all of these physician–hospital organizations can be examined by using the framework of health systems analysis. This approach analyzes both the parts and the total system. The analysis appraises the processes and technology of the organization, the environmental conditions, and the interrelationships among the components of the system. Effective management of any kind, but particularly health care administration, should use systems analysis to appraise the organization, and should be guided as well by the principles, processes, and theoretical foundations of scientific inquiry.

Types of Systems

A system is a set of resources that are organized to perform designated functions in order to achieve desired outcomes; health care systems use many types of resources, organized to accomplish a wide variety of outcomes. Before examining health care systems, further understanding of systems in general will be helpful.

Systems may be categorized by their origins. *Natural systems* arise from nature—for example, the solar system, an ecological food chain, or the human body. Man-made systems may take a number of forms. *Physical systems* are structures that perform a particular function; communication systems and transportation networks, such as the highway system, are physical systems. *Procedural systems* consist of rules, policies, and laws organized to accomplish particular objectives; our legal and political systems are examples, as are diagnostic algorithms. *Conceptual systems* are composed of well-defined concepts and relationships organized for some purpose, and take the forms of philosophy, cultures, mathematical models, and simulations.

One type of system in particular, the social system, provides a useful model for viewing health care organizations. Social systems are patterns of human activity; the interaction of the human members of the systems and the characteristics of this interaction comprise the structure of the systems. Social systems are rich and complex, because they reflect the values, beliefs, and attitudes of their members; furthermore, such attributes are important to the processes by which the social system accomplishes its goals and purposes.

An important differentiating feature of systems in general, and particularly social systems, is their complexity. In an organization, *complexity* refers to the number of employees, the characteristics of the organizational structure, and the organization's size. Systems are also differentiated by the characteristics of their boundaries. Closed systems have impenetrable boundaries and are completely self-contained, whereas open systems continually interact with their environments, exchanging materials, personnel, information, and resources. However, if there is turbulence or conflict in the environment, this may affect the functioning of an open system adversely. Protecting the technical core of the organization from environmental uncertainties through creation of appropriate boundaries and selected boundary-spanning activities is an important role of management.

The *adaptability* of a system is also an important attribute, encompassing the ability to change, grow, and survive. An adaptable system reacts to variations in the environment in a way that furthers its goals. Indeed, adaptability may be considered a useful indicator of a system's strength.

Components of a System

The essential concepts of general systems theory—input, throughput, and output—identify the essential components of systems. In health systems analysis, input consists of the raw materials, labor, effort, patients, capital, and equipment that the health care system uses to provide health care services. In evaluation and research, input may be symbolized as X, indicating that it is the exogenous or independent variable under study. Similarly, output for a health care system includes the products of service delivery, such as patient outcomes, mortality and morbidity rates, hospital days, or outpatient visits; output may be symbolized in research as Y, the dependent variable under study. Throughput, also referred to as process, is what is done to the input variable (X) to yield the resulting output (Y).

For the health care administrator, determining the relationship between input and output variables, as well as the effectiveness of process alternatives, is the major purpose of evaluation and research. Such knowledge about specific health care systems provides a sound basis for professional and rational decisions: selecting inputs and processes, and evaluating the quality, effectiveness, and success of the output. Furthermore, analysis of causal relationships allows an administrator to explain and predict to some degree the system's performance.

Input and output variables display one of two basic relationships: either recursive or nonrecursive. In a *recursive* relationship, an input variable either affects or causes the output variable, but the output variable has no effect on the input variable. This relationship may be noted as:

$$\text{Input} \rightarrow \text{Output, or } X \rightarrow Y, \text{ but not } Y \rightarrow X$$

A *nonrecursive* relationship is the opposite of a recursive relationship. Here, the two variables exert an effect on each other, in a loop fashion. This type of relationship, also called a feedback or reciprocal relationship, may be noted as:

$$\text{Input} \rightarrow \text{Output} \rightarrow \text{Next Input}$$

or:

$$X_{\text{time 0}} \rightarrow Y_{\text{time 1}} \rightarrow X_{\text{time 2}} \rightarrow Y_{\text{time 3}} \cdots$$

Identifying a recursive relationship is a critical part of the analysis of causal relationships. Nonrecursive relationships, however, raise the question of whether a variable is a cause or the effect of another variable.

An example of a nonrecursive relationship is helpful at this point. It is unclear whether a hospital's growth to a large size is the result or the cause of its participation in an integrated health delivery system. Here, the two variables, size and participation in the system, may have a nonrecursive relationship (i.e., each of the two variables may affect the other). Similarly, the health status of a community is both affected by and affects the types of intervention programs—preventive, treatment, or rehabilitation—provided by the health department. For both of these examples, establishing a cause-and-effect relationship is difficult; however, discovering which relationships are recursive, with clear direction of causality, is extremely useful in planning and managing health care services.

Analytical Perspectives in Health Systems Analysis

Systems analysis is the orderly and precise use of a variety of methods and methodologies to design, redesign, or control a large and complex set of resources in order to achieve the desired goals and outcomes of the system. The task is to identify, describe, and measure accurately 1) the input variables the system uses, 2) the processes and technologies that the system applies to inputs, and 3) the type and quality of outputs that result.

Thus, systems analysis requires a defined methodology and also a set of methods. The *methodology* refers to the underlying logic, assumptions, and theoretical framework chosen by the analyst. *Methods* are the techniques and procedures used, such as econometric analysis, scheduling, inventory control analysis, simulation, statistical analysis, forecasting, and experimental research methods for data collection and analysis.

Systems analysis is performed from one of two perspectives, which focus on different aspects of a system. The *structural–functional perspective* views the structure of the system, its purposes and objectives, and its activities, procedures, and functions. This approach is straightforward and relatively easy to apply; if an element of the system does not fit with the system objectives, it may simply be discarded. The structural–functional approach is congruent with the concept of rational bureaucracy, discussed earlier, which assumes that employees' roles are based on technical qualifications and that rules govern behavior. Missing, however, is a recognition of how individual attitudes, values, and beliefs, as well as the environment, affect organizational performance and behavior.

The alternative perspective, the *behavioral perspective*, attempts to deal with the role of individual attitudes and values by focusing on interpersonal aspects of the system, acknowledging that interactive human behavior is a critical factor in organizational performance and behavior. While a behavioral perspective is more consistent with analyzing a health care system as a social system, that perspective is also considerably more difficult to apply because individual behavior is extremely difficult to investigate, predict, or control, and the study of human interaction is complex.

To examine a situation thoroughly, health systems analysis often uses methods from both the structural–functional and behavioral approaches. An important criterion for systems analysis is that the methodology and the methods must be congruent with each other and also appropriate to the object of the analysis. For example, the use of a Theory Z framework for a descriptive analysis of the organizational chart, rules, policies, and procedures would be incongruent, because that type of method examines characteristics of a rational bureaucracy, rather than of a Theory Z organization. Alternatively, if the investigation focused on employee perceptions of job satisfaction and the relationship of satisfaction with productivity, then that method would not be terribly relevant for studying these variables. Instead, using surveys to collect and analyze data about factors contributing to or interfering with employee job satisfaction, and time–motion studies or other productivity measures would be more likely to illuminate the relationship between job satisfaction and productivity. These two types of method reflect the structural-functional and behavioral perspectives in health systems analysis.

Systems Modeling

When examining a complex social system such as a health care organization, it is helpful to describe the organization in a way that represents the essential attributes of the system without getting bogged down in detail. The technique of systems modeling can be used to do that. Systems modeling represents the real-life situation of the organization in abstract form. The model reduces the system to its skeletal features, concentrating on functions and behaviors. The goal is to understand the relationships between system components.

Five steps for model construction have been recommended by Morris (1967). The first step consists of identifying and conceptualizing the system and formulating it in writing, with particular attention to any problem areas. Quantification is the next step; here, the constant attributes of the system, their parameters, and pertinent variables are defined and are assigned symbols. A critical task here is selecting the most influential variables and distinguishing between those that are controllable and those that are not. Attributes that have little influence on the system or that cannot be controlled should be eliminated from the model to keep it as simple as possible.

The third step is modeling. Here, relationships among the variables are stated on the basis of known principles, specially gathered data, intuition, and reflection. Assumptions and predictions about the behavior of the noncontrollable variables also are stated at this point. Using these stated relationships, a model is constructed by combining all relationships into a system represented symbolically. Then symbolic manipulations can be performed to answer questions about the behavior of variables and the relationships among them, and a solution to the model can be derived.

In the final step of systems modeling, testing the symbolic model, the symbolic model is used to make predictions about the behavior or performance of the variables in the model. By collecting and analyzing data from the actual system being studied, these predictions are supported or rejected; the model then can be revised as indicated. The value of an accurate model is that it can be used for problem analysis, prediction, and planning for the real-world system.

The systems modeling technique applies systems analysis to problem solving. A problem is identified, quantified, and described in a symbolic model, which can be solved and revised as necessary. Ultimately, however, the solutions for problems derived from this modeling technique are implemented in a real-world system.

Types of Models

There are many types of models, which provide various levels of insight about the systems that they portray. A classification of models has been proposed by Murdick and Ross (1971) to include functional models, structural models, time-referenced models, uncertainty-referenced models, and generality-referenced models.

Functional models fall into three subgroups: descriptive, predictive, and normative. *Descriptive models* simply provide a picture of the situation, but do not predict or recommend. *Predictive models* identify relationships between dependent and independent variables and allow "What if?" questions about the model. *Normative models* can answer questions about the symbolic system, in particular with regard to the best answer to a problem. This group of models, the functional models, can recommend courses of action for specific problem situations.

Structural models are concerned with the component parts of the systems, and are constructed using one of three strategies. When some of the physical characteristics of the entities represented in the model are retained, an *iconic model* results. An *analogue model* substitutes for components or processes to provide a parallel to the system being modeled. In *symbolic modeling*, symbols represent aspects of the real world.

Models that are **time referenced** may be either static or dynamic. A *static model* has no mechanism to account for changes over time. *Dynamic models*, in contrast, use time as an independent variable.

An **uncertainty-referenced model** is considered to be either deterministic or probabilistic. For the *deterministic model*, there is a uniquely determined output for any specific set of input values; this represents the solution of the model. *Probabilistic models*, also referred to as *stochastic models*, involve probability distributions for specific inputs and provide a range of values for at least one of the outputs. An example of a probabilistic model is the decision tree.

Finally, models may be classified as either general or specific. *General models* are those that have applications in several functional areas: general systems theory, for instance. A *specialized model* is one that can be applied only to a particular and unique problem. A diagnostic algorithm for cardiovascular disease, or an expert system, would be an example of a specialized model.

Summary

Systems modeling is another valuable tool for examining the relationships and behavior of variables in complex systems. Planning and managing health care systems requires accurate knowledge and perspicacity, yet many variables and issues have yet to be described, explained, and predicted. The processes of scientific inquiry and the use of such techniques as systems analysis and systems modeling can provide essential information for problem solving, planning, and managerial decisions.

EXAMPLE OF USE OF SYSTEMS ANALYSIS IN HEALTH SERVICES ADMINISTRATION

A systems approach can be used as a framework for identifying the essential inputs, processes, and outputs of the health care system; in doing so, however, an important consideration is the level at which the analysis can be done, or should be done. Examination of a health care system may focus on patients/clients, providers, organizations, administrators, perceptions of health and health care, information systems, intervention and treatment modalities, aggregation of services, and types of services provided. Each of these areas may be analyzed at either the micro or macro level (see Table 1.1). At the micro level, the individual patient, provider, or organization is considered as the unit of analysis; at the macro level, analysis treats groups of organizations, a community, or a population. These two models, which have been described by Tilquin (1976), represent parallel but very different aspects of study.

Once the level of analysis has been determined, a systems approach can be used to identify, describe, and measure the inputs of the system, the processes and technologies used, and the outputs that the system produces. An example of the inputs, processes, and outputs for a health care organization is presented in Figure 1.4. Here, inputs include material resources, such as equipment, capital, and facilities; personnel resources consist of health care providers, administrators, and support staff; moreover, patients/clients are also considered to be inputs for a health care organization. Processes include the delivery of services by various health care professionals, administrative and management activities, and various technical support operations. Outputs of this system include health care outcomes for specific patients and organizational performance. Clearly, all the elements of this system would require more precise definition and measurement before they could be used as variables in a study of health care management; however, this example does demonstrate a systems analysis framework in use.

CONCLUSION

The remaining chapters of this book describe specific methods available to the health care manager who is applying a systems approach to management studies in health services administration. Strategies are outlined for selecting meaningful problems to examine, identifying and quantifying relevant variables, and using statistical analyses; specific examples of these strategies are presented. Managerial epidemiology, evaluation research methods, and the issues of cost-effectiveness and cost–benefit analysis are discussed. Finally, some future directions for health services evaluation and research are examined. The world of health care is changing rapidly. A principal goal of health care organizations is to provide the services needed by their patient/client population effectively and efficiently. To do that requires accurate and reliable information about the needs of the population, the systems for providing care, and the larger social system or environment of the organization. Equally essential is an ability to analyze and inter-

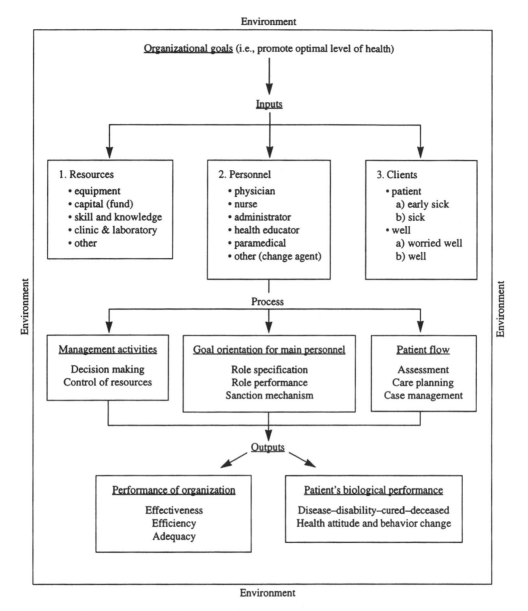

Figure 1.4. Schematic model of a health care system.

pret the meaning of that information. The use of health care services evaluation and research methods, grounded in the scientific process and relevant theoretical foundations, can provide many of the answers to the challenging questions that health care administrators confront.

REFERENCES

Aday, L.A., Begley, C.E., Laison, D.R., & Slater, C.H. (1993). *Evaluating the medical care system: Effectiveness, efficiency, and equity.* Ann Arbor, MI: Health Administration Press.

Aldrich, H.E., & Pfeffer, J. (1976). Environments of organization. *Annual Review of Sociology, 2,* 79–105.

Anderson, G.F., Alonso, J., Kohn, L.T., & Black, C. (1994). Analyzing health outcomes through international comparisons. *Medical Care, 32,* 526–534.

Bader, B.S. (1992). *Rediscovering quality.* Rockville, MD: Bader & Associates, Inc.

Begun, J.W., & Lippincott, R.C. (1993). *Strategic adaptation in the health professions.* San Francisco: Jossey-Bass.

Deming, W.E. (1986). *Out of the crisis.* Cambridge, MA: Massachusetts Institute of Technology, Center for Advanced Engineering Study.

Galbraith, J. (1977). *Organization design.* Reading, MA: Addison-Wesley.

Gaucher, E.J., Coffey, R.J., Hannan, M.T., & Freeman, J. (1977). The population ecology of organizations. *American Journal of Sociology, 82,* 929–964.

Hannan, M., & Freeman, J. (1977). The population ecology of organizations. *American Journal of Sociology, 82,* 929–964.

Hersey, P., & Blanchard, K.H. (1982). *Management of organizational behavior: Utilizing human resources* (4th ed.). Englewood Cliffs, NJ: Prentice Hall.

Herzberg, F. (1966). *Work and the nature of man.* Cleveland, OH: World Publishing.

Howland, D., & McDowell, W.W. (1964). The measurement of patient care: A conceptual framework. *Nursing Research, 13*(1), 4–7.

Hyman, H.H. (1975). *Health planning: A systematic approach.* Germantown, MD: Aspen Systems Corporation.

Knox, P. (1979). Medical deprivation, area deprivation, and public policy. *Social Science and Medicine, 130,* 111–121.

Lawrence, P.R., & Lorsch, J.W. (1967). *Organization and environment: Managing integration and differentiation.* Boston, MA: Graduate School of Business Administration, Harvard University.

Lewin, K. (1947). Frontiers in group dynamics: Concept, method, and reality in social sciences, social equilibrium, and social change. *Human Relations, 1*(1), 5–41.

Lippit, R., Watson, J., & Westley, B. (1958). *The dynamics of planned change.* New York: Harcourt, Brace, and World.

March, J.G., & Simon, H.A. (1958). *Organizations.* New York: John Wiley & Sons.

Melum, M.M., & Sinioris, M.K. (1992). *Total quality management: The health care pioneers.* Chicago: American Hospital Association.

McFarland, G.K., Leonard, H.S., & Morris, M.M. (1984). *Nursing leadership and management: Contemporary strategies.* New York: John Wiley & Sons.

McGregor, D. (1960). *The human side of enterprise.* New York: McGraw-Hill.

Morris, W. (1967, August 9). On the art of modeling. *Management Science, 13*(2), B707–717.

Murdick, R.G., & Ross, J.E. (1971). *Information systems for modern management.* Englewood Cliffs, NJ: Prentice Hall.

National Center for Health Statistics. (1993). *Healthy people 2000 review, 1992.* Hyattsville, MD: Public Health Service.

Newell, A., & Simon, H. (1972). *Human problem solving.* Englewood Cliffs, NJ: Prentice Hall.

Ouchi, W. (1981). *Theory Z.* New York: Avon Books.

Reinhardt, U.E. (1975). *Physician productivity and the demand for health manpower.* Cambridge, MA: Ballinger Publishing Company.

Rogers, E.M. (1962). *Diffusion of innovations.* New York: The Free Press.

Schieber, G.J., Poullier, J., & Greenwald, L.M. (1993). Healthy spending delivery and outcomes in OECD countries. *Health Affairs, 12,* 120–129.

Scott, W.R. (1992). *Organizations: Rational, natural, and open systems* (3rd ed.). Englewood Cliffs, NJ: Prentice Hall.

Shortell, S.M. (1990). Sustaining a competitive advantage in the '90s. *Hospitals, 64,* 72.

Shortell, S.M., Morrison, E.M., & Friedman, B. (1990). *Strategic choices for America's hospitals.* San Francisco: Jossey-Bass.

Silver, M. (1972). An econometric analysis of spatial variations in mortality rates by race and sex. In V. Fuchs (Ed.), *Essays in the economics of health and medical care* (pp. 161–227). New York: Columbia University Press.

Simon, H.A. (1957). *Administrative behavior* (2nd ed.). New York: Macmillan.

Spath, P.L. (Ed.). (1989). *Innovations in health care quality management.* Chicago: American Hospital Association.

Spiegel, A.D., & Hyman, M.H. (1991). *Strategic health planning: Methods and techniques applied to marketing and management.* Norwood, NJ: Ablex Publishing Corporation.

Tausky, C. (1970). *Work organizations: Major theoretical perspectives.* Itafca, IL: F.E. Peacock Publications, Inc.

Tausky, C. (1976). Theories of organization. In W. Nord (Ed.), *Concepts and controversy in organizational behavior* (2nd ed., pp. 275–304). Santa Monica, CA: Goodyear Publishing Company.

Thompson, J.D. (1967). *Organizations in action*. New York: McGraw-Hill.

Tilquin, C. (1976). Modeling health services systems. *Medical Care, 4*, 223–230.

von Bertalanffy, L. (1950). The theory of open systems in physics and biology. *Science, 111*, 23–28.

von Bertalanffy, L. (1956). General systems theory. *General Systems, 1*, 1–10.

Wan T.T.H., & Broida, J.H. (1983). Indicators for planning of health services: Assessing impacts of social and health care factors on population health in Quebec, Canada. *Socio-Economic Planning Sciences, 17*, 225–234.

Weber, M. (1947). *The theory of social and economic organization* (edited by A.H. Henderson & T. Parsons). Glencoe, IL: Free Press.

Zelman, W. (1994). The rationale behind the Clinton health care reform plan. *Health Affairs, 13*(1), 9–29.

2

Selection and Formulation of a Research Problem for Management Study

A problem clearly defined is a problem half solved.

Anonymous

The quotation above highlights the importance of identifying a problem before trying to study or solve it. Indeed, it is impossible to solve a problem if you do not know what it is! Health services managers confront challenging and complex problems every day; often a management study can identify the scope or significance of the problem, the possible factors causing the problem, or the effects of the solutions undertaken. However, launching a management study before understanding exactly what the problem is can waste time and effort, produce incorrect information, and fail to solve the problem. Because no one likes to fail, accurate identification of the problem before subsequent efforts to solve it must be part of any useful management study.

This chapter discusses techniques for selecting and formulating a problem for management study. They include 1) describing the problem area, 2) narrowing the focus or scope of the problem, 3) assessing the significance of the problem, 4) ascertaining the feasibility of studying the problem, and 5) identifying the resources needed to conduct the study. The decisions made about these issues play a critical role in the actual execution of the management study. The second section of this chapter describes the procedures for conducting a management study, with examples to illustrate their application.

ISSUES IN SELECTING AND FORMULATING THE STUDY PROBLEM

For the busy manager in health services, selecting and formulating a problem for management study can present difficulties—not from a dearth of matters to be studied, but from the wide range of questions about the delivery of health care services and their complex interrelationships, and the rapid changes in the health care environment. On any given day, a health services manager must think about the volume, type, and quality of services provided; the different types of health care providers and support staff and their work; and, ultimately, the effectiveness and success of the health care organization. A problem in any of these areas can be studied effectively only after it has been identified and defined accurately.

Sources of Researchable Problems

Where do ideas about subjects for management study come from? Personal experience, professional literature, relevant theory, and conceptual models are common sources. Often, however, a

23

curious and astute observer may identify a problem worth studying: An immediate difficulty in need of a solution, a recurring situation with a discernible pattern, an irksome aspect of one's work, or a novel approach to an everyday problem can stimulate critical analysis that identifies a question for management study. Beyond the existence of observable problems, however, are other opportunities for worthwhile research. Although managers and decision makers often have used management study to correct an unsatisfactory situation, this reactive habit of mind has drawbacks. Problems must have occurred, and damage appeared, before anything is done to change the process. In today's turbulent environment of competition and change, organizations must deal with *potential* problems (i.e., be *proactive*) in order to flourish. Better ways of doing things must be sought *before* problems arise; instead of awaiting a negative development and then searching for its solution. Managers who continually look for better ways of doing things not only avoid the costs of "damage" but also improve their products or services, and thus strengthen the position of their organizations.

Remember, however, that a situation that to one person requires management study may appear differently to another. As in the story of the blind man and the elephant, each observer's perspective transforms the definition of the situation. It is therefore essential for the investigator to recognize his or her perspective as unique, and to recognize as well the perspectives of all the other individuals or groups affected by the management issue. If the investigator is also a member of the management team, this aspect of the analysis especially should be borne in mind.

An example of the complexity and interrelated aspects of a management study problem, as well as the possible variety of perspectives, will be helpful at this point. Let us consider a community general hospital that faces a high demand for ambulatory services, but is concerned about their cost-effectiveness. Already, two related issues, high demand for services and cost-effectiveness, are apparent; using a successful ambulatory services program as a strategy to attract patients to the hospital is another significant issue.

To study this problem, the health services manager must examine a complex variety of issues from a number of perspectives. Physicians, for example, may want more office space for examining patients or performing procedures. The nursing department may call for more patient education and home care follow-up services if patient care is to shift more to outpatient services. Managers may deplore additional ambulatory services as inefficient in both managerial and budgetary terms when the pediatric and obstetrical services are currently underutilized. The hospital's board of directors may question whether outpatient surgical services are compatible with the organization's traditional acute care mission. Finally, community planners and public health officials may urge the addition of ambulatory services, as an effective way to meet the primary care needs of the community and reduce costly inpatient services.

This example shows how much the definition of a problem for management study depends on the perspective of the investigator and the perspectives of key groups in the environment. Each group identified in the preceding paragraph could develop an appropriate and useful research question based on its unique perspective on the ambulatory surgical service. However, posing five research questions to reflect all these perspectives is not a feasible way to decide whether this community general hospital should expand its ambulatory care services. What is required is to narrow the topic area to a manageable research question that reflects the priorities of the organization.

Developing and Refining a Research Problem

Selecting a research topic is essentially a creative process, so it is sometimes helpful to begin in an unstructured manner, by jotting down general ideas and queries of interest. Once these broad topic areas have been identified, they can be sorted in terms of interest, importance, knowledge available, and relevance as topics of investigation. Then the topic that holds the most promise can be selected. The list of other ideas generated in this process should not be discarded, however, because those ideas may be useful in the future.

Once a general topic of interest has been selected, the next step is to narrow the focus to a problem statement that is amenable to research, by moving from the general to the specific. Questions such as: What causes . . . ?, What is the extent of . . . ?, What characteristics are associated with . . . ?, or What is the relationship between . . . ? are useful. The transformation of a general topic into a workable problem usually is accomplished through a series of uneven steps, successive approximations that focus the scope of the problem more exactly as the pertinent concepts are defined more sharply. In the process, one or more potential questions will emerge as most significant or intriguing.

Another important task when identifying a research question for management study is deciding on the type of approach to use. The two approaches most frequently used are the descriptive approach and the analytical approach. The purpose of **descriptive research** is primarily the accurate portrayal of characteristics of persons, situations, or groups, and of the frequency with which specified phenomena occur. The descriptive approach is therefore inclusive of qualitative research methods (Cassell & Symon, 1994; Patton, 1990).

Descriptive research uses classification and a variation of classification termed *typology*. *Classification* describes a system, entity, person, or attribute by classifying it into some category along one dimension. The classification of multihospital arrangements presented in Table 2.1 is an example of this approach. In the *typological approach*, a system, entity, person, or attribute is categorized along more than one dimension (Table 2.2).

As a descriptive approach, the main purpose of qualitative research methods is to describe phenomena via observation, or to discover meaning rather than cause and effect (Strauss & Corbin, 1990). Most qualitative research designs are distinguished from quantitative research designs by the use of ideas that are collected and analyzed in the form of words, instead of the use of variables that are analyzed as numbers (Roberts & Burke, 1989). Three main features distinguishing qualitative research are the emic perspective, the holistic perspective, and an inductive and interactive process of inquiry. First, the *emic perspective* means that the researcher focuses on experience or perception from the participant's point of view, rather than that of the researcher. Second, the *holistic perspective* is an approach that considers and includes the underlying values and context of the phenomena as a part of the phenomena rather than removing them. Third, there is an *inductive and interactive inquiry* between the researcher and the data, with the researcher moving the analytical process as he or she gains insight about the phenomena of interest. The researcher moves from specific subjective observations to general concepts or theories. Techniques of information gathering and analysis commonly used in qualitative research include interviews, intuition, observation, and linguistic analysis (Morse, 1992).

Qualitative research may be applied to the health care setting in numerous ways. One example is the recent emergence of qualitative methods in nursing research. Qualitative approaches often allow nurses to understand the experiences and the meaning of dysfunctions to their patients. As a result, nurses may become more aware of human responses to health and illness (Habermann-Little, 1991). Another example of a qualitative research study is historical research on medicine (Stevens, 1971). The purpose of this type of research is to study past events in order to gain a better understanding of events in the present. In her study, Stevens (1971) researched the history of the medical care system in the United States in order to identify and tie together the elements of today's health care crisis.

Although the advantages of qualitative research are many, there are also certain limitations to the design of qualitative research methods. Unfortunately, qualitative research methods have a low potential to explain causality, therefore making qualitative studies low on internal validity. Furthermore, qualitative research methods have limited potential to generalize the findings.

Table 2.1. Classification of multihospital arrangements

Types or categories

Less commitment, more institutional autonomy → ... → More commitment, more system control

CONTINUUM

Characteristics	I	II	III	IV	V	VI	VII
	Formal affiliation	Shared or cooperative services	Consortia for planning or education	Contract management	Lease	Corporate ownership but separate management	Complete ownership
Descriptions, definitions, terms	Patient transfer agreements, house officer affiliations, referral agreements	Financial, political commitment over time for selected products or services	Voluntary health planning council for a specific geographic area; Area Health Education Centers (AHECs)	Corporate management; full management without ownership	Policy as well as management provided by a single board	Owners do not interfere in the management of hospitals even though they have legal authority; absentee ownership	1. Mergers, consolidations 2. Satellites, branch operations 3. Authorities, chains 4. Holding companies
Corporate ownership	No	No	No	No	No	Yes	Yes
Corporate management	No	No	No	Yes	Yes	No	Yes
System influence on major policy decisions	No	No	Yes	Minor	Yes	Maybe	Yes

Adapted from Devries (1978).

Table 2.2. Typological approach to categorizing management style by geographic location

Management style	Centralized	Decentralized
Contract managed	Shared service organization model	Functional (referral hospital model)
Owned/controlled	Centralized corporate model	Decentralized corporate model

Hence, the external validity is very poor. However, qualitative studies yield high content validity that may enhance the meaningfulness of observations (Roberts & Burke, 1989).

Analytical research tests relationships between variables using complex models, experimentation, and statistical tests. In analytical research, the intent is to organize data to answer research questions. Two approaches generally are used, the associative approach and the causative approach. An *associative approach* assumes that there is a linear relationship between variables, and data analysis measures the strength and direction of the relationship; however, this approach cannot draw conclusions about causality.

The *causative approach* is used to find and specify causal relationships between variables. The concept of causation seems implicit in human thought; indeed, our observations often link action and outcome, producing irresistibly the notion of cause and effect. In many areas of management study, it often seems that there is a web of multiple, interrelated factors that could be regarded as causative. Although this may make it hard to find solutions, a number of statistical and econometric methods can verify the validity of causal models.

A *causal relationship* is one such that the presence or absence of one variable determines the presence, absence, or value of another. Five kinds of information are considered to be criteria for causation, according to Susser (1973):

1. Time sequence of variables
2. Consistency of association on replication
3. Strength of association
4. Specification of association
5. Coherent explanation

Two broad categories of causative factors in medical practice are special and common causes. *Special causes* are those that occur infrequently and are unpredictable. Some examples of special causes are: when a patient experiences a rare illness and needs a prolonged inpatient stay, causing higher variation in the distribution of length of stay; or external environmental effects, such as extreme weather conditions and other natural disasters, that cause sharp increases in the use of health care services for a short period of time. *Common causes* are those involving a lack of training, experience, or control, which are due to faults in the organization. These faults can be eliminated by managers through changes in processes. The search for cause-and-effect relationships in health services research is an important area with exciting challenges. Recently, for example, the adoption of total quality management (TQM) or continuous quality improvement (CQI) in health care has broadened the search for causes of variation in medical practice.

Criteria for Evaluating a Research Problem

Although there are no hard and fast rules for making a final selection of a research question, there are three important criteria: the significance of the problem, the feasibility of studying the problem, and the resources needed to conduct the study. These criteria not only shape the final question, but also guide many of the choices made during a management study.

A crucial factor in selecting a problem for management study is the **significance** of the problem. How is this evaluated? Often it is evaluated from the perspective of the researcher and from the perspectives that are dominant either within the organization or in the environment where the organization exists. Other determinants of the problem's significance include the immediacy of the problem, the implications of leaving a problem unsolved, the practical applications of a solution, the theoretical relevance of the problem, and the impact of the problem on the community and on society.

At this point, useful questions are: Will patients, providers, health care organizations, the community, or society benefit from the study of this problem? Will the results lead to practical applications? Will this study lead to the formulation or alteration of existing policy, procedure, or practices? Will anyone *care* what the findings of this study would show? If the answer to these questions is "no," that study problem probably should be abandoned. The time, energy, and resources that a management study requires should not be wasted.

Once it is decided that the study problem is significant, the next question is the **feasibility** of conducting the study. The issue of feasibility is complex; considerations include time and timing, the availability of subjects, the cooperation of others, the experience of the investigator, and ethics.

A pragmatic aspect of management studies is that there is usually a deadline of some kind; therefore, the problem must be one that can be studied adequately within the limited time available. This consideration often restricts the scope of the question. A related issue is timing. Certain aspects of the study problem may occur more frequently at particular times during the year, or day. Moreover, the individuals who would participate in the study may be unavailable at certain times. For example, a study of the types of trauma services most often utilized at a medical center would provide more useful data if it were done in the summer months, when the incidence of traumatic injuries is higher. If the timing requirements of the study do not match the time period available to conduct it, the feasibility of the project may be in question.

A second aspect of feasibility has to do with the availability of subjects. When health services research focuses on human subjects, such as patients, clients, health care providers, and employees of health care organizations, difficulties include identifying and locating subjects with the necessary characteristics and then obtaining their cooperation. In addition to studying human subjects, health services research may examine information in existing records, such as balance sheets, inventories, staffing patterns, census data, and other management reports. If this information is unavailable, or if it is in a form that is difficult to access or interpret, then this information may be of little use in management studies. When subjects or information are unavailable, the feasibility of the study vanishes.

The cooperation of others is a third necessary aspect of feasibility. Certainly, the cooperation of human subjects in a study is indispensable. However, cooperation from a number of persons or groups also may be necessary, taking the forms of administrative permission and support, technical assistance, and allocation of resources. If the study requires informed consent from human subjects, obtaining the necessary approval from review boards requires not only the subjects' cooperation but that of the organization as well.

The experience of the investigator is another important aspect of a study's feasibility. Generally, an investigator should choose a problem from an area about which he or she has some prior knowledge and experience, because it will be more difficult and time consuming to prepare, design, and execute a management study about an unfamiliar topic. Technical expertise is also an important consideration, and this may include instrument development, statistical analysis, and presentation strategies. The beginning researcher should try to select a problem from a familiar topic area and identify consultants or resources who can provide any substantive or technical assistance needed.

A final factor in assessing the feasibility of a management study is the ethics of the study. Research questions or study methods that make unfair or unethical demands on participants cannot be considered feasible. Requirements to be met include informed consent; protection of the subjects from harm; and the preservation of privacy, anonymity, and confidentiality for those individuals who participate in the study. Beyond these, the ethical issues raised by scientific research are not always clear cut, and they often may pose major moral dilemmas for the researcher. Many health care organizations now have committees on bioethics that guide the conduct of any research that raises ethical issues.

Along with significance and feasibility, a third important concern about a possible study has to do with what **resources** it will require. Resources may include persons, equipment, facilities, and financial support. (In truth, financial support probably should be considered first rather than last.) Human resources could include consultants, interviewers, data entry personnel, students, researchers, librarians, and secretaries. The equipment and facility resources needed depend on the focus of the project. For example, if job satisfaction interviews are conducted, a quiet, private place to hold the interviews is necessary. The need for technical equipment varies with the specific study problem; most management studies, however, require office equipment and supplies, printing services, and computer access. Close attention to these resource requirements at the beginning can greatly enhance the planning and execution of the project.

Research Questions in Health Services Management

Selecting a meaningful question for management study may seem like an arduous process, but a carefully selected and framed research question is the essential foundation for a successful study. In health services, the investigator may choose questions for management study at the internal, or intraorganizational, level, or questions pertaining to groups of organizations at the system-wide, or interorganizational, level. Health services managers with specific concerns about their own organizations often focus on the intraorganizational level, which is also termed micro-level organizational analysis. The interorganizational level for research questions, in contrast, is used more by health planners, community leaders, multihospital corporations, and academicians.

Whether intra- or interorganizational, management studies in health services share the goal of scientific inquiry: to generate a set of hypotheses, which are then verified in repeated observations, so that theory can be derived, tested, and confirmed or rejected. This goal is pursued using either a principally inductive approach, moving from specific information to generalizations, or a more deductive approach, using theory as a starting point to identify and examine specific expectations. Each of these approaches to scientific inquiry, together with its relationship to the level of analysis (intra- or interorganizational), lends itself to the study of certain elements of health care systems (Table 2.3).

The health services manager who has specific observations and information about scheduling, staffing patterns, or resource decisions will undertake an intraorganizational study and will use an inductive method to arrive at the research question. For example, noticing that referrals for home visits to postoperative patients dramatically increase on Fridays might lead the director of community health nursing services to ask questions such as: Is there an increase in the number of patients requiring weekend home visits for wound care? Do we have adequate resources to meet this demand? What is the cost of providing these services? In this situation, specific observations lead to questions about the activities of the particular organization.

In a somewhat different approach, a professor of health administration, using a theoretical framework of population ecology, might decide to study the fit between health care organizations and their environments. This deductive strategy might begin with identifying key concepts of the theory: organizational structure, the environment, and the fit between these two. Through a process of moving from theoretical tenets to specific expectations, a question about the impact of a new management structure on the fit between organizations and their environments could be posed and then studied.

Table 2.3.   Scientific inquiry and focus of management studies

	Logic of inquiry	
	Inductive	Deductive
Focus of management study	From specific information to generalization	From theory to specific expectations
Intraorganizational or internal level	Scheduling Staffing patterns Inventory control Resource-size decisions Procedure decisions	Human motivation and productivity Leadership and control Morale and satisfaction
Interorganizational or system-wide level	Competition Market share Technological assessment Coordination	Exchange relations Organizational innovation Adoption of innovation Assessment of impacts of new management systems (i.e., centralization, ownership, management style, location, governance, etc.)

The management study is a useful and effective strategy to begin answering the many challenging and important questions in health services management. To conduct a management study that is meaningful and provides useful information to the manager, it is essential to understand the problem clearly, arrive at a realistic assessment of its significance, the feasibility of studying it, the necessary resources, and the appropriate level of organizational analysis and framework for inquiry. The development of a research problem is a creative endeavor; an open, curious mind can find the process stimulating.

RESEARCH PROCEDURES

With the problem for study determined, the next step is the design and execution of the management study. This process, which follows the stages of scientific inquiry, consists of six steps (Table 2.4): 1) identification and specification of the study problem, 2) selection of a theoretical framework to guide the research process, 3) quantification of the study variables, 4) carrying out the research project, 5) program development based on the study results, and 6) implementation of the program, with appropriate evaluation. The six steps are described in this section; more detailed discussions of techniques that can be used at various points in the procedure appear in later chapters.

Table 2.4.   The six stages of scientific inquiry

1. Identification of problem
2. Selection of theoretical framework
3. Quantification of study variables
4. Execution of research project
5. Development of program based on results
6. Implementation of program

Step 1: Identification and Specification of the Study Problem

Once a research question has been developed, it is necessary to state the study problem in clear, precise terms and to specify the salient aspects of the problem. A useful problem statement should guide the investigator in the design and execution of the study.

The starting point for this process is to identify the key issues and variables contained in the problem. Every problem affects three dimensions—persons, time, and place—so the persons involved, the place or location, and the time element or causal chains must be stated clearly.

The next step is to specify the variables of the problem. Specification of the study problem means elucidating the precise attributes of the problem. Attributes of particular importance are the magnitude and significance of the study problem, its location and boundaries, and its determinants and consequences. Magnitude and significance refer to two important statistics: the incidence of the problem and the prevalence of the problem. The **incidence** of a problem is the number of new episodes of the problem that occur within a certain time *interval*, while **prevalence** is the number of old and new episodes of a problem existing at a given *point* in time. Incidence refers to the timing of the problem, while prevalence refers to the sheer numbers of events. Considered together, these two aspects of the problem provide a good picture of its seriousness.

The specification process must provide operational definitions for these attributes, so they can be understood and interpreted clearly. An *operational definition* describes a variable or concept in terms of procedures by which it can be measured. For example, if the study problem is an examination of whether patients are being discharged too soon, the variable of early discharge could be defined as "discharged on the first or second postoperative day." This type of definition is essential for the quantification step, which is discussed later.

Step 2: Selection of a Theoretical Framework to Guide the Research Process

Theories can be defined as abstract generalizations that present systematic explanations about the relationships among phenomena; theories also knit together observations and facts into an orderly system (Polit & Hungler, 1987). A theoretical framework is a statement by the researcher of the assumptions and beliefs that guide the research process. Theory also provides an analytical framework through which to form logical interpretations of the facts collected in the study, and guides the search for new information. Selecting a theoretical framework consists of five stages: conceptualization, model selection, critique of previous work in the field, review of evidence, and reformulation of the model.

The conceptualization stage expresses the issues of the problem in relation to clear principles. The investigator formulates the study problem in abstract, conceptual terms. This formulation ultimately will help to explain the data. It is important to remember, however, that conceptual thought is a deductive process, and so requires testing in the real world.

After the relevant concepts have been distinguished separately, the next stage is developing a theoretical model of the study problem. The model gives the real-world attributes and manifestations of the study problem an abstract representation. Portrayed that way, relationships between variables can be examined and analyzed readily. This abstract representation of variables and relationships is the basis for proposing hypotheses later in the research procedure.

In the first two stages of selecting a theoretical framework, the investigator reformulates the study problem in abstract terms. Once this has been accomplished, it is helpful to examine work by other researchers or managers on the same or similar issues. This review of the literature can include research findings, theory, methodological information, opinions, and viewpoints, as well as anecdotes and experiential descriptions. Often there is a wealth of available literature, and the investigator must use good judgment in deciding how relevant particular material is to the study problem.

After the review of the pertinent literature, the evidence that led to the selection of the study problem is reexamined. For example, if the quarterly audit of patient incident reports at a general hospital indicates that there has been an increase in patient falls, it would be useful to compare data from the audit with information in the literature. While the literature suggests that elderly patients are high-risk candidates for falls while in the hospital, the audit data show that the majority of patients who fell were middle-aged postoperative patients who were receiving narcotics for pain relief. Thus, both age and the effects of medications should be included as variables in a theoretical framework for a management study about the causes of patient falls. Such an analysis ties the development and choice of a theoretical framework to the existing experimental data in the management study (i.e., to the real world).

To summarize the process of selecting a theoretical framework that will guide the management study, the investigator conceptualizes the problem, develops an abstract model of the problem that describes the relationships between concepts, performs a critical review of previous work in the field, and then reviews existing evidence about the problem. This process should produce an understanding of the problem that is both conceptually clear and grounded in reality. Although the process may seem laborious, it has much to offer the busy health services administrator. The initial work of carefully defining a problem and the theoretical basis for studying it can save an administrator from expending resources on poorly conceived or planned projects, and can focus time and energy instead on significant problems and their solutions.

Step 3: Quantification of the Study Variables

A *variable* can be defined as a characteristic of a person or object that varies within the population under study. The problem statement and the theoretical framework for a management study identify variables. The study variables can be measured at the individual (patient) or aggregate (organization or community) level (Marks, 1982). If the results of the study are to be meaningful to the investigator and communicate clearly to those who use them, the variables must be defined clearly. This clarity of communication is achieved by using operational definitions and measurement techniques.

Operational definition links the abstract concept found in the problem statement and theoretical framework to a variable that can be measured and quantified. For very broad concepts, *proxy measures* are used; for example, job turnover often is used as a proxy measure for job satisfaction, a much more ambiguous concept. Once variables have been operationalized, propositions stating the relationships between the variables are presented as theoretical hypotheses.

Important steps in operationalizing a variable are specifying how the variable will be observed and how it will be measured. Variables differ considerably in the ease with which they can be described, observed, and measured. Even something as seemingly simple as body weight can be measured in pounds or kilograms, as well as fractions of either. In addition, body weight may show diurnal variation, which suggests that the time of day when the weight is determined should be specified in the operational definition. Furthermore, body weight also may be examined using anthropomorphic measurements to determine the percentage of lean muscle mass and body fat.

To explore the example further, an operational definition of body weight will depend on the problem under study and where it fits in a theoretical framework. If the problem concerns overall population health, then a random weight to the nearest pound is adequate. In a weight reduction clinic, in contrast, detecting small weight losses might be of concern and so the operational definition might specify weights taken first thing in the morning. Another example would be an exercise physiologist studying long-distance runners, whose research requires more precise anthropomorphic measurements.

This example of body weight describes a number of options for linking that concept with measurements. The most precise observations and measurements must be chosen to describe the attributes, magnitude, and significance of variables, as well as to identify causal relationships between them. Beyond that, the validity and reliability of the measurement techniques used to arrive at an operational definition must be established.

Only if a measurement is both valid and reliable can it be depended on as an accurate representation of a concept or attribute. **Validity** is the degree to which the tool or technique actually measures what it is supposed to measure. **Reliability** refers to the extent to which a tool or technique will yield the same results every time it is used to measure the same response. Furthermore, validity and reliability cannot be considered as independent qualities; a measuring device that is not reliable cannot possibly be valid. Validity and reliability are important criteria both for existing measurement tools and for the development of new instruments. Issues of quantification, measurement, reliability, and validity are discussed further in Chapter 3.

Step 4: Carrying out the Research Project

Now is the time to execute the management study. This step consists of data collection, data analysis, and testing and verification of the study hypotheses using statistical methods. Although this step may seem like the meat of the research project, the ability to carry out the research project depends entirely on the quality and thoroughness of the work done in the preceding steps.

Data collection procedures are shaped by the variables identified in the problem statement and theoretical framework, and by the operational definitions that tell how the variables will be measured. Data collection strategies include review of existing documents, surveys, questionnaires, structured or unstructured interviews, and direct observations. A management study about job satisfaction, for example, could employ unstructured and structured interviews as a data collection method, but a study of financial performance would examine existing documents, such as balance sheets, budgets, utilization data, and other management reports.

After the required data have been collected, the next step is data analysis, which will be guided by the study questions and the theoretical framework. For example, in a large study of population health and utilization of community health services, data analysis will focus on statistical descriptions of the population characteristics and utilization indicators. A study of nurse turnover might examine the study data for qualitative characteristics in order to "understand human beings and the nature of their transactions with themselves and with their surroundings" (Benoliel, 1984, p. 3).

Data analysis using statistics reduces, summarizes, organizes, interprets, and communicates numerical data. Basic arithmetic and logical thought are the major skills needed to apply and interpret statistics. Research statistics are classified as either descriptive or inferential statistics.

Descriptive statistics describe and synthesize data obtained from empirical observations and measurements, including averages, percentages, frequency distributions, measures of central tendency, and measures of variability. The mode, median, and mean, indices of *central tendency* that are drawn from the center of a distribution, can be used as an overall summary. *Variability* refers to the degree to which the subjects in the study are similar to one another with respect to the attribute under study; indicators of variability are the range and standard deviation. The role of descriptive statistics in health services research, as well as appropriate statistical procedures, can be found in the texts by Lay and Broyles (1980) and Longo and Bohr (1991).

Inferential statistics are used to draw conclusions about the study group, and to make generalizations about a large class of subjects on the basis of data from a limited number of subjects.

Although it is possible to generalize (i.e., draw conclusions about a larger group) through ordinary thought processes, the application of inferential statistical methods provides an objective, systematic framework that ensures that researchers working with identical data would be likely to come to the same conclusions. Examples of inferential statistical methods include estimation of population parameters, hypothesis testing, and tests of statistical significance. The role of inferential statistics in research and appropriate statistical procedures are presented in Chapters 3 and 4.

An important part of the data analysis process is comparing the study results to the proposed hypotheses. **Hypothesis testing** helps the researcher make objective decisions about the results of the study. Statistical methods allow the researcher to decide whether the study results reflect chance differences between groups or true differences. Hypothesis testing follows the rules of negative inference, in which a contradictory, or null, hypothesis is proposed. The *null hypothesis* states that there is no relationship between the variables, and that any observed relationship is due to chance. For example, an investigator believes that a certain drug is effective in treating a specific disease. The process of determining if the drug is indeed helpful would begin with the null hypothesis (H_0) that the drug does not treat the disease, but that the illness is cured for reasons other than the use of the drug. Tests then would determine if the null hypothesis was correct (accept H_0), or if it was incorrect and the drug does have an effect in treating the disease (reject H_0); this rejection or acceptance of the null hypothesis is decided by statistical analysis of the study data. The two types of errors in testing hypotheses are: rejecting a null hypothesis as false when it is actually true (*Type I error*) and accepting a null hypothesis as true when it is actually false (*Type II error*). The term *level of significance* is used to describe the probability of committing a Type I error, and this can be controlled by the researcher; the level of significance is also referred to as alpha (α). The probability of committing a Type II error is beta (β), and its complement, ($1 - \beta$) is referred to as the *power* of a statistical test (see Figure 1.1). Procedures for hypothesis testing, determining the level of significance, and using tests of statistical significance are described in Chapter 4.

Hypothesis testing verifies the model that was specified in the theoretical framework through procedures that analyze the attributes and relationships of the variables described in the study problem. For example, if a management study on the utilization of emergency services examined whether certain age groups were more likely to use certain types of services, one hypothesis might be that young adults, middle-aged adults, and the elderly have similar requirements for emergency services. Suppose that descriptive statistical analysis of the data on these three age groups shows that 1) young adults and the elderly have similar utilization patterns for skeletal trauma and head injuries, although the main cause for young adults is motor vehicle accidents, whereas for the elderly it is falls; and 2) middle-aged adults' emergency service use is more for medical problems such as myocardial infarction and hypertension. Using inferential statistics, the health administrator would decide whether these differences were statistically significant and whether they could be generalized to the larger community served by the hospital.

	H_0: Null hypothesis	
	H_0 true	H_0 false
Accept null hypothesis		Type II error (Beta)
Reject null hypothesis	Type I error (Alpha)	

Figure 1.1.   Type I and Type II errors.

Step 5: Program Development Based on the Study Results

A principal purpose of a management study is to find solutions for the study problem. However, simply identifying a possible solution is not enough. Solutions must be put into effect in the real world, and the results evaluated.

The data analysis portion of the management study provides information about the attributes and relationships of the variables, which then can be used in designing programs to improve the situation. Issues such as the timing or immediacy of the problem, implications of leaving the problem unsolved, practical applications of the problem solution, theoretical relevance of the problem, and the impact of the problem in the broader arena of the community and society influence program development. Information about the actual conditions and the significance of the problem also should be integrated in program development and evaluation.

Let us return to the example of a study of the utilization of emergency services by age group discussed in the preceding section. Although the data analysis might suggest that there are statistically significant differences in utilization patterns among young adults, middle-aged adults, and the elderly, the decision about development of a program based on this analysis would have to consider the significance of the problem as well. If existing resources met the needs of each group, new programs would not be indicated. Conversely, if the resources for the medical emergency conditions seen in the middle-aged group were well developed, but fewer facilities and specialists for comprehensive management of traumatic emergencies were available, then a new program in the latter area would be appropriate. Factors such as timing, the implications of *not* developing such a program, and the practical aspects of developing a major trauma service also would be considered.

The goal of program planning is an effective program. This process begins with precise determination of the problem to be solved or the purpose to be accomplished. Then it identifies the goals, objectives, and activities of the program in a clear and measurable way. Objectives are particularly important in program planning because evaluations are based on them. The planning process is highly detailed and so requires a great deal of information. However, effective program planning also requires being able to see beyond the numbers and understand the complicated interactions among the program's internal components and with its external environment. According to Nutt:

> Planning is more than an analytical process. The most important activity in planning is *synthesis*, putting ideas together. . . . Successful planning is often mysterious to both the manager who carries it out and the researcher who studies it. The successful planning process takes creative leaps which draw on mental processes that people find hard to articulate. These creative leaps are stimulated by synthesis, which draws on intuitive rather than analytical skills. (1984, p. 4)

Thus managers and decision makers should develop their intuition as well as their analytical skills. Otherwise, the effectiveness of the programs they plan will suffer.

Evaluation, a critical aspect of program planning and implementation, generally is defined as a process that assesses a given action or intervention. Program evaluation assesses the activities of the program (McKenzie & Jurs, 1993). The many types of design that can be used to evaluate program outcomes are presented in Chapter 9.

Step 6: Implementation of the Program

A management study concludes with recommendation of a program and the strategies to implement it. The results of a management study and the conditions in the health care organization often offer several possibilities for new programs. As with the selection of the study problem, considerations of feasibility and resources influence choices about program implementation. Of particular concern are timing, cost-effectiveness, acceptability of the program to the organization, and the urgency of solving the problem.

Implementation puts the strategies and activities of the program into effect. However, it is not enough simply to start a program; only if the new activities and systems are monitored, reinforced, and evaluated continually can implementation be successful. Evaluation, then, is a part of a program from the beginning, rather than something that occurs only at the end.

The evaluation of health services is a challenging area of research. The evaluation of a program often serves as the basis of a management study question, and the whole process begins again. A discussion of evaluation research methods is presented in Chapter 9.

CONCLUSION

A management study is an effective way to identify and examine questions and issues in health services delivery, and to explore and evaluate strategies for possible solutions to problems. Conducting a successful management study depends on a clear understanding of the problem and its salient aspects. By using the principles and procedures of scientific inquiry, it is possible to approach complex, interrelated issues in health care services in an organized and productive manner.

REFERENCES

Benoliel, J.Q. (1984). Advancing nursing science: Qualitative approaches. *Western Journal of Nursing Research, 6,* 1–8.

Cassell, C., & Symon, G. (1994). *Qualitative research methods in organizational psychology.* Thousand Oaks, CA: Sage Publications.

Devries, R. (1978). Health care delivery strength in numbers. *Hospitals, 52*(6), 81–84.

Habermann-Little, B. (1991). Qualitative research methodologies: An overview. *Journal of Neuroscience Nursing, 23,* 188–190.

Lay, C.M., & Broyles, R.W. (1980). *Statistics in health administration* (Vol. I). Germantown, MD: Aspens Systems Corporation.

Longo, D.R., & Bohr, D. (1991). *Quantitative methods in quality management.* Chicago: American Hospital Publishing.

Marks, R.G. (1982). *Designing a research project: The basics of biomedical research methodology.* Belmont, CA: Lifetime Learning Publications.

McKenzie, J.F., & Jurs, J.L. (1993). *Planning, implementing, and evaluating health promotion programs.* New York: Macmillan.

Morse, J.M. (1992). *Qualitative health research.* Newbury Park, CA: Sage Publications.

Nutt, P.C. (1984). *Planning methods for health and related organizations.* New York: John Wiley & Sons.

Patton, M.Q. (1990). *Qualitative evaluation and research methods.* Thousand Oaks, CA: Sage Publications.

Polit, D.F., & Hungler, B.P. (1987). *Nursing research: Principles and methods.* Philadelphia: J.B. Lippincott.

Roberts, C.A., & Burke, S.O. (1989). *Nursing research: A quantitative and qualitative approach.* Boston: Jones and Bartlett.

Stevens, R. (1971). *American medicine and the public interest.* New Haven, CT: Yale University Press.

Strauss, A., & Corbin, J. (1990). *Basics of qualitative research.* Thousand Oaks, CA: Sage Publications.

Susser, M. (1973). *Causal thinking in the health sciences.* New York: Oxford University Press.

3

Quantification of Variables and Measurement Issues

Whatever exists, exists in
some amount and can be measured.

L.L. Thurstone

A major activity in scientific inquiry is the quantification of concepts. To measure something for the purposes of a management study means describing and measuring real-world phenomena so that their attributes can be characterized and their relationships with other phenomena identified. The first step in this process is to select phenomena as variables; quantification and measurement constitute the second step.

A **variable** is an attribute of a person or object under study that varies. Another way to define variables is to say they represent concepts in operation. The process of linking an abstract concept with methods for its observation and measurement is referred to as *operationalizing the variable*, or defining it operationally; an operational definition is a specification of the operations the investigator must perform to observe and measure the variable.

Measurement and quantification procedures are central to the use of scientific methods. The rules for measuring things, however, are neither unanimously agreed on nor intuitively obvious, a quandary especially perplexing when abstract variables are being quantified and measured. For example, although the measurement of length of employment may be fairly straightforward, attempts to quantify the factors influencing length of employment, such as job satisfaction, motivation, organizational loyalty, or professional commitment, face formidable and enduring problems.

Measurement may be defined as the "rules for assigning numbers to objects to represent quantities of attributes" (Nunnally, 1978, p. 2). One attribute of variables is their variability; this variability can be given a numerical expression, which signifies how much of any particular attribute is present in the subject or object measured. **Quantification** determines the differences in the amount of an attribute and communicates them through numerical expression. More simply put, measurement tells us how much, while quantification tells us how much more or how much less.

In measurement and quantification of variables, it is useful to begin by distinguishing the variable in terms of its purity. *Purity* refers to whether the variable represents a unitary attribute or a conglomeration of interrelated concepts. A useful measurement tool is one that yields a quantitative score for a single, unitary attribute; complex variables may require several measurement tools for their various facets.

Numerical values or numbers are assigned to variables according to specified rules; the measurement and quantification process in a study specifies those rules and the criteria for their application in that study. These specifications are especially important when new measurement tools are used and when complex variables are measured.

Measurement and quantification are essential to scientific inquiry. They remove much of the guesswork from collecting and analyzing data. They provide objectivity, because numerical measures can be verified by other investigators. An additional advantage of quantification is that, when abstract concepts are transformed into numerical results, they can be subjected to statistical analysis.

Quantitative measures also make it possible to obtain data that are reasonably precise. This accuracy and rigor make the task of establishing the different degrees of an attribute much easier; furthermore, this precision also provides consistency and a recognized framework for communicating information to a broad audience. Rather than saying that a 250-bed hospital is "always full," for example, the utilization of services can be described precisely as an average inpatient census of 222 and an occupancy rate of 88%.

To measure and quantify variables is an important, challenging role of a management study. Unless the variables are defined, measured, and quantified clearly, the results of the study will have little use for planning programs and evaluating their success. This chapter describes methods for classifying variables, types of measurement scales, and issues of measurement, and will introduce strategies for constructing measurement scales.

CLASSIFICATION OF VARIABLES

Variables can be classified in a number of ways; the classification helps determine what type of measurement technique to use. This classification is based on the characteristics of the variable. Variables are classified according to gappiness, descriptive orientation, randomness, or fixity.

Gappiness

Variables may or may not have gaps between their successive observations. A **discrete variable** is one with gaps between its values. That is, representatives of the variable fall into one place or another; there are no intermediate positions. Examples of discrete variables include sex, race, group identification (Group A, Group B), and diagnostic category (pneumonia, brain tumor). A **continuous variable** is one with no gaps between values; the values progress fractionally, without any breaks. Some examples of continuous variables are age, blood pressure, height, number of inpatient beds, and organizational size.

Descriptive Orientation

This refers to the function of the variable in describing the situation under study; the designations of **independent variable** and **dependent variable** are used to identify the function. These terms also may suggest directionality of influence, rather than a causal connection.

Other terms for an independent variable are causative, explanatory, or *exogenous variable*. This is the variable believed to cause or influence the outcome variable; in experimental research, the independent variable is the one the researcher manipulates. A dependent variable is the outcome variable being studied (i.e., the effect, result, or outcome of the independent variable). The term *endogenous variable* also is used to refer to the dependent variable.

Note, however, that variables are not inherently dependent or independent. These descriptions reflect the situation under study. A variable may be classified as dependent in one study but be considered the independent variable in another. For example, one management study may treat job satisfaction as an independent variable influencing length of employment, the dependent or outcome variable. Another management study might examine how leadership style as an independent variable affects job satisfaction, a dependent variable.

Randomness

The characteristic of randomness means that the occurrence of the variable cannot be predicted or anticipated with any certainty. A **random variable**, then, is one whose values can be known only as the result of an experiment. For example, the prevalence of a disease, a random occurrence, can be estimated; however, the actual number of cases can be determined only after a count is taken.

Fixity

A **fixed variable**, or **nonrandom variable**, has a known value before experimentation is done. An example of a fixed variable is the number of hospitals in an area, because this fact would be known to the investigator at the beginning of the management study.

TYPES OF MEASUREMENT SCALES

Measurement scales are tools used to collect data about an attribute, object, system, or person; a scale is designed to assign numerical scores that will place subjects along a continuum with respect to the attribute being measured. A common example of a measurement scale is the bathroom scale, which assigns a numerical value to one's weight; a ruler is also a measurement scale that provides quantifiable values for the height and length of an object. Measurement scales may be categorized by their levels of precision in measurement. Differing scales of measurement are used for variables with differing characteristics.

   A comparison of the four types of measurement scales (nominal, ordinal, interval, and ratio), the types of variables with which they are used, their statistical properties, and the required level of analysis is presented in Table 3.1.

Nominal Scales

This is the simplest level of measurement scale: naming or classifying of variables according to a common characteristic. A basic requirement of the nominal scale is that the classifications must be mutually exclusive and collectively exhaustive; each subject must be classified into one, and only one, category. If a nominal scale uses numerical values, they do not have any quantitative implications and cannot be used mathematically. An example of a nominal scale is a classification of hospital type, such as for-profit, not-for-profit, and voluntary. Other common examples of nominal scales are gender, race, religion, nationality, medical diagnosis, and blood type.

Ordinal Scales

Ordinal measurement goes a step further than categorization. An ordinal scale consists of categories, but the relationships between categories are ordered in terms of their relative importance. However, an ordinal scale does not indicate how much more or less (quantity) of the attribute is found at each level.

Table 3.1.   Management scales and their statistical properties

Variable type	Measurement level	Statistical property	Level of analysis required
Discrete	Nominal (sex, race) Ordinal (socioeconomic status)	Discrete categories Rank ordering	Proportion Chi-square test
Continuous	Interval (thermometer) Ratio (bed size)	Ranking with equal intervals Equal intervals with real zero	Parametrics, regression, correlation, variance, multiple regression, etc.

The types of mathematical operations that can be done with ordinal data are limited. Averages, for example, are generally meaningless with rank-order measures. Frequency counts, percentages, and nonparametric statistical tests, in contrast, can be used for data measured on an ordinal scale. An example of an ordinal scale is a survey that allows responses of strongly agree, agree, undecided, disagree, and strongly disagree. These responses can be assigned numerical values of 1 (strongly disagree) to 5 (strongly agree); however, there is no uniform or measurable distance between categories, nor is there a real zero point.

Interval Scales

When both the rank ordering and the equivalent distances between attribute values can be specified, this is an interval scale. Thus, interval measures are more informative than ordinal measures; they allow the use of addition, subtraction, and averages, as well as some parametric statistical tests. However, an interval scale does not possess a real or rational zero point, so multiplication and division are meaningless. The Fahrenheit and Celsius temperature scales are familiar examples of the interval scale. While the differences in temperature are uniform, a zero on the thermometer does not mean a total absence of heat.

Ratio Scales

Ratio scales provide the greatest precision in measurement, because they have equidistant points that correspond to real empirical distances and a real zero point. Measures on a ratio scale provide information about the rank ordering of objects according to the critical attribute, the intervals between the objects, and the absolute magnitude of the attribute for each object. For data measured on a ratio scale, the presence of a real zero makes it possible to perform all arithmetic operations as well as parametric statistical tests. Ratio measurement is the ideal measurement, but is probably unobtainable for many types of variables. The bathroom scale is a common example of a ratio scale. Unless someone is standing on the scale, it registers zero, indicating an absence of weight. A measurement of 200 pounds is exactly twice the weight of 100 pounds.

MEASUREMENT ISSUES

Measurement of variables is a critical component of a management study. Unless variables are observed, measured, and quantified accurately and precisely, the study will yield little useful information. In using existing measurement tools or in devising new tools, an investigator must evaluate their transferability, unidimensionality, reliability, and validity.

Transferability

The term *transferability* means the extent to which a measurement scale developed in one setting can be used in other similar settings for the same purpose. This is an important consideration for using an existing measurement scale. If a measurement scale was developed to measure the intensity of nursing care required by patients in an acute care setting, it would not be appropriate for an outpatient setting. In another example, a measurement tool that was developed and tested using male respondents might not be transferable to female respondents.

Unidimensionality

A desirable characteristic of a measurement tool is that it measures only one concept, or one dimension of that concept. This provides a much clearer representation of the concept under study than would measuring several concepts together. To conduct a management study about job satisfaction, for example, it might be necessary to use several measurement tools to examine several aspects of job satisfaction; this process would provide unidimensional measures of the factors that constitute job satisfaction. Deciding which factors to measure and the appropriate measurement techniques for each is a process guided by the nature of the study problem and the choice of theoretical framework.

It is often necessary to study a problem along multiple continua, because many problems in health services research have several interrelated aspects. A statistical technique called factor analysis can be used in this situation to isolate the factors, or to develop subscales in a measurement tool. The uses of and methods for factor analysis are discussed later in this chapter.

Reliability

Two important qualities of a measurement instrument are reliability and validity (Table 3.2). The reliability of an instrument is the extent to which a tool will yield the same results every time it is used to measure the same response. Reliability is an essential characteristic of a useful measurement tool, although it is not by itself a sufficient condition for effective research.

Three aspects of reliability are stability, internal consistency, and equivalence. The **stability** of a measure is the extent to which the same results are obtained on repeated applications. One procedure for evaluating stability is *test–retest reliability*, accomplished by administering the instrument on two separate occasions for the same study subjects. The two sets of scores are compared, and a reliability coefficient is computed, which gives a numerical index of how reliable the test is. Assessments of test–retest reliability may be influenced by several factors. Repeated use of a measurement device in an organization makes it likely that measures of its reliability will be inaccurate (Kaluzny & Veney, 1980, p. 134). Another factor to be considered is that, when the interval between test administrations is longer than 1–2 months, test–retest reliability tends to be higher for short-term retests than for long-term retests (Polit & Hungler, 1987, p. 319). Inaccurate results also can occur when respondents attempt to remember and conform to their original answers, or when they think about their previous answers and change their responses deliberately.

Internal consistency is the degree to which the subparts of an instrument all measure the same attribute. One procedure for evaluating internal consistency is the *split-half method*, which pairs each question on the instrument with an item elsewhere in the test. This can result in a lengthy instrument; if the test procedure exhausts the respondent, that can affect the results.

Table 3.2.   Summary of reliability and validity

Characteristic	Reliability	Validity
Definition	The degree to which the same measure yields consistent results on repeated application	The degree to which a particular measure reflects what it is supposed to measure
Nature of error measured	Chance or random error	Systematic error—i.e., natural variation in the phenomenon under study
Relationship	Reliability is necessary for validity	Validity is not necessary for reliability
Types	Interrater, intrarater, split-half, test–retest	Face, content, concurrent (convergent), predictive, construct
Sources	Subjects, observers, situations, instruments, processing	Same as for reliability; in addition, errors due to sampling, data collection, administration, and analysis
Level of significance necessary	Depends on the degree of validity required; the greater the degree of validity required, the greater the need for higher reliability coefficients	If the program results are to be used for internal improvement only, one might accept somewhat lower validity coefficients; if the program is to be generalized to other settings and be given wide exposure, more stringent (higher) validity coefficients are needed

The correlation coefficient computed on split halves of a measure tends to underestimate the reliability of the instrument systematically; furthermore, this method is handicapped by the fact that different "splits" of the items produce different results (Polit & Hungler, 1987, p. 320). The difficulty can be avoided by determining the intercorrelations between all of the questionnaire items. This is the *coefficient alpha*, also known as *Cronbach's alpha* (Kaluzny & Veney, 1980, p. 135). This method is preferable to the split-half method because it estimates the split-half correlations for all possible ways of dividing the items into two halves.

The relative contribution of each item to internal consistency is shown by the *item–total score correlation*. This technique isolates the items that do not pertain to the total scale, or construct, under investigation. Each item's score is correlated with the summed score of the whole scale. A cutoff point of correlation, usually .71, is the criterion for discarding items. The remaining items in the instrument measure the critical attribute and nothing else.

The **equivalence** aspect of reliability is important in two situations. The first is when different observers use an instrument to measure the same phenomenon at the same time. *Interobserver reliability* is another way of describing this. The second situation occurs when two presumably parallel instruments are used at the same time; concerns about this type of reliability often occur in educational research (Polit & Hungler, 1987, p. 321).

Polit and Hungler summarized the basic point about reliability: "The reliability of an instrument is not a property of the instrument, but rather of the instrument when administered to a certain sample under certain conditions" (1987, p. 316).

Three methods for determining the reliability of a measuring instrument have been discussed: the test–retest technique, the coefficient alpha, and the item–total score analysis. The procedure chosen for assessing reliability will depend on the nature of the measurement tool and on which aspect of reliability is most relevant.

Validity

Along with reliability, validity is a major criterion that a measurement tool must meet. Validity is the degree to which the instrument actually measures what it purports to measure. As with reliability, several techniques can evaluate the validity of an instrument. However, there is an important difference; the validity of an instrument may be very difficult to establish, particularly if the attribute measured is highly abstract.

There are three types of validity: content, construct, and criterion. **Content validity** is the adequacy of the sample representing the content area being measured; it is essential in tests that measure specific content areas. The two aspects of content validity are face validity and consensual validity. *Face validity* is the extent to which the instrument makes sense in terms of the issue being measured, and it is evaluated in terms of *consensual validity* (i.e., the agreement of experts). Thus, content validity clearly is a matter of judgment (Polit & Hungler, 1987, p. 324).

Construct validity is the measurement instrument's actual ability to measure the selected construct. A construct is an operationally defined concept, so the question is how well the operations used to observe and measure it actually do so. Construct validity is essential as the link between theory and empirical investigation. A technique known as factor analysis is one method to determine construct validity.

Factor analysis is a correlation technique that is useful when the instrument is multidimensional. In factor analysis, a large set of variables is reduced to a smaller, more manageable set of measures with a common underlying dimension, which is termed a *factor*. Each factor or subscale of the instrument can be analyzed for its relationship to a construct of interest to the investigator. Once the factors have been revealed by this method, their correlation can be examined. High correlation of items within a similar domain indicates *convergent validity*; low correlation of the items from different domains shows *discriminant validity*.

The third type of validity is **criterion validity**. This is a pragmatic approach that applies a known criterion to the measurement instrument. This approach assumes the known criterion is valid—that is, the researcher must have available a reasonably reliable criterion. Criterion validity can be evaluated in two ways: as concurrent validity and as predictive validity. *Concurrent validity* compares the measurement instrument with some other criterion at the same point in time. *Predictive validity*, however, compares the performance of the measurement instrument with another measure taken over time. In fact, predictive validity can be tested only over time, making this the most stringent of the tests of validity. Predictive validity also can be evaluated using a *general linear model of regression*. This is a statistical procedure that predicts values of a dependent variable according to the values of one or more independent variables.

Correlation

In evaluating both reliability and validity, an essential method is correlation, which describes the relationship between two measures. The relationship is expressed by a *correlation coefficient*, a mathematical term that states the extent to which one variable is related to another.

A correlation coefficient (r) is an index that can range from $+1.00$ (for a direct or positive relationship), through 0.0 (no relationship), to -1.00 (for an inverse relationship). Correlations ranging from .20 to .35 show a very slight relationship between variables, although they may be statistically significant. A correlation coefficient in the .35–.65 range indicates moderate strength in the relationship between variables. For most variables of a social–psychological or social nature, a correlation coefficient of .70 or higher indicates a strong relationship (Polit & Hungler, 1987, p. 387).

Summary

An ideal measurement instrument yields measures that are valid, reliable, unidimensional, sensitive, relevant, efficient, and transferable to similar groups. This is no small challenge. Daunting as the requirements for a measurement tool may seem, however, it is essential to meet them. Only reliable and valid instruments can describe, measure, and quantify usefully the many complex and interesting variables in health services research.

INTRODUCTION TO SCALE CONSTRUCTION AND VALIDATION

Because the field of research in health services is relatively new and the issues it presents vary widely, in any given area of research a reliable and valid measurement tool for a given situation may not be available, or the available instrument may have to be adapted. However, designing and testing a new research scale or instrument can be difficult and time consuming, so the researcher should examine existing scales and instruments thoroughly before deciding to develop a new one.

Scale construction has several steps. The first step is to decide on the concept to be measured and the types of observation or measurement that are appropriate. A review of the pertinent literature is helpful, as is consultation with both theoretical and technical experts. Deciding which type of scale is most suitable for the measurement instrument is the next step. A description of various scales and criteria for their use are presented here.

Differential Scale (Thurstone's Scale)

This type of scale generally is used to measure attitudes; originally developed in the 1920s, it is named after the psychologist L.L. Thurstone. This type of scale, which is an ordinal scale, is made by creating several hundred statements to describe the construct being measured. A large number of expert judges then independently classify these statements by using a scoring system of 1–11, where 1 is the least extreme statement and 11 the most extreme statement about the concept. Each statement is then given a score based on the median score, and items with widely differing scores from the judges are discarded as ambiguous. Those items that show agreement by the judges are included in the measurement scale.

Summated Scale (Likert Scale)

One of the most commonly used scales, a summated, or Likert, scale, is also an ordinal scale, meaning that categories of responses are ranked. Like the Thurstone scale, it often is employed to measure attitudes. Summated scales are constructed by summing the item scores to derive a composite score. A summated or Likert scale consists of several declarative statements expressing viewpoints on a particular topic, and respondents are asked to indicate the degree to which they agree or disagree with each viewpoint.

Such a scale is created by developing a large pool of items that express favorable, unfavorable, or neutral attitudes toward the issue under consideration. Usually 10–20 items are included in the scale. It is important to focus on a single concept, rather than including items about several concepts. If it is necessary to measure more than one concept in a scale, then the items about each concept should be separated in the scoring procedure.

An advantage of the summated scale is that it provides a single numerical representation of the attitude under study. The score for a summated scale is found by summing the numbers chosen for each response. An example of a summated scale would be a six-item questionnaire about patients' attitudes toward the nursing care they received during their hospitalization. Such a questionnaire is presented in Table 3.3. In this six-item scale, two items are worded as positive statements, two are worded negatively, and the final two statements are neutral. Each item can be scored and recoded so that a high score represents a positive perception of nursing care quality. A score of 30 on this scale would indicate that the patient had very positive feelings about the nursing care, while a score of 6 would indicate a profoundly negative response.

Summated or Likert scales, which are useful in examining attitudes, are actually quite powerful. However, their drawback is that the scale may include several dimensions of a concept, and therefore produce ambiguous results. In the example above, although scores of 30 and 6 strongly suggest, respectively, a positive and a negative attitude, other factors that influenced the patient's attitude may not have been measured on this scale. With this in mind, mid-range scores must be interpreted with caution.

Table 3.3.   Questionnaire items to examine patients' perceptions about their nursing care

Answer the following questions using this scale:
    5 = Strongly Agree
    4 = Somewhat Agree
    3 = No Opinion
    2 = Slightly Disagree
    1 = Strongly Disagree

1. The nurses were helpful in bathing, hygiene, and other physical care activities. _____
2. The nurses gave me an opportunity to explain my feelings about being in the hospital. _____
3. There was not an adequate carryover of nursing care when the shifts of nurses changed. _____
4. The nurses did not display adequate concern about me and my well-being. _____
5. The nurses responded to my calls for assistance. _____
6. My therapeutic needs were considered by the nurses. _____

Cumulative Scales

Cumulative scales attempt to avoid some of the difficulties encountered with summated scales; they are useful for measuring multidimensional constructs. There are three different methods for constructing cumulative scales: item-to-scale correlation, factor analysis, and Guttman scaling.

Item-to-Scale Correlation   The item-to-scale correlation technique was discussed earlier as a way to evaluate the reliability of a measurement tool. It also may be used in developing a scale. The advantage is that the scale is likely to "hang together" and measure a single, unidimensional construct; furthermore, mid-range scores will not be as ambiguous as with a summated scale.

The item-to-scale technique isolates the items that do not pertain to the total scale. As is done for reliability, each item's score is correlated with the summated score of the whole scale; a cutoff point of correlation, usually .71, is used to discard items. When only those items with high intercorrelations with the total score remain, those items constitute the measurement instrument. Thus the instrument measures the critical attribute and nothing else.

Factor Analysis   Factor analysis is a correlation technique, useful when the scale is intended to be multidimensional. As in the differential, or Thurstone, scale, items are grouped together according to similarity by correlating each item to each other item. This item-to-item correlation reveals clusters of items that are related to each other, enabling the researcher to identify subscales within the larger measurement tool. When an instrument is used to formulate subscales that are highly correlated with each other, it is appropriate to employ a factor analysis using an oblique rotation rather than an orthogonal varimax rotation (Carey & Seibert, 1993). As discussed earlier, factor analysis is also useful in establishing the construct validity of an instrument. A further discussion of factor analysis and its statistical procedures is presented later in this Chapter.

Guttman Scales   This type of cumulative scale was developed by Louis Guttman in the 1940s. Guttman scales are highly sophisticated tools that capitalize on the intercorrelation between items. To construct a Guttman scale, many items are developed that reflect increasing intensity of feeling about an attitude. The items on a Guttman scale are ordered by the degree of intensity. The purpose is to form a hierarchical structure such that, when a respondent endorses the most extreme statement in the hierarchy, all less extreme statements are endorsed as well. This then permits the prediction of responses.

An example of a Guttman scale is the Index of Activities of Daily Living, developed by Katz, Ford, Moskowitz, Jackson, and Jaffe (1963) and used to classify nursing home residents and severely ill persons. The scale measures functional ability and disability based on the capacity to use six self-care skills: feeding, bathing, dressing, transfer ability (the ability to move from bed to a chair), toileting, and continence. In this scale, the hierarchy is based on the complexity of each self-care skill, and the levels of dependency are scored on six levels, from "A" for complete independence, to "G" for total dependence on assistance. If a patient is scored "G" on feeding, for example, he or she must be fed by an assistant. This highest level of dependency reflects the need for assistance in all functional areas. The Guttman scale is used to classify the dependency needs of patients, but it also can be used to predict physical status and expected progress.

MEASUREMENT OF HEALTH STATUS: AN EXAMPLE

An instrument to measure health status is needed at both the population and the individual level. At the population, or macro, level, the epidemiologist could use such an instrument with individuals in a population sample and take an average score to estimate the general well-being of the population. On the micro, or individual, level, a physician could use the instrument in patient care. Previous work has shown the usefulness of the General Well-Being (GWB) index as a reliable and valid instrument for such a purpose. Here, the primary purpose of this example is to show its reliability and validity from a sample of 38 students. Other indicators for measuring personal and community health are given in Appendix A.

Data and Methods

The GWB index is a self-administered test consisting of 18 questions in the form of a Likert scale (Wan & Livieratos, 1978) (Table 3.4). Each respondent is asked to answer each question on the basis of how he or she has been feeling in the past month. The numerical values of all 18 questions (items) then are summed to give a total score for general well-being. Each item is given a score based on a scale; for the first 14 items, possible scores range from 1 to 6, while items 15–18 are scored from 1 to 10. A low score indicates positive responses for some items and negative responses for others. The same is true of higher scores. An advantage of this type of scoring, then, is that it eliminates possible patterning of responses, thus improving the quality of the instrument.

The 38 students given the test comprised 20 men and 18 women. The education level throughout the group was relatively uniform.

Reliability

This study uses three reliability tests: test–retest reliability, item-to-scale correlation, and the overall reliability coefficient.

Test–Retest Reliability   The GWB test was given to the group twice, with a 1-week interval between tests. Responses from the second test were correlated with those of the first as a measure of the instrument's stability. This technique is limited in that respondents may remember their original answers and repeat them. Test–retest reliability coefficients were calculated for the total group and then separately for men and women (see Table 3.5).

Item-to-Scale Correlation   Item-to-scale correlation measures the individual reliability of each item in a scale, and points out those items or questions in the test that do not pertain to the total scale. In item-to-scale correlation, each item score is correlated against the score of the total scale. These correlation coefficients then may be examined to determine the reliability of each item as well as the internal consistency of the scale (see Table 3.6).

Overall Reliability Coefficient   Another measure of internal consistency of a scale is the overall reliability coefficient (r_{kk}). It is computed as follows:

$$r_{kk} = \frac{k\,\overline{r_{ij}}}{[1 + (k - 1)\,\overline{r_{ij}}]}$$

where k = number of items in the scale (18) and r_{ij} = average intercorrelations of all items. As the reliability coefficient increases toward 1.0, the internal consistency of the scale improves. Results of this measure appear below.

Validity

Reliability is not by itself a sufficient condition for validity. Further tests are therefore necessary to verify the validity of the GWB index (i.e., to show whether it truly measures what it is intended to measure).

Content Validity   Two types of content validity are face validity and consensual validity, each of which is simply a statement of opinion. An instrument is said to have face validity if it makes sense in terms of the issue it is intended to measure. Face validity is attributed by an individual's opinion (e.g., by the reader or the investigator). An instrument is said to have consen-

Table 3.4.   General well-being index

Circle the letter of the response that seems closest to how your life has been generally during the past month.

1. How have you been feeling in general?
   a. In excellent spirits
   b. In very good spirits
   c. In good spirits mostly
   d I have been up and down in spirits a lot
   e. In low spirits mostly
   f. In very low spirits

2. Have you been bothered by nervousness or your "nerves"?
   a. Extremely so—to the point where I could not work or take care of things
   b. Very much so
   c. Quite a bit
   d. Some—enough to bother me
   e. A little
   f. Not at all

3. Have you been in firm control of your behavior, thoughts, emotions, or feelings?
   a. Yes, definitely so
   b. Yes, for the most part
   c. Generally so
   d. Not too well
   e. No, and I am somewhat disturbed
   f. No, and I am very disturbed

4. Have you felt so sad, discouraged, or hopeless, or had so many problems that you wondered if anything was worthwhile?
   a. Extremely so—to the point that I have just about given up
   b. Very much so
   c. Quite a bit
   d. Some—enough to bother me
   e. A little bit
   f. Not at all

5. Have you been under or felt you were under any strain, stress, or pressure?
   a. Yes—almost more than I could bear or stand
   b. Yes—quite a bit of pressure
   c. Yes—some, more than usual
   d. Yes—some, but about usual
   e. Yes—a little
   f. Not at all

6. How happy, satisfied, or pleased have you been with your personal life?
   a. Extremely happy—could not have been more satisfied or pleased
   b. Very happy
   c. Fairly happy
   d. Satisfied—pleased
   e. Somewhat dissatisfied
   f. Very dissatisfied

7. Have you had any reason to wonder if you were losing your mind, or losing control over the way you act, talk, think, or feel, or of your memory?
   a. Not at all
   b. Only a little
   c. Some—but not enough to be concerned or worried about
   d. Some and I have been a little concerned
   e. Some and I am quite concerned
   f. Yes, very much so and I am very concerned

(continued)

Table 3.4.   (*continued*)

---

8. Have you been envious, worried, or upset?

    a. Extremely so—to the point of being sick or almost sick
    b. Very much so
    c. Quite a bit
    d. Some—enough to bother me
    e. A little bit
    f. Not at all

9. Have you been waking up fresh and rested?

    a. Every day
    b. Most every day
    c. Fairly often
    d. Less than half the time
    e. Rarely
    f. None of the time

10. Have you been bothered by any illness, bodily disorder, pains, or fears about your health?

    a. All the time
    b. Most of the time
    c. A good bit of the time
    d. Some of the time
    e. A little of the time
    f. None of the time

11. Has your daily life been full of things that were interesting to you?

    a. All the time
    b. Most of the time
    c. A good bit of the time
    d. Some of the time
    e. A little of the time
    f. None of the time

12. Have you felt downhearted and blue?

    a. All of the time
    b. Most of the time
    c. A good bit of the time
    d. Some of the time
    e. A little of the time
    f. None of the time

13. Have you been feeling emotionally stable and sure of yourself?

    a. All of the time
    b. Most of the time
    c. A good bit of the time
    d. Some of the time
    e. A little of the time
    f. None of the time

14. Have you felt tired, worn out, used up, or exhausted?

    a. All of the time
    b. Most of the time
    c. A good bit of the time
    d. Some of the time
    e. A little of the time
    f. None of the time

(*continued*)

Table 3.4. *(continued)*

For each of the four scales below, note that the words of each end of the 0–10 scale describe opposite feelings. Circle any number along the bar that seems closest to how you have felt generally during the past month.

15. How concerned or worried about your health have you been?

Not concerned at all _____ Very concerned

0 1 2 3 4 5 6 7 8 9 10

16. How relaxed or tense have you been?

Very relaxed _____ Very tense

0 1 2 3 4 5 6 7 8 9 10

17. How much energy, pep, vitality have you felt?

Lifeless _____ Dynamic

0 1 2 3 4 5 6 7 8 9 10

18. How depressed or cheerful have you been?

Very depressed _____ Very cheerful

0 1 2 3 4 5 6 7 8 9 10

sual validity if a panel of experts in the subject agree on the instrument's face validity. The face validity of the GWB index developed by The National Center for Health Statistics is obvious, and no panel was needed.

Construct Validity Factor analysis was applied to the data to determine the construct validity. Factor analysis is a technique that is useful for a scale that is clearly or intentionally multidimensional. The data obtained through factor analysis were intended to verify the multidimensional nature of the GWB index in terms of physical, psychological, and social well-being. The analysis demonstrated how well each item is associated with the underlying dimensions (factors). It is assumed that the true attributes of people cannot be measured directly, so it is necessary to pool the results of several observable variables that relate to an underlying assumption of the index.

Factor analysis began with the intercorrelation matrix from all of the questions on the GWB index, and then through mathematical operations assigned values, called *factor loadings*, to each item. Factor loadings for each item are interpreted in the same fashion as correlation coefficients (-1 to $+1$), with items having a loading close to $+1$ being indicators of the true attribute represented by that dimension (factor). Communality values for a given item represent how much of the variance in the item is accounted for by the underlying factors, while the eigenvalues divided by the number of items give the proportion of total variance accounted for by each factor (see Table 3.7).

Predictive Validity It is not possible to test the predictive validity of the GWB index without collecting data in a follow-up study to examine how well future health status is related to the results of the GWB index. That investigation would determine the predictive validity of the index.

Results

Table 3.5 contains a summary of test–retest reliability coefficients for the GWB instrument. Correlations are given for each of the items between Test 1 ($V_1 - V_{18}$) and Test 2 ($V_{19} - V_{36}$). Total scores are given for the entire group of 38 students, and then for men and women separately. For the group as a whole, all items were significantly correlated at the .05 or lower level, and all but two had p values of .0001. The two items with larger yet still significant p values were items 11 (interesting daily life: $p = .0082$) and 14 (tired, exhausted: $p = .0020$). Item 11 (interesting

Table 3.5.   Test–retest reliability coefficients of the GBW scale items by gender

Variable	GWB item	Total ($n=38$)	Males ($n=20$)	Females ($n=18$)
V1 & V19	General feeling	0.822	0.721	0.868
V2 & V20	Nervousness	0.744	0.514	0.904
V3 & V21	Control of emotions	0.692	0.473	0.823
V4 & V22	Sad, discouraged	0.982	0.061	0.915
V5 & V23	Stress level	0.791	0.738	0.829
V6 & V24	Satisfied with life	0.705	0.578	0.768
V7 & V25	Afraid of losing mind	0.817	0.840	0.802
V8 & V26	Anxious, worried	0.640	0.429	0.734
V9 & V27	Wake up rested	0.624	0.582	0.725
V10 & V28	Bothered by bodily disorders	0.723	0.755	0.693
V11 & V29	Interesting daily life	0.423	0.517	0.332
V12 & V30	Downhearted, blue	0.765	0.742	0.769
V13 & V31	Emotionally stable	0.581	0.242	0.725
V14 & V32	Tired, exhausted	0.486	0.217	0.600
V15 & V33	Concerned or worried for health	0.694	0.751	0.623
V16 & V34	Level of tension or relaxation	0.811	0.579	0.925
V17 & V35	Energy level	0.786	0.681	0.860
V18 & V36	Depressed or cheerful	0.833	0.636	0.923
GWB Test 1 vs. Test 2: Total Score		0.888	0.762	0.934

Note: Boldfaced figures are significant at the .05 level or lower.

Table 3.6.   Item–score total coefficients for GWB items by gender and time

Variable	Test 1			Test 2		
	Total	Males	Females	Total	Males	Females
V1 & V19	0.794	0.752	0.826	0.802	0.702	0.862
V2 & V20	0.658	0.674	0.699	0.525	0.431	0.622
V3 & V21	0.672	0.502	0.742	0.725	0.681	0.745
V4 & V22	0.656	0.523	0.700	0.575	0.463	0.626
V5 & V23	0.715	0.654	0.732	0.867	0.745	0.927
V6 & V24	0.585	0.483	0.620	0.778	0.596	0.841
V7 & V25	0.594	0.202	0.723	0.456	0.141	0.532
V8 & V26	0.569	0.385	0.646	0.786	0.701	0.818
V9 & V27	0.546	0.441	0.690	0.475	0.480	0.495
V10 & V28	0.480	0.562	0.527	0.340	0.473	0.310
V11 & V29	0.436	0.264	0.518	0.548	0.558	0.580
V12 & V30	0.776	0.655	0.816	0.843	0.698	0.914
V13 & V31	0.674	0.389	0.810	0.806	0.718	0.832
V14 & V32	0.660	0.373	0.758	0.722	0.619	0.778
V15 & V33	0.527	0.611	0.532	0.495	0.269	0.763
V16 & V34	0.794	0.731	0.817	0.812	0.729	0.839
V17 & V35	0.589	0.542	0.619	0.769	0.674	0.790
V18 & V36	0.855	0.774	0.890	0.870	0.707	0.935

Note: Boldfaced figures are significant at the .05 level or lower.

Table 3.7.   Factor analysis of 18 GWB items ($n = 38$)

Variable item	GWB item	Factor 1	Factor 2	Factor 3	Communality
V1	General feeling	0.57875	0.61952	−0.02101	0.71918
V 2	Nervousness	0.23489	0.64317	0.29359	0.55505
V3	Control of emotions	0.72657	0.21349	0.26079	0.64150
V4	Sad, discouraged	0.50051	0.45501	0.24736	0.51873
V5	Stress level	0.14924	0.83572	0.14743	0.74243
V6	Satisfied with life	0.49227	0.50624	−0.13191	0.51601
V7	Afraid of losing mind	0.64141	0.09474	0.48984	0.66033
V8	Anxious, worried	−0.12433	0.82730	0.26881	0.77213
V9	Wake up rested	0.71457	0.14393	−0.01242	0.53148
V10	Bothered by bodily disorders	0.02709	0.20668	0.81917	0.71450
V11	Interesting daily life	0.65839	−0.07443	0.19428	0.47677
V12	Downhearted, blue	0.70088	0.45954	−0.07349	0.70788
V13	Emotionally stable	0.52969	0.50974	0.04808	0.54272
V14	Tired, exhausted	0.54942	0.18514	0.45356	0.54185
V15	Concerned or worried for health	0.06380	0.18688	0.84062	0.74564
V16	Level of tension or relaxation	0.26547	0.75608	0.27935	0.72017
V17	Energy level	0.67947	0.21202	−0.11838	0.52065
V18	Depressed or cheerful	0.60428	0.67581	0.00794	0.82194
Variance explained by each factor					Total (Σ) or (Sum)
Total eigenvalue		4.779856	4.380701	2.288285	11.448842
% Total variance accounted for by each factor		27	24	13	
% Common variance explained		42	38	20	

Note: An underscore denotes a strong relation between an item and a common factor.

daily life) was unreliable for the female group, and four items were unreliable for the male group: 4 (sad, discouraged, hopeless), 8 (anxious, worried), 13 (emotionally stable), and 14 (tired, exhausted). The reliability coefficients for total scores were significant and verify the overall stability of the GWB index.

Table 3.6 contains a summary of the item–score total coefficients for both test times and for the total group, men, and women. All the GWB Test 1 items are grouped together at a significance level lower than .05, to verify the internal consistency of the index. All the GWB Test 1 items are statistically significant for females, but the following six items fail to conform to the construct for the male group: 7, 8, 9, 11, 13, and 14. The second test for GWB fares better in the male group, with only three items not significant (2, 7, and 15); item 10 is not significant in Test 2 for the female group or for the total group. An overall reliability coefficient was calculated for the GWB index, using the first test's information. The average intercorrelation of all items was $r_{ij} = .3881$, and the overall reliability coefficient was $r_{kk} = .9194$; that further verifies the internal consistency of the index.

In addition, alpha values for the two test times were $\alpha_1 = .8894$ at time 1, and $\alpha_2 = .9194$ at time 2, indicating a higher level of internal consistency. Because internal consistency has been verified through three different methods and stability through the test–retest method, we can say that GWB is, without doubt, a reasonably reliable instrument.

Table 3.7 contains the results of the factor analysis. One can see that factors 1 (Life Satisfaction and Emotional Stability) and 2 (Depressive Mood) are heavily loaded, while factor 3 (Health Concern) is weaker yet significant. The three factors together account for 64% of the total variance in the GWB index. It therefore can be said that these three factors make up the primary constructs of the health index.

Factor analysis should verify construct validity as being discriminant. That is, it should demonstrate how an item is able to discriminate between underlying dimensions and load heavily on the one to which it is most related. In this example, factor analysis did verify construct validity, but not as being discriminant. In Table 3.7, the underlined factor loadings are those that are deemed significant. Eight of the 18 items are loaded heavily in more than one factor. For example, item 6 is the question "How happy, satisfied, or pleased have you been with your personal life?" It is apparent that this would relate to factor 1 (Life Satisfaction and Emotional Stability), yet it is almost equally loaded in two dimensions. The items pertaining to "general feeling," "downhearted and blue," "emotionally stable," and "depressed or cheerful" also are loaded heavily. Only one of the three factors is clearly defined—factor 3, which is called Health Concern—even though only two items load heavily in it. The 10 items with significant loadings in only one dimension are listed in Table 3.8 along with their corresponding factors.

Discussion

In relation to the reliability of the GWB index, the study found that, overall, the responses of the 38 students were reliable; however, as a group, the women's responses were more reliable in both stability and internal consistency than those of the men, or of the group as a whole. The weakest part of the reliability testing was the men's performance item–score total for the first test, where six items failed to correlate with the total.

Some of the failure of correlation on test–retest for the men may be due to the conditions under which the tests were given. The first GWB test was given to a class of graduate students in their first week of classes; therefore, many of the respondents may have been anxious or lacking in self-confidence, and others overconfident. Test 2 was administered after 1 week of classes and assignments. Those who were anxious and unsure may have found the classes less demanding than anticipated, while those who were overconfident may have lost their confidence. These changes in their psychological well-being obviously would affect their responses to the GWB test.

The methods for improving the reliability of the GWB index can be addressed more effectively after it has been tested under more favorable conditions. Even though there is room for

Table 3.8.   Items with significant loadings in only one dimension

Item	Dimension
Factor 1	
Firm control of emotions	Life satisfaction
Wake up fresh, rested	Health concern
Interesting daily life	Life satisfaction
Energy level	Health concern
Factor 2	
Nervousness	Depressive mood
Stress level	Depressive mood
Anxious, worried	Depressive mood
Relaxed	Health concern
Factor 3	
Bothered by bodily disorders	Health concern
Health concern, worried	Health concern

improving the reliability of the GWB, however, the results of these tests are acceptable to verify the overall reliability of the GWB instrument.

Differences in factor loadings, as seen in Table 3.8, are likely to be due to the unreliability of the male group; if the factor analysis were applied to the female group only, it might discriminate more effectively.

Overall, this example illustrates the reliability and validity of the GWB index as a measure of general health status.

CONCLUSION

This chapter has discussed the issues in measurement and quantification of variables in the area of health services research. Although the variables that would concern health services managers and administrators may appear straightforward, many represent multidimensional, intricate conglomerations of attributes, characteristics, and systems. Concepts such as health status (Huber, 1994; Patrick & Erickson, 1993; Ware, 1993), severity of illness (Horn & Hopkins, 1994), quality of life (Bungay & Ware, 1993), patient satisfaction (Ho, Stegall, & Wan, 1994), and provider productivity (Lanthrop, 1993; Moskowitz, 1994) require painstaking and meticulous definition, measurement, and quantification. Careful attention to measurement and quantification in health services research can significantly affect the success of a management study and the usefulness of its results.

REFERENCES

Bungay, K.M., & Ware, J.E. (1993). *Measuring and monitoring health related quality of life: Current concepts.* Kalamazoo, MI: The Upjohn Company.

Carey, R.G., & Seibert, J.H. (1993). A patient system to measure quality improvement: Questionnaire reliability and validity. *Medical Care, 31,* 834–845.

Ho, P.S., Stegall, M.B.H., & Wan, T.T.H. (1994). Modeling two dimensions of patient satisfaction-A panel study. *Health Service Management Research, 6*(4), 1–11.

Ho, P.S., Stegall, M.B.H., & Wan, T.T.H. (1994). Modeling two dimensions of patient satisfaction: A panel study. *Health Service Management Research, 6*(4), 1–11.

Horn, S.D., & Hopkins, D.S.P. (1994). *Clinical practice improvement: A new technology in developing cost effective quality health care.* New York: Faulkner and Gray.

Huber, M. (1994). *Measuring medicine: An introduction to health status assessment and a framework for application.* New York: Faulkner and Gray.

Kaluzny, A.D., & Veney, J.E. (1980). *Health services organizations: A guide to research and assessment.* Berkeley, CA: McCutchen Publishing Corp.

Katz, S., Ford, A.B., Moskowitz, R.W., Jackson, B.A., & Jaffe, M.W. (1963). Studies of illness in the aged: The index of ADL: A standardized measure of biological and psycho-social function. *Journal of the American Medical Association, 185,* 914–919.

Lanthrop, J.P. (1993). *Restructuring health care.* San Francisco: Jossey-Bass.

Moskowitz, D.B. (1994). *Ranking hospitals and physicians: The use and misuse of performance data.* New York: Faulkner and Gray.

Nunnally, J.C. (1978). *Psychometric theory.* New York: McGraw-Hill.

Patrick, D.L., & Erickson, P. (1993). *Health status and health policy: Allocating resources to health care.* New York: Oxford University Press.

Polit, D.F., & Hungler, B.P. (1987). *Nursing research: Principles and methods* (3rd ed.). Philadelphia: J.B. Lippincott.

Wan, T.T.H., & Livieratos, B. (1978). Investigating a general index of subjective well-being. *Milbank Memorial Fund Quarterly, 5-6,* 531–556.

Ware, J.E. (1993). *SF-36 health survey: Manual and interpretation guide.* Boston: The New England Medical Center Health Institute.

4

Cross-Sectional
Study Design and Analysis

*The most merciful thing in the world, I think, is the
inability of the human mind to correlate all its contents.*
Howard P. Lovecraft, *The Call of Cthulhu* (1928)

DEFINITIONS

To obtain data for managerial studies, investigators can choose from among a variety of study
designs; most can be classified as either time-span study designs or cross-sectional study designs. A *time-span study* makes a longitudinal investigation. For example, an analysis of factors
that affect the demand for hospital care can use data collected over several years either retrospectively or prospectively, or in both ways.

A study of a particular time, analyzing a sample selected to be a representative cross section of the population in terms of relevant variables (i.e., age, gender, race, ethnic group, education, occupation, etc.), is called a *cross-sectional study* design. Cross-sectional studies are
too limited to allow causal inferences, because the sequences of the variables over time are not
known. However, several statistical methods can provide precise information about the association between the variables when other variables are taken into account simultaneously. Health
care researchers often use cross-sectional studies, because they cost much less than time-span
studies.

SURVEY METHODS AND THEIR
APPLICATIONS TO HEALTH CARE RESEARCH

Health surveys are an important way to obtain valid and reliable information about health status,
health care use, and medical costs. Refinements of survey methodology have made it possible to
estimate health-related events from a survey of a representative sample with increasing accuracy. Sample surveys serve several purposes: 1) identifying health care needs, 2) identifying
health service utilization patterns, 3) measuring medical care costs, 4) assessing health care programs, and 5) developing targeted intervention programs.

Survey methods rely heavily on self-reported information from interviews or questionnaires. An interviewer elicits information or responses from the interviewee directly in a face-to-
face interview or by telephone. The *interview* is an appropriate technique for obtaining or prob-
ing the sentiments and perceptions that may underlie an expressed opinion (Kinsey, Pomeroy, &
Martin, 1948; Selltiz, Wrightsman, & Cook, 1976). A *questionnaire*, in contrast, gathers written

responses to prearranged and precoded questions. Questionnaires can be administered to a large sample with a minimum of explanation; sometimes the questionnaire simply can be mailed to the sampled respondents. Thus, the questionnaire survey is relatively inexpensive. It also maintains the respondent's anonymity, can reach a large sample of the population, and can obtain data on attitudes. Although the cost of an interview survey will be higher than that of a questionnaire survey, the interview is a more flexible and powerful technique, enabling one to ask more in-depth, complex questions than with a mailed questionnaire. A detailed comparison of the two survey methods can be found in Table 4.1.

In the United States, several national health surveys are conducted routinely by the National Center for Health Statistics and the Agency for Health Care Policy and Research under Congressional mandates to study illness and health care in the nation (Gable, 1990). Since 1956, the National Health Survey has become the umbrella title of several surveys: the Health Interview Survey (HIS), the Health and Nutrition Examination Survey (HANES), the National Ambulatory Medical Care Survey, the Hospital Discharge Survey, the Survey of Institutionalized Population, and the National Medical Care Utilization and Expenditure Survey. Detailed design information and descriptions of these surveys can be found in the documents listed in Table 4.2.

Table 4.1. Advantages of various survey methods

	Survey methods				
Advantages	Mailed	Mass-administered questionnaires	Face-to-face interviews	Self-administered questionnaires in face-to-face contexts	Telephone interviews
Low cost	3	2	1	1	2
Speed	1	3	1	1	3
Anonymity	3	2	1	2	1
Lack of pressure on respondent for an immediate response	3	2	1	2	1
Likelihood of obtaining a good sample from the population	1[a]	1	3	3	2[b]
Avoidance of interviewer bias	3	2	1	2	1
Lack of dependence on motivation and ability of respondents to read questionnaires and write responses	1	2	3	2	3
Likelihood of establishing rapport with respondent	1	2	3	2	2
Ability to ask complex questions at length and in depth	1	2	3	2	2
Ability to get full, detailed answers through clarification and probing	1	1	3	1	2
Ability to use visual aids	1	3	3	3	1

Note: Scale: 3 = relatively good, 2 = intermediate, 1 = relatively poor.

[a]Unless a relatively high response rate can be obtained.

[b]Unless no-phone and unlisted-phone households are dealt with.

RELATIONSHIPS BETWEEN VARIABLES

In analyzing cross-sectional data, the investigator should examine the association between multiple variables. The interrelations among these variables can be expressed by three approaches: the symmetrical, reciprocal, and asymmetrical relationship.

Symmetrical Relationship

A symmetrical relationship exists when neither variable is caused by the other. For example, X_1 (hospital age) and X_2 (hospital bed size) are structural variables that are symmetrically related to each other. A symmetrical relationship exists when:

Two variables are viewed as alternative indicators of the same concept (e.g., both palmar perspiration [X1] and heart pounding [X2] indicate anxiety).

Two variables are *effects of a common cause* (e.g., poor physical health can cause both frequent hospitalization and frequent physician visits).

Variables are *parts of a common system* or complex phenomenon (e.g., hospital performance can be measured by quality of care, access, and efficiency).

There is a *functional interdependence* between variables (e.g., the heart and lungs are two interdependent organ systems).

Reciprocal Relationship (Feedback or Nonrecursive Relationship)

This is a circular relationship between variables. For instance, an organization's structure and its performance may have a reciprocal relationship, where the physical layout of a hospital affects the quality of care, which increases hospital use and thus creates demand for a larger structure.

Table 4.2.   Sources for descriptions of the National Health Interview Survey components

Survey component	Source of description
Health Interview Survey	Health Interview Survey Procedure, 1957–1974. *Vital and Health Statistics, Series 1: Programs and Collection Procedures,* No. 11 (1975).[a]
	Current estimates: National Health Interview Survey, 1989. *Vital and Health Statistics, Series 10: Data from the National Health Survey,* No. 176 (1990).[a]
National Ambulatory Medical Care Survey	National Ambulatory Medical Care Survey: Background and Methodology, United States, 1972. *Vital and Health Statistics, Series 2: Data Evaluation and Methods Research,* No. 61 (1974).[a]
National Medical Care Expenditure Survey	National Center for Health Services Research. (1981). NMCES Estimation and Sampling Variances in the Household Survey. Hyattsville, MD: Author.
National Nursing Home Survey	The National Nursing Home Survey: 1985 Summary for the United States. *Vital and Health Statistics, Series 13: Data from the National Health Survey,* No. 97 (1989).[a]
National Hospital Discharge Survey	The National Hospital Discharge Survey: Annual Summary, 1987. *Vital and Health Statistics, Series 13: Data from the National Health Survey,* No. 99 (1989).[a]
National Health and Nutrition Examination Survey	Plan and Operations of the Second National Health and Nutrition Examination Survey, 1976–1980. *Vital and Health Statistics, Series 1: Programs and Collection Procedures,* No. 15 (1981).[a]

[a]Document is available in library periodical or government documents section, or from the Superintendent of Documents, U.S. Government Printing Office, Washington, DC 20402.

Asymmetrical Relationship

In an asymmetrical relationship, the set of causal relationships between variables operates in one direction over time. For example, contextual variables affect the design of an organization, and design in turn affects performance.

TESTING A RELATIONSHIP BY THE USE OF A TEST VARIABLE

To test the relationship between the independent and dependent variables, the researcher introduces a third variable: the test, or control, variable. The test variable can take one of the following roles:

Extraneous variable or control variable: a third variable controlled for (i.e., held constant) to see whether it affects the relationship between two other variables. When this control variable (X_2) is associated with both the dependent variable (Y) and a primary independent variable (X_1), the relationship between Y and X_1 is said to be confounded.

Intervening variable: a third variable (Z) that intervenes between an independent variable (X) and a dependent variable (Y), so that X affects Y only (through) Z:

$$X \longrightarrow Z \longrightarrow Y$$

Antecedent variable: a third variable (Z) that precedes the independent variable (X) and the dependent variable (Y):

$$Z \longrightarrow X \longrightarrow Y$$

In this case, all three variables are related; however, when X is controlled, the relationship between Z and Y disappears, and when the antecedent variable (Z) is controlled, the relationship between X and Y remains.

Suppressor Variable

The absence or presence of a relationship between X and Y may appear real, whereas in fact the relationship may be due to the intrusion of a variable (Z). To discover whether the relationship between X and Y is real, it is necessary to control the suspected variable (Z). For example, suppose the correlation between X and Y is .78 and that, when the third variable (Z) is introduced, the correlation between X and Y becomes weaker (.01). This shows that the Z variable is a suppressor variable of the real relationship between X and Y.

Distorter Variable

A distorter variable is a third variable that converts the observed relationship between two variables so that it diverges from the real one. If r_{XY} is .45 and, when Z is introduced as a control variable, the relationship changes to a negative one ($r_{XY} = -.50$), then Z is a distorter variable of the real relationship between X and Y. For example, patient satisfaction with acute care hospitals is found to be related positively to the quality of food served. However, when this relationship is examined further by hospital ownership status, we observe a startling result: an inverse relationship between patient satisfaction and the quality of food services. In the public hospitals, those who report high satisfaction with food services are less likely to favor the quality of health care, and the same is true for the patients from private hospitals. Thus, the use of hospital ownership as a control variable distorts the real relationship between patient satisfaction and quality of food services; the reason for this distortion may not be apparent, and the distortion may lead to misinterpretation of results.

DESCRIBING RELATIONSHIPS AMONG MULTIVARIATES (MULTIPLE VARIABLES)

Partial Correlation Coefficient

A partial correlation coefficient provides a single measure of the association between two variables, while adjusting for the effects of one or more additional variables. In other words, partial correlation removes the effects of a control variable from the relationship between the independent and dependent variables. In this way, a researcher can detect any spurious relationship between two variables. A *spurious relationship* is one in which, for example, X's correlation with Y is solely the result of X varying along with some other variable, Z, which is indeed the true explanatory variable of Y. For example, hospital size (X) is found to be associated with efficiency level (Y): $r_{xy} = .78$. If we introduce a control variable, the level of specialization of the hospital (Z), we find the correlation between X and Y (r_{xy}) diminishes to a very small correlation or zero. This implies that there is a spurious relationship between X and Y when Z is controlled.

The computational formula for a partial correlation coefficient for variables X and Y when Z is a control variable is:

$$r_{XY.Z} = \frac{r_{XY} - (r_{XZ})(r_{YZ})}{\sqrt{1 - r_{XZ}^2}\sqrt{1 - r_{YZ}^2}}$$

Figure 4.1 contains correlation coefficients of four variables.

Contingency Relationship

In a contingency relationship, the relationship between two variables is contingent on a third variable. In the example above, the relationship between hospital size (X) and efficiency (Y) is contingent on specialization (Z).

STATISTICAL TEST OF SIGNIFICANCE OF ONE OR MORE FACTORS ON A DEPENDENT VARIABLE

Now that we have an idea of the ways in which independent variables can affect the dependent variable, we need to know how to test whether such a relationship is statistically significant. There are three ways to do that. Each serves a different purpose. Detailed statistical procedures may be found in the texts by Lay and Broyles (1980), Hanke and Reitsch (1991), Siegel (1988), and Selvin (1991).

Testing a Hypothesis on One Parameter in a Single Population

Z Value (When the Variance Is Known)

Problem   Examine whether or not there is a mean increase or decrease in productivity by a total of 25 employees in a multihospital system. The average number of tasks completed by

Variable	X	Y	Z	W
Bed size (X)	1.00	0.78	0.90	0.50
Efficiency level (Y)		1.00	0.65	−.30
Specialization (Z)			1.00	0.20
% Medicaid patients (W)				1.00

Figure 4.1.   A hypothetical example of correlations.

these employees is 15 ($\bar{x}$), with a variance of 4 tasks (σ^2). Because the variance is known, the Z distribution is the appropriate test statistic.

Solution $H_0: \mu = 0$

$\qquad$ $H_a: \mu \neq 0$

If we set α at .05, $Z_{\alpha/2}$ is 1.96. Then

$$Z_0 = \frac{\bar{x} - \mu}{\sqrt{\dfrac{\sigma^2}{n}}} = \frac{15 - 0}{\dfrac{2}{\sqrt{25}}} = 37.5$$

Because $Z_0 > Z_{\alpha/2}$, we find that H_0 is rejected, and conclude there is a mean change in (increase or decrease) productivity at the $\alpha = .05$ level.

T Test (When the Variance Is Unknown)

Problem   Evaluate a new management program in a random sample of 25 hospitals selected from the VHA-affiliated hospitals in Virginia. Each hospital has kept a record of the turnover resulting from the new program. It is expected that the mean percentage (probability) of turnover will be 60%. In the sample you find the mean percentage to be 52% and the standard deviation to be 12%. Are there grounds for concluding that, in this sample, the level of turnover of employees is below the standard expected? The variance is unknown; thus the t distribution is the appropriate test statistic.

Solution $H_0: \mu = 60\%$

$\qquad$ $H_a: \mu \neq 60\%$

If $\bar{x} = 52, s = 12\%, n = 25$ ($df = n - 1 = 24$), and we set $\alpha = .05$, then

$$t = \frac{\bar{x} - \mu}{\dfrac{s}{\sqrt{n}}} = \frac{52 - 60}{\dfrac{12}{\sqrt{25}}} = 3.33$$

Because the t value for a two-tailed test at the .05 level is 2.064, we reject H_0 and conclude that the actual level of turnover in these hospitals is below the standard expected.

Multiple Sample Tests: Difference of Means and Proportions

T Test (Variances Unknown but Assumed Equal)

Problem   Compare teaching and nonteaching hospitals in terms of the efficiency of patient care. The average occupancy rate (percentage) is used as the indicator of efficiency; the comparison is based on the information presented in Table 4.3. Assuming the hospitals are selected randomly, can you conclude that there is a significant difference in hospital efficiency as shown by occupancy rate?

Solution $H_0: \mu_1 = \mu_2$

$\qquad$ $H_a: \mu_1 \neq \mu_2$

Table 4.3.   Comparison of occupancy rate between teaching and nonteaching hospitals

	Teaching hospitals	Nonteaching hospitals
Sample	$n_1 = 33$	$n_2 = 19$
Average occupancy rate	$\bar{x}_1 = 57\%$	$\bar{x}_2 = 52\%$
Standard deviation	$s_1 = 11\%$	$s_2 = 14\%$

If we set $\alpha = .05$ ($t_{\alpha/2} = 2.0$) and $df = [(n_1 + n_2) - 2] = 50$, then

$$t_0 = \frac{\bar{x}_1 - \bar{x}_2}{\sqrt{\dfrac{(n_1 - 1)s_1^2 + (n_2 - 1)s_2^2}{n_1 + n_2 - 2}} \sqrt{\dfrac{n_1 + n_2}{n_1 n_2}}} = \frac{57 - 52}{3.50} = 1.43$$

Because t_0 is smaller than $t_{\alpha/2}$, we fail to reject H_0 and conclude that there is no statistically significant difference in the efficiency level (percentage of occupancy) between teaching and non-teaching hospitals.

T Test (for Variances Unknown and Assumed Unequal) To test the difference between two means when variances are unknown and assumed unequal, a t test may be used with the population standard deviation estimated as:

$$t = \frac{\bar{x}_1 - \bar{x}_2}{\hat{\sigma}\bar{x}_1 - \bar{x}_2}$$

The degrees of freedom are also estimated:

$$\hat{\sigma}\bar{x}_1 - \bar{x}_2 = \sqrt{\frac{s_1^2 + s_2^2}{(n_1 - 1)(n_2 - 1)}}$$

Testing the Significance of the Difference Between Two Proportions (Large Sample) An important problem that occurs regularly in statistical analysis is to find out whether two populations differ with respect to a certain attribute. For example, we may be interested in whether the proportion of the patients having surgery performed in one hospital is significantly different from the proportion of the patients having surgery in another hospital.

In testing the difference between two proportions, the null hypothesis is $H_0: P_1 = P_2$, and the alternative hypothesis is $H_a: P_1 \neq P_2$.

The appropriate test statistic is the Z distribution, provided that n_1 and n_2 are both sufficiently large:

$$Z_0 = \frac{P_1 - P_2}{\text{Standard error}}, \text{ if } Q_1 = 1 - P_1 \text{ and } Q_2 = 1 - P_2$$

The standard error of the difference between two proportions is represented by the following formula:

$$\sqrt{\frac{P_1 Q_1}{n_1} + \frac{P_2 Q_2}{n_2}} \text{ or } \sqrt{(P^*)(1 - P^*)\left(\frac{1}{n_1} + \frac{1}{n_2}\right)}$$

Because the population proportions are unknown to us, we take the weighted mean of the two sample proportions as the estimate of the population proportion. We refer to P^* as the *pooled estimate of the population proportion*:

$$P^* = \frac{n_1 P_1 + n_2 P_2}{n_1 + n_2}$$

We can now substitute P^* into the Z statistic:

$$Z_0 = \frac{P_1 - P_2}{\sqrt{(P^*)(1 - P^*)\left(\dfrac{1}{n_1} + \dfrac{1}{n_2}\right)}}$$

Problem   A study of two types of direct patient care by nurses, team care and primary care, has reported the information shown in Table in 4.4 about the proportion of direct care given by nurses under each approach. Is this 13% difference in the amount of direct patient care by nurses statistically significant? What can one conclude from this analysis?

Solution $H_0: P_1 = P_2$ (There is no difference between the amounts of direct patient care given by the two different nursing care approaches.)

$H_a: P_1 \neq P_2$ (There is a difference between the amounts of direct patient care given by the two different nursing care approaches.)

If $\alpha = .05$, P = percentage of direct patient care given, $P_1 = .70$ (team nurse), $P_2 = .83$ (primary care nurse), $n_1 = 500$, and $n_2 = 600$, then

$$P^* = \frac{n_1 P_1 + n_2 P_2}{n_1 + n_2} = \frac{500(.70) + 600(.83)}{500 + 600} = \frac{848}{1100} = .771$$

$$Z_0 = \frac{P_1 - P_2}{\sqrt{(P^*)(1 - P^*)\left(\dfrac{1}{n_1} + \dfrac{1}{n_2}\right)}} = \frac{.70 - .83}{\sqrt{(.771)(.229)\left(\dfrac{1}{500} + \dfrac{1}{600}\right)}} = \frac{-.13}{.025} = -5.2$$

The Z value at the .05 level is 1.96 for a two-tailed test. Because $|Z_0| > Z_{\alpha/2}$, we conclude that the difference between the two nursing approaches is statistically significant.

Analysis of Variance

Analysis of variance (ANOVA) is an extension of the *t* test. Whereas a *t* test examines the difference between the means of two groups, ANOVA tests for differences among the means of *more* than two subgroups. An *F test* is the statistic that tests an ANOVA hypothesis.

One-Way Analysis of Variance   For a one-way ANOVA, it is simplest to present the data in an array of the type shown in Table 4.5. Using this notation, the total variation in a set of data (*total sum of squares*), the differences between the population sample means (*between-group sum of squares*), and the variation within the populations (*within-group sum of squares*) can be determined using the following equations.

Total sum of squares:

$$SS_T = \sum_{i=1}^{nj}\sum_{j=1}^{k}(x_{ij} - \bar{x}_{..})^2 = \sum_{i=1}^{nj}\sum_{j=1}^{k} x_{ij}^2 - \frac{\left(\sum_{i=1}^{nj}\sum_{j=1}^{k} x_{ij}\right)^2}{n}$$

Between-group (regression) sum of squares:

$$SS_R = \sum_{i=1}^{nj}\sum_{j=1}^{k}(\bar{x}_{.j} - x_{..})^2 = \frac{\left(\sum_{i=1}^{n_1} x_{i1}\right)^2}{n_1} + \frac{\left(\sum_{i=1}^{n_2} x_{i2}\right)^2}{n_2} + \cdots + \frac{\left(\sum_{i=1}^{n_k} x_{ik}\right)^2}{n_k} - \frac{\left(\sum_{i=1}^{n}\sum_{j=1}^{k} x_{ij}\right)^2}{n}$$

Table 4.4.   Comparison of proportions of direct patient care by nurses under two approaches

	Team	Primary	Difference
Proportion of direct patient care given	70%	83%	13%
Number of nurses sampled	500	600	100

Table 4.5. Data array format for one-way ANOVA

Scores	Symbolic representations of ANOVA data categories				Totals
	A_1	A_2	$\cdots$	A_k	
	x_{11}	x_{12}	$\cdots$	x_{1k}	Σx_{1j} (for $j = 1$ to k)
	x_{21}	x_{22}	$\cdots$	x_{2k}	Σx_{2j} (for $j = 1$ to k)
	.	.		.	.
	.	.		.	.
	.	.		.	.
	x_{n1}	x_{n2}	$\cdots$	x_{nk}	Σx_{nj} (for $j = 1$ to k)
Sums	Σx_{i1} (for $i = 1$ to n)	Σx_{i2} (for $i = 1$ to n)	$\cdots$	Σx_{ik} (for $i = 1$ to n)	$\Sigma \Sigma x_{ij}$ (for $i = 1$ to n; $j = 1$ to k)
Means	$\bar{x}_{.1}$	$\bar{x}_{.2}$	$\cdots$	$\bar{x}_{.k}$	$x_{..}$
Total number	n_1	n_2	$\cdots$	n_k	n

Within-group (error) sum of squares:

$$SS_E = \sum_{i=1}^{nj}\sum_{j=1}^{k}(x_{ij} - \bar{x}_{.j})^2 = \sum_{i=1}^{n_1}(x_{i1} - \bar{x}_{.1})^2 + \sum_{i=1}^{n_2}(x_{i2} - \bar{x}_{.2})^2 + \cdots + \sum_{i=1}^{n_k}(x_{ik} - \bar{x}_{.k})^2$$

Note that the total sum of squares = between-group sum of squares + within-group sum of squares:

$$SS_T = SS_R + SS_E$$

Problem Information about nurse turnover rates was collected for 8 months in three local hospitals. Can you draw any conclusions from the information presented in Table 4.6? Is there any significant difference in nurse turnover rates among the three hospitals?

Solution Hypothesis (H_0): Population means are equal ($\mu_1 = \mu_2 = \cdots = \mu_k$).

$$SS_T = \sum\sum x_{ij}^2 - \frac{\left(\sum x_{ij}\right)^2}{n} = 1453.58 - \frac{(161.0)^2}{24} = 373.54$$

Table 4.6. Nurse turnover rates in three area hospitals over the span of 8 months

Month	Hospital A	Hospital B	Hospital C	Total
1	4.3	5.1	12.5	21.9
2	2.8	6.2	3.1	12.1
3	12.3	1.8	1.6	15.7
4	16.3	9.5	6.2	32.0
5	5.9	4.1	3.8	13.8
6	7.7	3.6	7.1	18.4
7	9.1	11.2	11.4	31.7
8	10.2	3.3	1.9	15.4
Sum	68.6	44.8	47.6	161.0
Mean	8.58	5.6	5.95	6.71
Number of months	8.0	8.0	8.0	24.0

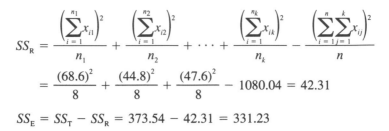

$$SS_R = \frac{\left(\sum_{i=1}^{n_1} x_{i1}\right)^2}{n_1} + \frac{\left(\sum_{i=1}^{n_2} x_{i2}\right)^2}{n_2} + \cdots + \frac{\left(\sum_{i=1}^{n_k} x_{ik}\right)^2}{n_k} - \frac{\left(\sum_{i=1}^{n}\sum_{j=1}^{k} x_{ij}\right)^2}{n}$$

$$= \frac{(68.6)^2}{8} + \frac{(44.8)^2}{8} + \frac{(47.6)^2}{8} - 1080.04 = 42.31$$

$$SS_E = SS_T - SS_R = 373.54 - 42.31 = 331.23$$

The ANOVA computations are shown in Table 4.7. Using the F value shown there, $F_{(2,21)}$, at the .05 level, is 3.47; therefore we fail to reject the null hypothesis (H_0) that the means are equal.

SAMPLING DESIGN

In the course of a managerial study, an investigator may collect information by using sampling. Study samples are obtained by applying nonprobability sampling or probability sampling procedures. In nonprobability sampling, an element of a universe or population has no known chance of being selected. Therefore, there is no assurance that the sample selected represents the population under study. In contrast, with probability sampling, each of the elements has a known probability of being selected.

Nonprobability Sampling

Nonprobability samples often are biased in the sense of being nonrepresentational of the population studied. Nonprobability is not a scientific procedure. There are two major types of nonprobability samples: quota samples and purposive samples.

    Quota sampling seeks to include sufficient cases from different subgroups or strata in the selected sample. For example, in a study of job satisfaction of nursing staff in different units, an investigator may specify the number of registered nurses (RNs) and licensed practical nurses (LPNs) in terms of the proportional distribution in each unit. Let us say that the total sample consisted of 100 nurses, of whom 80 were RNs and 20 were LPNs. Suppose we asked this sample whether they were satisfied with their work, and their responses were as shown in Table 4.8.

    The data show that one tenth of the LPNs and one half of the RNs were satisfied with their work. If we are interested in presenting the job satisfaction of nurses for each group separately, no adjustment is needed. However, if we use this sample to estimate the total percentage of nurses who were satisfied with their jobs, we find 42 percent classified in the category of "satisfied." That figure is very misleading, because the study sample oversampled RNs and undersampled LPNs. If the sample were corrected for the true distribution of RNs and LPNs in the nursing units, we would derive a different estimate of the percentage of nurses who were satisfied with their work.

    Purposive samples, a second type of nonprobability sample, are those for which a researcher deliberately handpicks the sample members. For example, a researcher interested in demonstrating the difference in quality of care between public and private hospitals might delib-

Table 4.7.   ANOVA computations for nurse turnover rates

Source	(1) Sums of squares (SS)	(2) df	(3) Mean SS (MS) (1)/(2)	F value
Total (T)	373.54	n − 1 = 23		
Between group (R)	42.31	k − 1 = 2	21.16	21.16/15.77 = 1.34
Within group (E)	331.23	n − k = 21	15.773	

Table 4.8. Nursing job satisfaction across skill levels

Job satisfaction	RNs	LPNs	Total
Satisfied	40	2	42
Not satisfied	40	18	58
Total	80	20	100

erately handpick certain teaching hospitals to identify nosocomial diseases and mortality. However, the selectivity of patients at the different hospitals could bias the study results.

Probability, or Random, Sampling

A probability sample is defined as any sample in which every unit has a chance of being selected that is different from 0 or 100%, and the chance of being selected is a known probability. In the selection of random samples, investigators need to know the sampling frame, which is a list of units in the universe.

Simple Random Sample Simple random sampling selects a sample from a universe with every unit having an equal chance of being selected. Every unit is assigned a number, and then a series of numbers is drawn from a table of random numbers.

Formulas for estimating the population mean ($\bar{x}$) and the standard error (SE) of the mean are presented below:

$$\bar{x} = \frac{\sum_{i=1}^{n} x_i}{n}$$

where x_i is the measurement on the ith individual included in the sample, n is the sample size.

$$\text{Var}\ (\bar{x}) = SE_{\bar{x}}^2 = \left(\frac{s^2}{n}\right)\left(\frac{N-n}{N-1}\right)$$

where N is the population size

$$s^2 = \frac{\sum_{i=1}^{n} x_i^2 - \frac{\left(\sum_{i=1}^{n} x_i\right)^2}{n}}{n-1}$$

and

$$\frac{N-n}{N-1}$$

is used to correct the standard error for a finite population without replacement.

Application To assess the general well-being of students, a simple random sample of 15 students was selected from a population of 31 students, using the procedures listed above. Their scores on the GBW index (see Chapter 3) are shown in Table 4.9.

The sample mean ($\bar{x}$) is computed as follows:

$$\bar{x} = \frac{\sum x_i}{n} = \frac{1{,}273}{15} = 84.9$$

Table 4.9.   General well-being scores for 15 students in a simple random sample drawn from 31 students

Observation ID number	GWB score (x_i)	$(x_i)^2$
1	67	4,489
4	68	4,624
7	85	7,225
8	73	5,329
9	100	10,000
11	99	9,801
13	68	4,624
15	67	4,489
16	102	10,404
17	77	5,929
18	94	8,836
19	94	8,836
21	97	9,409
25	97	9,409
26	85	7,225
n = 15	$\Sigma(x_i) = 1,273$	$\Sigma(x_i)^2 = 110,629$

The sample variance is computed as follows:

$$s^2 = \frac{\sum x_i^2 - \dfrac{\left(\sum x_i\right)^2}{n}}{n-1} = \frac{110,629 - 108,035}{15 - 1} = 185.27$$

$$VAR\,(\bar{x}) = \left(\frac{s^2}{n}\right)\left(\frac{N-n}{N-1}\right) = \frac{185.27}{15}\,\frac{31-15}{31-1} = 6.59$$

$$SE_{\bar{x}} = \sqrt{6.59} = 2.57$$

The sample mean can be compared to the population mean, using the t test of the hypothesis $H_0: \bar{x} = \mu$.

$$t_0 = \frac{\bar{x} - \mu}{\sqrt{\dfrac{s^2}{n}}} = \frac{84.9 - 85.4}{\sqrt{\dfrac{185.27}{15}}} = -.14$$

The t value for a two-tailed test at the .05 level of significance ($df = 14$) is 2.145. Since t_0 is smaller than $t_{\alpha/2}$, we can conclude that there is no significant difference between the sample mean and the population mean. Therefore the sample mean can be considered an unbiased estimate of the population mean, although they are not precisely equal.

Estimates of confidence intervals $\bar{x} \pm 2(SE_{\bar{x}})$:

Upper 95%: $\bar{x} + 2(SE_{\bar{x}}) = 84.9 + 2(2.57) = 90.04$
Lower 95%: $\bar{x} - 2(SE_{\bar{x}}) = 84.9 - 2(2.57) = 79.76$

Systematic Sampling   In systematic sampling, samples are taken for every nth unit after a randomly chosen starting unit. For instance, suppose we select three items from a total of 12 units by sampling every fourth one; we would randomly choose a number between 1 and 4 and thereafter choose every fourth unit. If "2" was the random starting unit, we would have the following three units in our sample:

$$1 \quad \underline{2} \quad 3 \quad 4 \quad 5 \quad \underline{6} \quad 7 \quad 8 \quad 9 \quad \underline{10} \quad 11 \quad 12$$

This procedure can generate representative samples as long as the numbered units have no built-in pattern. For example, suppose systematic samples are chosen from a series of monthly data of patient admissions in a given hospital, using April as the random starting month of every year. If April has shown a cyclical pattern of admissions, we will draw a biased sample. Nevertheless, a systematic sampling procedure is a relatively simple, economic, direct sampling approach, and can be used effectively providing that the units in a universe are thoroughly mixed or shuffled (Kish, 1965). The sample mean and variance can be estimated using the formulas for simple random samples.

Stratified Sampling In stratified sampling, a sample is selected randomly from each of the homogeneous subgroups or strata so that the group of representative samples can estimate the parameters of a universe efficiently. The population first is classified into strata according to variables that could be related to the dependent variable under study. A simple random sample then is chosen from each stratum.

A stratified sample is either proportionate or disproportionate. In *proportionate stratified sampling*, the sampling fraction is the same for all strata ($n_i / N_i = n/N$). If the sample is drawn disproportionately from the various strata, that is called *disproportionate stratified sampling*.

Statistical procedures in computing the sample mean for strata ($\bar{x}st$) and the standard error of the means for the proportionate stratified sampling are presented below.

Sample mean ($\bar{x}st$):

$$\bar{x}_{st} = \frac{\sum (n_i \bar{x}_i)}{n}$$

where

N = total population
N_i = population size for ith stratum
n = total sample size
n_i = sample size from ith stratum
x_{ij} = the measurement on jth unit of the sample from the ith stratum

Variance and standard error:

$$SE_{\bar{x}_{st}} = \sqrt{\frac{\sum \left(n_i s_i^2\right)}{n^2} \left(\frac{N-n}{N-1}\right)}$$

where

$$s_i^2 = \frac{\sum x_{ij} - \frac{\left(\sum x_{ij}\right)^2}{n_i}}{n_i - 1}$$

Application To continue with the previous example using GWB scores, we first stratify the total population ($N = 31$) into two strata, men ($N_1 = 17$) and women ($N_2 = 14$). In drawing 15 sample persons from the two strata, we must randomly select 8 men from the male stratum and 7 women from the female stratum. Their scores are shown in Table 4.10.

Table 4.10.   Stratified random sample of 15 students

Observation ID number	GWB score (x_i)	$(x_i)^2$
Male		
1	67	4,489
9	100	10,000
10	95	9,025
11	99	9,801
12	80	6,400
13	68	4,624
14	78	6,084
17	77	5,929
Subtotal	$\Sigma x_i = 664$	$\Sigma (x_i)^2 = 56{,}352$
Female		
2	76	5,776
3	85	7,225
6	83	6,889
7	85	7,225
16	102	10,404
18	94	8,836
24	83	6,889
Subtotal	$\Sigma x_i = 608$	$\Sigma (x_i)^2 = 53{,}244$

M = Male; F = Female.

The mean of the stratified sample is calculated by first computing the mean of each stratum:

Male students:

$$\bar{x}_1 = \frac{\sum x_{ij}}{n_1} = \frac{664}{8} = 83$$

Female students:

$$\bar{x}_2 = \frac{\sum x_{ij}}{n_2} = \frac{608}{7} = 86.85$$

Mean of the stratified sample:

$$\bar{x}_{st} = \frac{\sum n_i \bar{x}_i}{n} = \frac{(8)(83) + (7)(86.85)}{15} = 84.74$$

Computation of the standard error proceeds in the same manner, calculating each stratum separately using the formula:

$$s_i^2 = \frac{\sum x_{ij}^2 - \dfrac{\left(\sum x_{ij}\right)^2}{n_i}}{n_i - 1}$$

For the male sample:

$$s_1^2 = \frac{56,352 - \dfrac{440,896}{8}}{8 - 1} = 177.14$$

For the female sample:

$$s_2^2 = \frac{53,244 - \dfrac{369,664}{7}}{7 - 1} = 72.48$$

Variance for the stratified sample is computed as follows:

$$VAR\ (\bar{x}_{st}) = \left[\left(\frac{n_1 s_1^2}{n^2}\right) + \left(\frac{n_2 s_2^2}{n^2}\right)\right]\left[\frac{N - n}{N - 1}\right] = \left[\frac{8(177.14)}{15^2} + \frac{7(72.48)}{15^2}\right]\left[\frac{31 - 15}{31 - 1}\right] = 4.56$$

$$SE_{\bar{x}} = \sqrt{4.56} = 2.14$$

Solution   A comparison between the stratified sample mean ($\bar{x}st$) and the population mean (μ) is made as follows (H_0: $\bar{x}st = \mu$):

$$t_0 = \frac{\bar{x}_{st} - \mu}{\sqrt{\dfrac{s^2}{n}}}$$

where

$$s^2 = \frac{\sum x_{ij} - \dfrac{\left(\sum x_{ij}\right)^2}{n}}{n - 1}$$

Thus

$$s^2 = \frac{(56,352 + 53,244) - \dfrac{(1,617,984)}{15}}{15 - 1} = 123.6$$

$$t_0 = \frac{84.74 - 85.4}{\sqrt{\dfrac{123.6}{15}}} = -.23$$

The t value for a two-tailed test at the $\alpha = .05$ level is 2.145. Because $|t_0|$ is smaller than $t_{\alpha/2}$, we conclude that there is no statistically significant difference between the sample mean and the population mean.

Estimates of Confidence Intervals

Upper 95%: $\bar{x}_{st} + 2(SE_{st}) = 84.74 + 2(2.14) = 89.02$
Lower 95%: $\bar{x}_{st} - 2(SE_{st}) = 84.74 - 2(2.14) = 80.46$

Advantages and Disadvantages in Sampling Designs

There are many ways to select representative samples. A detailed comparison of the major advantages and disadvantages of types of sampling designs is presented in Table 4.11.

Estimation of Sample Size

Four basic rules guide an investigator in choosing a sample size to ensure a given probability of accuracy for using sample statistics to estimate population parameters:

1. The sample size is minimally affected by the population size when the population size is reasonably large.
2. The sample size varies positively with the confidence coefficient $(1 - \alpha)$; the higher the confidence coefficient desired, the greater the sample size required.
3. The sample size is affected by the power necessary to detect the difference between two means or two proportions. Generally, we can assume the ideal power $(1 - \beta)$ is approximately equal to $1 - 4(\alpha)$. When α is smaller than .05, it seems safe to consider $(1 - \beta) = .75$ or larger.
4. The more the characteristics of a population vary, the larger the sample size required.

Two examples of an estimation of sample size are listed below.

    Calculating Sample Size for the Difference Between Two Proportions   The first thing that must be done is to specify the likely proportion of events in each of the two groups being compared. Events may be a response to treatment, death, or recovery. Sample size then may be calculated using the equation:

$$n = \frac{(p_1 q_1) + (p_2 q_2)}{(p_2 - p_1)^2} \times f(alpha, power)$$

where

p_1 = rate in group 1
p_2 = rate in group 2
$q_1 = 1 - p_1$
$q_2 = 1 - p_2$
alpha = significance level
power = $1 - \beta$

The values for the $f(alpha, power)$ for a two-tailed test can be obtained from Table 4.12 [*note:* n is roughly inversely proportional to $(p_2 - p_1)^2$].

    Suppose you need to know the sample size required to detect a difference from 25% to 30% between two groups, if power = .90 and alpha significance level = .05. Therefore, using the values:

p_1 = .30
p_2 = .25
q_1 = .70
q_2 = .75
alpha = .01
power = .90
$f(alpha, power)$ = 14.9 (from Table 4.12)

$$n = \frac{(.30)(.70) + (.25)(.75)}{(.30 - .25)^2} (10.5) = 1,667$$

Table 4.11. Summary of major sampling designs: Advantages and disadvantages

Type of sample and brief description	Advantages	Disadvantages
A. Simple Random Assign to each population member a unique number; select the sample by using a table of random numbers.	1. Requires minimum advance knowledge of the population. 2. Free of possible classification errors. 3. Easy to analyze data and compute errors.	1. Does not make use of knowledge of the population that the researcher may have. 2. Larger errors for the same sample size than are found in stratified sampling.
B. Systematic Use natural ordering or order population; select a random starting point between 1 and the nearest integer to the sampling ratio (N/n); select items at the interval of near integer–to–sampling ratio.	1. If the population is ordered with respect to a pertinent property, the stratification effect reduces variability as compared to a simple random sample. 2. Simplicity of drawing sample; easy to check.	1. If the sampling interval is related to a periodic ordering of the population, variability may be increased. 2. Estimates of error are likely to be high where there is stratification effect.
C. Multistage Random When there are at least two stages, use a form of random sampling in each of the sampling stages.	1. Sampling lists; identification and numbering required only for the members of sampling units selected for the sample. 2. If sampling units are geographically defined, cuts down field costs (i.e., travel).	1. Errors are likely to be larger than with **A** or **B**. 2. Errors increase as the number of sampling units selected decreases.
D. Stratified *(1) Proportionate:* Select from every sampling unit at other than last stage a random sample proportionate to the size of the sampling unit.	1. Assures representativeness with respect to the property that is the basis of classifying units; therefore yields less variability than **A** or **C**. 2. Decreases failure to include members of population because of classification process. 3. Characteristics of each stratum can be estimated, and hence comparisons can be made.	1. Requires accurate information on the proportion of the population in each stratum; otherwise error rises. 2. If stratified lists are not available, may be costly to prepare; possibility of faulty classification and hence increase of variability.
(2) Optimum Allocation: Similar to **D***(1)* except that the sample is proportionate to the variability within strata as well as to their size.	1. Less variability for the same sample size than in **D***(1)*.	1. Requires knowledge of variability of pertinent characteristics within strata.
(3) Disproportionate: Similar to **D***(1)* except size of sample is not proportionate to size of sampling unit, but is dictated by analytical considerations or convenience.	1. More efficient than **D***(1)* for comparison of strata or where different errors are optimum for different strata.	1. Less efficient than **D***(1)* for determining population characteristics (i.e., more variability for same sample size).

(continued)

Table 4.11.   *(continued)*

Type of sample and brief description	Advantages	Disadvantages
E. Cluster Select sampling units by some form of random sampling; ultimate units are groups; select these at random and take a complete count of each.	1. If clusters are geographically defined, yields the lowest field costs. 2. Requires listing only individuals in selected clusters. 3. Characteristics of clusters as well as those of population parameters can be estimated. 4. Can be used for subsequent samples because clusters, not individuals, are selected and substitution of individuals may be permissible.	1. Larger errors for comparable size than other probability samples. 2. Requires ability to assign each member of population uniquely to a cluster; inability to do so may result in duplication or omission of individuals.
F. Stratified Cluster Select clusters at random from every sampling unit.	1. Reduces variability of plain cluster sampling.	1. Disadvantages of stratified sampling added to those of cluster sampling. 2. Because cluster properties may change, the advantage of stratification may be reduced and make the sample unusable for later research.
G. Repetitive *(1) Multiple* or *(2) Sequential:* Two or more samples of any of the above types are taken; results from earlier samples are used to design later ones, or to determine if they are necessary.	1. Estimates the population characteristics that facilitate efficient planning of a succeeding sample, therefore reduces error of final estimate. 2. In the long run, reduces the number of observations required.	1. Complicates administration of fieldwork. 2. More computation and analysis required than in nonrepetitive sampling. 3. Sequential sampling can be used only where a very small sample can approximate representativeness and where the number of observations can be increased conveniently at any stage of the research.
H. Judgment Select a subgroup of the population that, on the basis of available information, can be judged to be representative of the total population; take a complete count of this subgroup.	1. Reduces cost of preparing a sample and fieldwork, because ultimate units can be selected so that they are close together.	1. Variability and bias estimates cannot be measured or controlled. 2. Requires strong assumptions or considerable knowledge of populations and the subgroup.
(1) Quota: Classify population by pertinent properties; determine the desired proportion of sample from each class; fix quotas for each observer.	1. Same as above. 2. Introduces some stratification effect.	1. Introduces bias of observers' classification of subjects and nonrandom selection within classes.

Adapted from Ackoff (1953).

Table 4.12. Values of f(*alpha, power*) for a two-tailed test

		Power			
		.95	.90	.80	.50
Alpha	.10	10.8	8.6	6.2	2.7
significance	.05	13.0	10.5	7.9	3.8
level	.01	17.8	14.9	11.7	6.6

In order to be 90% sure of detecting this difference, you would need 1,667 people in each of the groups to detect a difference from 25% to 30% at the .05 significance level.

Calculating Sample Size for Testing the Difference Between Two Means The following formula is used to determine the sample size necessary to test for a difference between two means (given that there is an equal number in each group).

$$n = \frac{k \times 2\sigma^2}{E^2} = \textit{number in each group}$$

where

σ^2 is the error variance
E is the minimum difference to be detected or expected
k depends on significance level and power desired

Values for k are given in Table 4.13.

For example, to detect a difference in mean wage of 10 dollars between two groups of people, where variance is $200 and level of significance is .05 with a power of .90, the number of participants required is

$$n = \frac{10.507 \times 2(200)}{(10)^2} = 42 \text{ people}$$

for each of the two groups.

Table 4.13. Values for k according to significance level and power

Significance level	Power	k
.05	.99	18.372
	.95	12.995
	.90	10.507
	.80	7.849
.01	.99	24.031
	.95	17.814
	.90	14.879
	.80	11.679

CONCLUSION

There are many study designs managers may choose from when performing managerial studies. Cross-sectional study designs are studies of particular points in time, analyzing samples selected to be representative cross sections of a population in terms of relevant variables. Cross-sectional studies do not permit causal inferences, but precise information about associations between variables can be obtained through the use of several statistical methods (Kleinbaum, Kupper, & Morgenstern, 1982; Longo & Bohr, 1991). These methods include the partial correlation coefficient, Z values, t tests, and ANOVA. Researchers may utilize a variety of statistical packages, a few of which are STORM, SAS, SPSS, EXCEL, EPI-5, and EPI-STAT, in employing these statistical methods. Different methods of collecting samples for managerial studies, such as nonprobability sampling and probability sampling, are also important tools for managers. These methods allow for the selection of samples appropriate for a managerial study. Finally, the four basic rules of estimating sampling size to ensure a given probability of accuracy for a study are important for any manager performing a managerial study.

REFERENCES

Ackoff, R.L. (1953). *The design of social research*. Chicago: University of Chicago Press.

Gable, C.B. (1990). A compendium of public health data sources. *American Journal of Epidemiology, 131,* 381–394.

Hanke, J.E., & Reitsch, A.G. (1991). *Understanding business statistics*. Boston: Richard D. Iresin.

Kinsey, A.C., Pomeroy, W.B., & Martin, C.E. (1948). *Sexual behavior in the human male*. Philadelphia: W.B. Saunders.

Kish, L. (1965). *Survey sampling*. New York: John Wiley & Sons.

Kleinbaum, D.G., Kupper, L.L., & Morgenstern, H. (1982). *Epidemiologic research*. Belmont, CA: Lifetime Learning Publications.

Lay, C.M., & Broyles, R.W. (1980). *Statistics in health administration, Vol. II: Advanced concepts and applications*. Germantown, MD: Aspens Systems Corporations.

Longo, D.R., & Bohr, D. (1991). *Quantitative methods in quality management*. Chicago: American Hospital Publishing.

Selltiz, C., Wrightsman, L.S., & Cook, S.W. (1976). *Research methods in social relations*. New York: Holt, Rinehart, and Winston.

Selvin, S. (1991). *Statistical analysis of epidemiologic data*. New York: Oxford University Press.

Siegel, A.F. (1988). *Statistics and data analysis: An introduction*. New York: John Wiley & Sons.

5

Time-Span or Longitudinal
Study Design and Analysis

Time is the greatest innovator.

Francis Bacon, *Of Innovations*

USES OF LONGITUDINAL STUDIES

Time-span studies are longitudinal studies that trace the possible causative factors of a specific problem. A longitudinal study looks at a series of past events, or follows a series of events into the future, and, by ascertaining the sequence of those events, discovers their causal direction. Longitudinal studies have several important uses.

Identification of Cause–Effect Relationship

A longitudinal study can ascertain the sequence of events and thus establish the causal direction. In problem-oriented audit studies of a medical practice, for example, longitudinal design has been used to set up data bases, formulate the study problems, plan actions, and conduct follow-up audits of patient care. Time-span audits of patient care can identify the causes of problems and lead to changes in the way healthcare professionals provide care (Guccione et al., 1994; Tufo et al., 1977).

Assessment of Effectiveness of Management Tools

Longitudinal design is used in procedures for performance appraisal. If the introduction of a management tool such as incentive payments is being studied, time-span observations of employee productivity assess the effect of the change.

Examination of Theoretical Constructs and Formulations

Theoretical constructs can be tested empirically in a longitudinal study, and the predictive validity of a test instrument established. For instance, in a panel group study of the General Well-Being (GWB) index cited previously (see Chapter 3), the GWB scores were collected at time 1 and psychological symptoms were identified at time 2, in order to analyze the relationship between the GWB scores and the number of psychological symptoms. If a strong inverse relationship is found, the predictive power of GWB scores for psychological symptoms is demonstrated. Thus the predictive validity of the construct "general well-being" is confirmed.

Decisions About Resources and Size

There are many uses for time-span data on, for example, the demand for hospital beds: 1) to identify trends in demand for care, 2) to estimate hospital use, 3) to project the resources needed to deliver services, 4) to determine bed needs, and 5) to evaluate the hospital's financial condition.

Evaluation of Program Impacts

A longitudinal study can provide valuable data for evaluating a program. For example, data from preadmission screening in a health care facility (e.g., skilled nursing facility or nursing home) yield information about patient status (e.g., activities of daily living functions or mental functioning status) that guides appropriate placements. Careful assessment of the levels of care for geriatric patients can reduce inappropriate placements, and thus contain the cost of long-term care.

RETROSPECTIVE STUDY DESIGN AND ANALYSIS

Definition of Retrospective Study Design

A retrospective study examines past events and their effects on a present situation (Breslow & Day, 1980; Gold, Kitz, Lecky, & Neuhaus, 1993; Shapiro, 1989; Wacholder, Silverman, McLaughlin, & Mandel, 1992). Organizations (e.g., hospitals) seen as having a management problem are known as the *cases* and are compared to those without the problem (the *controls*). Past data on the two groups are compared with regard to their use of a specific mechanism, such as auditing or managerial controls. Differences in the number of instances of the study problem are examined to see whether they can be attributed to the presence or absence of this mechanism. A retrospective study can be diagrammed as shown in Figure 5.1.

A highly precise retrospective study design is the *case–control matching design*, in which for each "case" there is a nearly identical "control"—that is, the two are identical in as many areas as possible, except for the tested variable. For example, if a hospital with a management problem (e.g., high staff turnover) is the case, the control should be a hospital without that management problem (e.g., high staff turnover) that is similar in size, ownership, location, occupancy rate, and other characteristics. Then only the differences in management control mechanisms will be compared.

Analysis of Relative Risk in Retrospective Studies of Management Problems

Once different incident rates (e.g., staff turnover rates) have been found in the case and in the control group, we can analyze the data to see if the differences are related to the type of managerial control each group uses. Retrospective studies can measure the relationship between, for example, a managerial control mechanism and incidents of managerial problems; this concept is termed *relative risk*. Table 5.1 demonstrates this concept, using a hypothetical situation with samples from two categories of hospitals, those with and those without a managerial problem.

The proportion of hospitals with a managerial control mechanism and having the specific managerial problem is $a/(a + b)$, while the proportion of hospitals without a managerial control

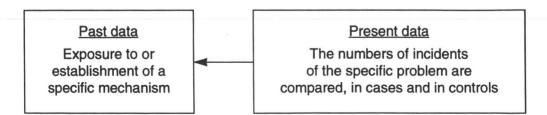

Figure 5.1.   Design of a retrospective study.

Table 5.1.　Distribution between cases and controls of hospitals with and without a managerial control mechanism

Managerial control mechanism	Number of hospitals		
	Cases (with a specific managerial problem)	Controls (without a specific managerial problem)	Total
With	a	b	$a + b$
Without	c	d	$c + d$
Total	$a + c$	$b + d$	N

mechanism and having the problem is $c/(c + d)$. Thus the relative risk (RR) of having the managerial problem reported is computed as follows:

$$RR = \frac{\left(\begin{array}{c}\text{Proportion of hospitals having a managerial} \\ \text{control mechanism and a specific managerial problem}\end{array}\right)}{\left(\begin{array}{c}\text{Proportion of hospitals not having a managerial} \\ \text{control mechanism but having the managerial problem}\end{array}\right)}$$

$$= \frac{\dfrac{a}{a + b}}{\dfrac{c}{c + d}} = \frac{a(c + d)}{c(a + b)}$$

Note, however, that, if the managerial problem is not frequent among the hospitals studied, we can estimate the relative risk in a simple procedure:

$$RR = \frac{a(c + d)}{c(a + b)} \cong \frac{ad}{cb}$$

A test of the difference between ad and cb resulting from sampling variation is calculated as follows (with one degree of freedom):

$$\chi^2 = \frac{N\left(|ad - cb| - \dfrac{N}{2}\right)^2}{(a + c)(b + d)(a + b)(c + d)}$$

If the χ^2 value is greater than 3.84, we can be 95% certain that the difference in risk between the case and the control hospitals is true.

Example　In a sample of hospitals with charity or free clinics and a sample of hospitals without such clinics, determine the relative risk of financial deficits and calculate the statistical significance using the data in Table 5.2.

The risk of having financial deficits among the hospitals with a free clinic relative to those without such an arrangement is estimated as:

$$\frac{ad}{bc} = \frac{(80)(250)}{(220)(50)} = 1.82$$

The χ^2 test of equal risk of having financial deficits is computed as:

$$\frac{N\left(|ad - bc| - \dfrac{N}{2}\right)^2}{(a + c)(b + d)(a + b)(c + d)} = \frac{600\left(|[(80)(250)] - [(200)(50)]| - \dfrac{600}{2}\right)^2}{(300)(300)(130)(470)} = 8.26$$

Table 5.2.   Distribution among cases (financial deficits) and controls (no financial deficits) of hospitals with and without charity or free clinics

| Charity or free clinics | Number of hospitals | | |
	(Cases) With financial deficits	(Controls) Without financial deficits	Total
With	$a = 80$	$b = 50$	$a + b = 130$
Without	$c = 220$	$d = 250$	$c + d = 470$
Total	$a + c = 300$	$b + d = 300$	$N = 600$

The above results show that the likelihood of having financial deficits is 1.82 times higher among the hospitals having a free clinic than among the hospitals without such an arrangement. The chi-square test ($\chi^2 = 8.26$) reveals that the difference in risk between the case group and the control group is also statistically significant at the .05 level.

Advantages and Disadvantages of Retrospective Studies

Advantages   Retrospective studies are relatively inexpensive, because they use existing pools of data obtained from the organization being studied; data collection is not complicated. One retrospective study can test several hypotheses, so new studies can be designed until ultimately the causal factors of the organizational problem are identified. Because information about past exposure to a suspect factor usually is obtained easily, studies can be completed quickly to help managers make decisions.

Disadvantages   If case and control groups are not selected carefully, selection biases threaten the validity of the retrospective study. For example, a study of case fatality rates (which are used as an indicator of the quality of care) compared cardiovascular mortality in 20 local hospitals, evenly divided into teaching and nonteaching hospitals. The results showed that the teaching hospitals had a higher case fatality rate than did nonteaching hospitals. These findings may mislead the investigator to generalize that the teaching hospitals delivered poorer care. In fact, however, other evidence from a careful assessment of these hospitals suggests just the opposite conclusion, that teaching hospitals deliver better care. The explanation is that selectivity biases in the admission processes made it likely that sicker patients or patients with special diagnoses of heart conditions were admitted to teaching rather than to nonteaching hospitals. Hence, comparative assessments of case fatality rates must take the case mix or severity difference of the study hospitals into account.

Retrospective studies use data from historical records or recalls; therefore, measurement errors are unavoidable. Moreover, because many other events also may affect the study problem, the presence or absence of a risk factor cannot be linked directly to the problem. Thus, a retrospective study is limited in its ability to attribute causation of the problem to the suspect factor directly. Furthermore, the chance of the risk factor being related to the observed problem can be overestimated if extraneous factors are not controlled. Many multivariate statistical procedures such as multiple regression analysis, multiple classification analysis and automatic interaction detector analysis can be used to separate out these confounding variables so that logical and realistic conclusions can be drawn.

PROSPECTIVE STUDY DESIGN AND ANALYSIS

Definition and Importance of a Prospective Study Design

A prospective study design is also called a *population-based study design* (Green & Wintfeld, 1993; Lakka et al., 1994; Lilienfeld, 1976; Norell, 1992). The normal subjects, either individuals or organizations, are selected and then exposed to a risk or an organizational control factor; the outcomes then are assessed over time. If significant differences in outcome measures are observed between those exposed and those not exposed to the study variable, researchers conclude that a cause–effect relationship exists between that risk or organizational control factor and organizational performance. A prospective study is designed as shown in Figure 5.2.

Practitioners and researchers in health care management have grown increasingly concerned with successful managerial control mechanisms and innovative organizational policies. Organizational research has developed many principles and theories; although they offer general insights, these principles provide little assistance to managers in the constant battle to contain costs and find effective organizational control mechanisms.

To pursue empirical solutions to these immediate problems, investigators could start with a study design using a cohort of hospitals that all are considered free of a particular management problem but that vary in their exposure to a specific innovative mechanism (e.g., organizational control). The study could follow the hospitals over time in order to measure differences in the rate at which management problems develop in relation to exposure to the organizational control. For example, it is believed that hospital utilization review and quality management programs have affected hospital operations positively by reducing unnecessary hospitalization and shortening average length of stay for surgical and medical patients (Borchardt, 1981; Gertman & Restuccia, 1981; Graham, 1982).

Analysis of Relative Risk in Prospective Studies of Managerial Problems

Hospitals are organizations based on strategy—that is, the efficiency of their operations depends on their use of innovative management strategies. Thus, assessment of relative risk for a strategy or management program (i.e., its chance of being successful or unsuccessful) is fundamental. For example, the "Economic Grand Rounds Program" of the American Medical Association tested the relative risk of a variety of demonstration projects to make physicians more aware of the cost of inpatient treatment and of approaches for minimizing those costs (American Medical Association, 1982).

The success or failure of a demonstration project or managerial study can be treated as a dependent variable (Y) that will be measured in a future observation, while the adoption of a specific strategy for containing costs is an independent variable (X). In a hypothetical study of a representative sample of hospitals, we can establish the distribution shown in Table 5.3. The proportion of hospitals that fail to meet a predetermined criterion for success is computed by $b / (a + b)$ for those adopting a strategy, and is computed by $d / (c + d)$ for those not adopting a strategy. The ratio of these two proportions is a measure of relative risk.

In reality, the presence of a given study characteristic (X) varies in magnitude, so that a continuous independent variable is used; similarly, the dependent variable (Y) also may be measured by a continuous variable. Therefore, it is appropriate to employ a simple regression analysis to estimate the effect of X on Y—for example, how the degree of exposure to a given control mechanism (X) affects the number of management problems encountered in a managed care or-

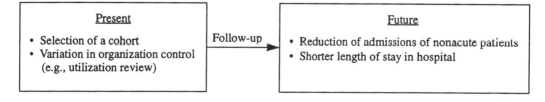

Figure 5.2. Design of a prospective study.

Table 5.3.   Results of hypothetical study of a cost containment strategy

	Number of hospitals		
	Success	Failure	Total
Adopting strategy	a	b	$a + b$
Not adopting strategy	c	d	$c + d$
Total	$a + c$	$b + d$	N

Note: A predetermined criterion should be used to determine success or failure.

ganization i (Y_i). We may use the level of patient audit systems as an independent variable (X), and use the number of people enrolled who dropout (resulting from the deficient patient management system) as a dependent variable (Y). The results of the analysis show that the average number of people enrolled who dropout is higher in the organizations with relatively less control (e.g., audit system) than in those with medium or higher levels of control (Table 5.4).

Advantages and Disadvantages of Prospective Studies

Advantages   Prospective studies more accurately estimate the risk of having a managerial problem for organizations with a specific characteristic (e.g., an organizational control mechanism). Selection biases are avoided because the organizations are selected according to specific criteria. The memory gaps or recall errors that plague retrospective studies are avoided. Prospective studies can establish cause–effect relationships firmly because many extraneous factors that may affect the measures of outcome (e.g., organizational performance) can be controlled.

Disadvantages   Prospective studies are usually more expensive and complicated, because they require long periods of observing the study subjects. Furthermore, a prospective study cannot be completed if a significant proportion of the study subjects refuse to participate in the course of the study. Prospective studies should not be used as exploratory investigations, because they require a highly specific theory or hypothesis to guide the investigation.

EXAMPLE OF A TIME-SPAN/LONGITUDINAL STUDY: COMORBIDITY INDEX

This example is taken from a study by Cornell University Medical College's Clinical Epidemiology Unit to develop and test a classification system for use in longitudinal studies of comorbidity (Charlson, Pompei, Ales, & MacKenzie, 1987).

The first part of the study developed a comorbidity classification system using empirical information from a population of 607 patients admitted to the Cornell Medical Center during a month-long period in 1984. The system was derived from this "training" population by using a 1-year follow-up study to determine the specifics of classification. This system then was applied

Table 5.4.   Average number of people enrolled who dropout by level of control in patient audit system ($N = 50$ managed care organizations)

X (level of control)	Y (number of dropouts)
Low ($X = 1$)	17.44
Medium ($X = 2$)	14.88
High ($X = 3$)	12.32

Note: $Y = a + bX_1 = 20 + (-2.56) X_1$
         $R^2 = 1.00$

to a "test" population of 685 women diagnosed as having breast cancer at Yale's New Haven Hospital between January 1962 and December 1969. Data were collected from medical records over a 10-year follow-up period (the remainder of the study) in order to ascertain the predictive validity of the instrument over long time periods.

The study used mortality data to develop a *comorbidity index*. Survival rates among the training population were used to determine the relative risk for each of the comorbid conditions and thus to create a weighted index of comorbidity. Annual mortality rates calculated by severity of illness and weighted index of comorbidity are illustrated in Table 5.5.

In the 1-year follow-up ("training"), age was not a predictor of death by comorbid disease, because the time span was brief. In longitudinal studies of 5 years or more, however, both age and comorbidity were predictive of death. A comparison of actual 10-year survival rates and predicted survival rates, after risk adjustment for age, is presented in Table 5.6.

The predictors of survival rates by combined risk score are very close to actual rates except in situations involving high risk scores. Overall, the combined comorbidity–age score is useful in predicting mortality rates for longer time frames (>5 years), while the weighted index of comorbidity alone is better suited to shorter follow-ups of around 1 year.

Table 5.5. Percentage of 1-year mortality among patients who survived hospitalization according to illness severity and weighted index of comorbidity

	Weighted index of comorbidity			
Severity	"0"	"1–2"	"3–4"	">5"
Not ill or mildly ill	7(97)	16(87)	41(17)	64(22)
Moderately ill	6(47)	17(63)	39(25)	76(17)
Severely ill	12(25)	30(57)	50(18)	100(15)
Total	7(169)	21(207)	43(60)	78(54)

Reprinted from the Journal of Chronic Diseases, 40, Charlson, M.E., Pompei, P., Ales, K.L., & MacKenzie, C.R., A New Method of Classifying Prognastic Comorbidity in Longitudinal Studies: Development and Validation, 373–383, Copyright 1987, with kind permission from Elsevier Science Ltd, The Boulevard, Langford Lane, Kidlington OX5 1GB, UK.

Table 5.6. Ten-year actual and predicted survival according to age–comorbidity in the test population

Comorbidity–age combined risk score*	Number of patients	Actual 10-yr survival (%)	Predicted 10-yr survival (%)
0	213	99	99
1	156	97	96
2	136	87	90
3	109	79	77
4	42	47	53
5	29	34	21

Reprinted from the Journal of Chronic Diseases, 40, Charlson, M.E., Pompei, P., Ales, K.L., & MacKenzie, C.R., A New Method of Classifying Prognastic Comorbidity in Longitudinal Studies: Development and Validation, 373–383, Copyright 1987, with kind permission from Elsevier Science Ltd, The Boulevard, Langford Lane, Kidlington OX5 1GB, UK.

* Each comorbidity rank was equivalent to 1 decade of age, with 40 year taken as the zero rank for age (e.g., a patient who was 50 who had a comorbidity index 2 would have a score of 3). The beta coefficient for the age–comorbidity combined score was 0.9 (e.g., < 40 coded as 0, 50 as 1, 60 as 2, 70 as 3, etc.).

The predicted survival was calculated from the 10-year survival of a theoretical low-risk population (0.983). Thus for a score of 70 the calculation was $0.983^{14.8}$, where $14.8 = e^{2.7} = e^{0.9(3)}$.

CONCLUSION

This chapter examined several types of study designs that health care managers can use in their analysis of various health care problems and/or situations. Longitudinal studies examine past events to discover their causal direction. One type of longitudinal study is the time-span study, which traces possible causative factors of a specific problem. A retrospective study examines past events and their impacts on a present situation. A prospective study, or a population-based study, exposes subjects to a risk or controlled factor and assesses outcomes over time. All of these types of studies are important means of analysis for health care managers.

REFERENCES

American Medical Association. (1982). *AMA cost effectiveness plan: 1982 and beyond.* Chicago: American Medical Association.

Borchardt, P.J. (1981, November). Non-acute profiles: Evaluation of physicians' non-acute utilization of hospital resources. *Quality Review Bulletin,* pp. 21–26.

Breslow, N.E., & Day, N.E. (1980). *Statistical methods in cancer research, Vol. 1: The analysis of case-control studies.* Lyon, Switzerland: International Agency for Research in Cancer.

Charlson, M.E., Pompei, P., Ales, K.L., & MacKenzie, C.R. (1987). A new method of classifying prognostic comorbidity in longitudinal studies: Development and validation. *Journal of Chronic Diseases, 40,* 373–383.

Gertman, P.M., & Restuccia, J.E. (1981). The appropriateness evaluation protocol: A technique for assessing unnecessary days of hospital care. *Medical Care, 19,* 855–871.

Gold, B.S., Kitz, D.S., Lecky, J.H., & Neuhaus, J.M. (1993). Unanticipated admission to the hospital following ambulatory surgery. *Journal of the American Medical Association, 62*(21), 3008–3010.

Graham, N.O. (Ed.). (1982). *Quality assurance in hospitals.* Rockville, MD: Aspen Systems Corporation.

Green, J., & Wintfeld, N. (1993). How accurate are hospital discharge data for evaluating effectiveness of care? *Medical Care, 31,* 719–731.

Guccione, A.A., Felson, D.T., Anderson, J.J., Anthony, J.M., Zhang, Y., Wilson, P.W.F., Kelly-Hayes, M., Wolf, P.A., Kreger, B.E., & Kannel, W.B. (1994). The effects of specific medical conditions on the functional limitations of elders in the Framingham Study. *American Journal of Public Health, 84,* 351–358.

Lakka, T.A., Venalainen, J.M., Rauramaa, R., Salonen, R., Tuomilehto, J., & Salonen, J.T. (1994). Relation of leisure-time physical activity and cardirespiratory fitness to the risk of acute myocardial infarction in men. *New England Journal of Medicine, 330,* 1549–1559.

Lilienfeld, A.M. (1976). *Foundations of epidemiology.* New York: Oxford University Press.

Norell, S.E. (1992). *A short course in epidemiology.* New York: Raven Press.

Shapiro, E.D. (1989). Analytic strategies in hospital epidemiology: Case-control studies. *Infection Control and Hospital Epidemiology, 10*(4), 167–169.

Tufo, H.M., Bouchard, R.E., Rubin, A.S., Twitchell, J.C., VanBuren, H.C., Weed, L.B., & Rothwell, M. (1977). Problem-oriented approach to practice. II. Development of the system through audit and implication. *Journal of the American Medical Association, 238,* 404–407.

Wacholder, S., Silverman, D.T., McLaughlin, J.K., & Mandel J.S. (1992). Selection of controls in case-control studies. II. Types of controls. *American Journal of Epidemiology, 135,* 1029–1041.

6

Managerial Epidemiology

The cause is hidden, but the result is known.

Ovid, *Metamorphoses IV*

A BRIEF HISTORY OF EPIDEMIOLOGY

Epidemiology, a word derived from Greek (*epi*, meaning thrust; *demos*, meaning population; and *logos*, meaning study), is the study of the determinants and distribution of diseases and disabilities in a population. Epidemiology, as a science, has roots going back to Hippocrates in the epic *On Airs, Waters, and Places*. Hippocrates sought to show that many environmental factors and living habits influence human disease (Lilienfeld, 1976). John Graunt furthered the study of epidemiology with his 1692 manuscript, *Natural and Political Observations Mentioned in a Following Index and Made upon the Bills of Mortality*. Graunt collected vital statistics and health statistics, from which he drew inferences about the morbidity, mortality, and fertility of different population groups (Lilienfeld, 1976).

John Snow's investigation of the occurrence of cholera in London from 1848 to 1854 is a landmark epidemiological study. Several water companies then were responsible for supplying water to different parts of London. Snow found that cholera rates were particularly high in areas of London served by water companies that took their water from the Thames River at a place heavily polluted by sewage (Lilienfeld, 1976). More historical examples of epidemiological studies are found later in this chapter.

TYPES OF EPIDEMIOLOGY

There are three basic types of epidemiology: clinical epidemiology, social epidemiology, and managerial epidemiology (see Table 6.1).

Clinical Epidemiology

Clinical epidemiology is the study of the natural history of a disease. Sometimes, experimental methods are used to conduct clinical trial studies to understand the casual link between etiological factors and the disease. Each disease has its own life history. The first stage in a disease's history is *susceptibility*, when the disease is not developed but the groundwork has been laid to favor its occurrence. The second stage is *presymptomatic disease;* although no disease symptoms have appeared yet, the disease is present. The third stage is *clinical disease*, when the symptoms are recognizable. The last stage is *disability*. Some diseases resolve completely, but others cause a residual defect of either short or long duration (Mausner & Bahn, 1974).

Table 6.1.　Types, aims, approaches, and methods of epidemiological investigation

Type	Aim	Approach	Method
Clinical	To study the occurrence, distribution, size, and progression of diseases in human populations	Descriptive	Analysis of morbidity and mortality data, collected either routinely or through special studies
Social	To provide data that contribute to understanding the etiology of ill health and disease	Descriptive	Same as above; such descriptive analyses help formulate hypotheses on the etiology of ill health and disease
		Analytical	Retrospective/case–control studies Prospective/cohort studies Cross-sectional/survey studies
		Experimental	Clinical/controlled study
Managerial	To promote the utilization of epidemiological concepts in the management of health services	Descriptive	Description of morbidity and mortality data: by service area, by diagnosis-related groups (DRGs)
		Analytical	Determination of patient flow by disease category (DRGs); determination of disease-specific rates; market penetration and market segmentation (age-specific rates)
			Identification of potential new markets, of research areas for expansion, and of demographic trends

Social Epidemiology

Social epidemiology is the study of factors in society and in the environment (e.g., the population's exposure to stress or the level of urban crowding), and how social factors affect the development and manifestation of disease.

Managerial Epidemiology

Managerial epidemiology applies epidemiological principles and methods to health administration. For example, epidemiology, coupled with the applied fields of social sciences and management sciences, provides the quantitative and analytical methods, principles of logical inquiry, and rules of evidence for:

Investigating the natural history of disease (Benenson, 1990; Caper, 1987)
Diagnosing, measuring, and projecting the health needs of communities and populations (Dever, 1991)
Determining health goals, objectives, and priorities (Shapiro, 1991)
Allocating and managing health care resources (Carson & Zucconi, 1993)
Assessing intervention strategies and evaluating the impact of health services on the health of the population (Filerman, 1982; Malcolm, 1993)
Linking the delivery of health services to population needs (Oleske, 1993)
Applying epidemiological indicators in assessment of managed care plans (MacDowell & Lutz, 1993)

Epidemiology is used *in* health administration to solve problems and analyze decisions; the epidemiology *of* health administration itself, however, is applied to test hypotheses and create theory. Thus, the process of epidemiology *in* health administration assesses service needs and assists planning and marketing, evaluation (diagnosis-related groups [DRGs], cost control, etc.), and implementation (Appropriateness Evaluation Protocols [AEPs], peer review organizations [PROs], risk management, etc.). In contrast, the epidemiology *of* health administration studies the relationship between contextual, design, and performance factors within a health care system.

Managerial epidemiology long has played a significant role in shaping medical care, service planning, and evaluation. Now, as competition for the health care market intensifies, epidemiology will be an even more useful study for managers.

DESCRIPTIVE AND ANALYTICAL USES OF EPIDEMIOLOGY

Epidemiology uses both a descriptive and an analytical approach. In observational studies, epidemiology is used descriptively to identify associations between several characteristics (independent variables) and a condition of interest (dependent variable). Independent variables may be personal, such as personal hygiene; environmental, such as climate; or, societal, such as the degree of occupational stress. The dependent variable is the health condition of interest (Burstin, Lipsitz, & Brennan, 1992; Ibrahim, 1983). An example of descriptive epidemiology is the association found between sunbathing and skin cancer.

Epidemiology is used analytically to test the hypotheses generated by observational studies. For example, to test the hypothesis that sunbathing causes skin cancer, data on the amount of sunbathing by a certain population and on the number of people in that population who contract skin cancer would be collected. These data then would be correlated to test the relationship between sunbathing and skin cancer. The descriptive use of epidemiology generates questions, whereas the analytical application of epidemiology provides the answers (Ibrahim, 1983).

EPIDEMIOLOGICAL METHODS

Epidemiological methods comprise: 1) the use of vital statistics; 2) the interpretation of mortality rates; 3) the use of surveys, including sampling and questionnaire techniques; 4) the study of outcomes for people with different characteristics; 5) the study of features commonly occurring in patients with certain diseases; 6) the use of multivariate risk models; 7) the study of the occurrence of disease over space and time; and 8) the interpretation of incidence and prevalence rates (Elwood, 1982). It is important to clarify the distinction between incidence and prevalence.

Incidence Versus Prevalence

Incidence refers to the number of new cases of a disease that occur in a community over a specific time span. *Prevalence*, in comparison, refers to the total number of cases of a disease existing at a particular time. The formulas below help clarify the difference between incidence and prevalence.

$$\text{Prevalence} = \text{Incidence} \times \text{Time (duration)}$$

$$\text{Prevalence Rate} = \frac{\text{Total Number of Cases (new and old)}}{\text{Total Population at Risk}}$$

$$\text{Incidence Rate} = \frac{\text{Number of New Cases}}{\text{Total Population at Risk}}$$

PRINCIPAL CONTRIBUTIONS OF EPIDEMIOLOGY TO HEALTH SERVICES ADMINISTRATION

Epidemiology has made three principal contributions to the teaching and practice of health services administration and to health institutional planning (Henderson & MacStravic, 1982):

1. Epidemiology offers a general approach that develops and employs causal models of disease, injury, and disability. These models, which vary from the simple to the complex, allow health administrators to discover and understand how disease develops and is distributed in the community.
2. Epidemiology offers a set of scientific methodologies for identifying the nature and distribution of specific diseases, tracing their origins, assessing their consequences, and testing the effectiveness of interventions to alter or stop their progress.
3. Epidemiology has accumulated a body of knowledge that can be used in planning interventions and in managing health problems.

MANAGERIAL APPLICATIONS OF EPIDEMIOLOGY

Many managerial applications of epidemiology have been listed by Filerman (1982) (Table 6.2). Those managerial applications discussed in this chapter are:

Assessing the health status of a community
Defining the need for health services within a community
Discovering what health services are used within a community (i.e., assessing the demand for health services)
Assessing an institution or organization's efficiency
Developing case-mix measures to describe the patient mix of an institution
Evaluating performance of hospitals and physicians
Analyzing variations in medical care

Table 6.2.   Examples of managerial applications of epidemiology

1. Deciding whether to begin a preventive program aimed at a particular problem. Deciding the range of services to be included. Evaluating the efficacy and use of the program.
2. Distinguishing services needed within the service area and within the greater community, compared to the services offered.
3. Identifying high-risk populations. Estimating their needs, designing services they can use, marketing the services to them, and evaluating the effectiveness of the services.
4. Evaluating alternative delivery modes, such as satellite practice groups, ambulatory surgical centers, emergency posts, and day surgery. Identifying alternative investment options, estimating use, and evaluating impact.
5. Analyzing use and cost of services used by specific populations or groups.
6. Evaluating the appropriateness of a health services research report and its applicability to a particular institution, system, or program.
7. Evaluating the effectiveness of a new configuration of tasks or a new profession such as nurse practitioners, and its applicability in a given situation.
8. Deciding on the effectiveness of organizational developments (e.g., HMO, CCUs, or change in practice). Specifying appropriate measures of health care outcomes to justify investments in organizational developments.
9. Evaluating steps to alleviate iatrogenic disease.
10. Deciding on the scope of the program, marketing to the populations at risk, and evaluating program outcomes.
11. Utilizing health data to justify or maintain the operating program.

Adapted from Filerman (1982).

ASSESSMENT OF A COMMUNITY'S HEALTH STATUS

The purpose of assessing the health status of a community is to work toward an optimal level of health in it. Epidemiological methods can measure the incidence and prevalence of disease in the community, which is the first step toward reducing disease.

To analyze the health of a community, one views it from an epidemiological perspective—in other words, from a systems perspective. The health of a community depends on the following factors (Figure 6.1):

1. *Population characteristics*, such as genetic factors, diet, and the utilization of health resources
2. The *effectiveness and efficiency* of the health care organization
3. *Environmental characteristics*, such as pollution, urban crowding, and food sources
4. *Technological characteristics*, such as new drugs, new medical equipment, and new medical techniques

One can measure the health status of a community by analyzing census data, vital statistics data, linked health records, and morbidity data (Mausner & Bahn, 1974). Morbidity data can be collected from reports of notifiable disease, hospital records, prepaid group practice insurance programs, private physicians, disease registers, morbidity surveys such as the National Health Survey, and from surveys for specific diseases (Mausner & Bahn, 1974). Examples of specific indices of community health are: 1) cause-specific indices, which approximate the risk of death from a specific condition; 2) infant and neonatal mortality rates; 3) fetal and perinatal mortality rates; and 4) maternal mortality rates, life expectancy statistics, and disability rates (obtained mostly from the National Health Survey) (Gable, 1990; Mausner & Bahn, 1974).

It should be noted that, although mortality data in the United States are very reliable as a measure of death and moderately reliable as to the cause of death, morbidity data are difficult to obtain and often unreliable, for several reasons. First, the definition of disease may vary depending on the source of the data and the perspective of the respondent (i.e., whether the person doing the defining is a medical professional or a patient). The frequency of a particular disease also may vary according to the information source, whether it be hospital discharge summaries, medical records from primary care physicians, or surveys of lay respondents (Hulka, 1976; Safran, 1991).

Besides determining the need for health services, another major reason for assessing the health status of a community is to evaluate interventions to improve health status. For evaluating an intervention, Ibrahim (1983) suggested several criteria:

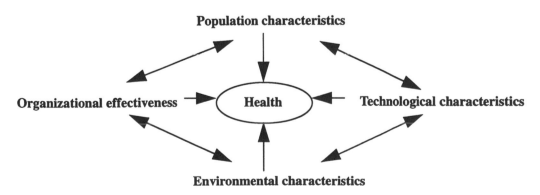

Figure 6.1.   A systems model of factors affecting the health of a community.

1. Have the services needed to bring about the desired changes been provided?
2. Did the changes needed to achieve the objectives of the program occur?
3. Have the objectives of the program been achieved?
4. Can the achieved objectives be attributed to the program?

Many programmatic interventions have as a goal the improvement of a community's health. If this improvement in health does not occur, other interventions should be considered.

ASSESSMENT OF COMMUNITY NEED FOR HEALTH SERVICES

Need for health care is synonymous with "biological urgency." The need for health services can be viewed from two perspectives. The first perspective is individual need, which in our system is decided by the physician's or other trained practitioner's diagnosis. Once the physician diagnoses a patient's problem, he or she understands that patient's need for health services.

The need for health services also can be viewed at the community level by using an epidemiological approach. The process parallels the determination of individual need by the physician: The epidemiologist makes observations and from them interprets the health needs of the community. The epidemiological study starts with an assessment of the community's health status, particularly the overall incidence and prevalence of disease. Areas of abnormally high mortality or morbidity rates need health services.

The need for health services in a community also is affected by the age distribution there; relatively older populations need more health services than do relatively young populations (Dever, 1991).

Another factor is income level. A population with a relatively high percentage of families below the poverty line is likely to need more health care services than do more fortunate populations, because people with low incomes tend to have poorer health and to lack a primary care physician; they simply cannot afford health care.

Once identified, the health needs of a community should be ordered by severity and the more severe needs given top priority.

The next step is to identify the possible interventions that would meet community health needs, evaluate them, and select the most effective and efficient alternatives to implement. Planning should specify achievable and measurable objectives for each program, and also the evidence required to prove a program is successful. Then the changes needed to meet the objectives of the new program can be outlined, and plans made for whatever services will be needed (Ibrahim, 1983).

The two applications of epidemiology discussed above—to assess the health status of the community and to identify its need for health services—are essential components of health services planning.

MEASURING A COMMUNITY'S USE OF HEALTH SERVICES

Epidemiological methods also can measure utilization (i.e., the demand for health services) (Goldberg, Hartz, Jacobsen, Krakauer, & Rimm, 1992; Wennberg, Freeman, Shelton, & Bubolz, 1989). Measurement of health services use usually is expressed as a rate or ratio. For instance, use of a hospital's inpatient services can be measured by the occupancy rate, such as:

$$\frac{\text{Total number of actual bed days per year}}{\text{Total number of available bed days per year}}$$

This gives the yearly occupancy rate; the formula can be adapted to find monthly, weekly, or daily rates. One also may change the unit of analysis from the entire hospital to a particular unit, such as the intensive care unit or a stroke unit.

Another utilization measure is the ratio of inpatient days to outpatient days, which provides a guide for resource allocation. For example, if the ratio of inpatient days to outpatient days declines, more resources can be devoted to outpatient services and fewer to inpatient services.

The application of epidemiology to measure utilization is also useful in evaluating programs. The impact of an intervention on health status often is measurable only in the long run. To assess more immediate effects, changes in utilization can be measured to provide an intermediate indicator (Hulka, 1976). A study by Okada and Wan (1980) used changes in utilization as an indicator of a program's effect, by examining how community health centers and Medicaid affected health services utilization by urban low-income populations. Follow-up health surveys collected data on access to care and also on physician, hospital, and dental services utilization 4–7 years after the community health centers had been established. The study found that the community health centers were serving a large proportion of the population in these low-income areas, and that the program was reaching the target population—poor black residents. The study also showed that access to health care had increased for this population. Use of physician and dental services had increased. Travel times to sources of care had been shortened dramatically because the community health centers were centrally located for these populations. Use patterns also had shifted, from hospital emergency rooms to the community health centers. These epidemiological measures of utilization gave early indications of the effect of community health centers on their target areas. In fact, 23% of the respondents reported that these community health centers were their primary source of care.

ASSESSING EFFICIENCY

A fourth managerial application of epidemiology is to measure efficiency, an increasingly urgent issue for managers as hospitals and other health care institutions compete more intensely. *Webster's Dictionary* defines efficiency as "the ratio of energy expended to power produced in a machine"; because health care is a service, however, managerial epidemiology views efficiency as outcomes per unit input (mostly labor). Because the efficiency of a health care institution involves the patient, the provider, and the organization itself, to analyze it requires a systems approach.

A major role of epidemiology in ensuring efficiency is in utilization management—that is, to review utilization patterns with the goal of making sure that patients and providers do not use expensive services unnecessarily. A study by Gertman and Restuccia (1981) exemplifies this use of epidemiology. They examined the efficiency of hospital utilization through a new clinical protocol, the AEP, for assessing possibly unnecessary hospital days of care. The AEP is composed of 27 objective criteria for medical services, nursing/life support services, and patient condition factors. The use of a preadmission screening strategy resulted in reduction of inappropriate hospital utilization.

DEVELOPMENT OF CASE-MIX MEASURES

Another major application of epidemiology by managers of health service institutions is in deriving case-mix measures, which analyze why some cases are more complex and require more resources than other cases.

Applications

Case-mix measures are useful in evaluating hospital performance, especially cost analysis. For instance, costs across several hospitals cannot be compared directly, because different hospitals produce different products; that is, different hospitals serve different types of patients and provide different services, and an average patient day in one hospital is apt to be very different from an average patient day in another hospital. Case-mix measures meet this difficulty in evaluating hospital costs across institutions, because they distinguish the cost variation caused by differences in product from the cost variation resulting from difference in operating efficiency.

Besides being used by administrators and planners to evaluate hospital performance, case-mix measures also are used by prospective reimbursement systems, which reimburse hospitals for the treated case (output) rather than, as formerly, for the costs of the inputs they consume. Case-mix measures are the tool used by prospective payment systems to take account of the variations in costs of different case treatments.

Case-mix measures also are useful in quality improvement programs. By controlling for case mix, one can compare mortality rates accurately among hospitals, or analyze differences in physician practice patterns (Iezzoni, 1992; Plomann, 1982).

Determinants of Case-Mix Complexity

The many determinants of hospital case-mix complexity have been outlined by Becker and Steinwald (1981). Their study found that teaching hospitals have a more complex case mix than do nonteaching hospitals, because complex cases provide teaching material and because teaching hospitals have the staff and resources to treat complex cases. Becker and Steinwald (1981) also found that hospitals performing research had greater case-mix complexity; research focused on the diagnostic and therapeutic problems of complex illnesses.

Occupancy rates also affect case-mix complexity. Because hospitals with low occupancy rates are more inclined to admit discretionary, nonurgent cases, they tend to have a less complex case mix (Becker & Steinwald, 1981). Becker and Steinwald (1981) showed that outpatient cases also affect case-mix complexity; hospitals with large outpatient departments are better able to provide continuous care to patients whose complex illnesses require extensive follow-up after discharge, and so those hospitals have a more complex case mix. (It should be noted, however, that another study [Lion, 1981] found no influence by outpatient departments on hospital case mix.)

Becker and Steinwald (1981) also found that the percentage of Medicare patients influences a hospital's case-mix complexity. The aged suffer more complex conditions than other age groups do, so a higher percentage of Medicare patients increases the complexity of the hospital's case mix.

Becker and Steinwald (1981) found that the per capita income of the community affects a hospital's case-mix complexity. They hypothesized that a community's affluence allows hospitals to purchase and staff the sophisticated facilities that treat more complex cases.

The Becker and Steinwald (1981) study discovered that the greater the proportion of general practitioners in the community, the lower the hospital's case-mix complexity. This was attributed to the fact that general practitioners have less specialized medical training, so patients who go to them are those with less complex illnesses.

The patient distribution within a hospital also, of course, affects the case-mix complexity (Becker & Steinwald, 1981). Cases involving surgery were found to be the most complex, and pediatric and obstetric cases to be the least complex. These results, however, are not consistent with another study by Becker and Sloan (1983), which found that surgical patients used fewer resources than did other types of patients.

Indirect and Direct Case-Mix Measures

Indirect case-mix measures are hospital bed size, average length of patient stay, teaching versus nonteaching hospitals, and the existence of rare clinical services (Plomann, 1982); however, these increasingly are being discarded in favor of direct case-mix measures, which are more accurate. Direct case-mix measures have gained importance because case mix affects the revenue a hospital receives under the Medicare Prospective Payment System (MPPS), and because volatility and competition in the health care industry have led hospitals to focus on controlling costs.

Direct case-mix measures include: the ICD-9-CM List A, DRGs, disease staging, patient management categories, Veterans Administration Multi-Level Care Groups, AS-SCORE, the Severity of Illness Index, MD-DADO, and other generic algorithms (Plomann, 1982).

The following sections give a brief overview of two of the above direct case-mix measures, DRGs and the Severity of Illness Index. DRGs are discussed more fully in a later section of this chapter. Information also is provided on what are known as risk-adjusted outcome measures, which include such direct case-mix measures as disease staging algorithms and patient management categories.

Sample Calculation of a DRG Case Mix   This section describes how to calculate a DRG-based case-mix index, as used by the MPPS. In Table 6.3, five hospitals are listed vertically and five hypothetical DRGs are listed horizontally. Within the matrix formed by the five hospitals and the five DRGs are listed the various percentages of Medicare discharge by DRG for each hospital. For instance, for hospital A, DRG 1 accounts for 2.5% of the total Medicare discharges, DRG 2 accounts for 27.3% of the total Medicare discharges, and so on. As can be seen in column 6, the five DRGs account for 100% of all Medicare discharges. At the bottom of Table 6.3, one finds the average percentage of Medicare discharges for which each DRG accounts. For instance, DRG 1 accounts for an average of 19.92% of all Medicare patient discharges over the five hospitals; DRG 2 accounts for, on average, 23.32% of all Medicare discharges over the five hospitals. Below these average percentage Medicare discharges are shown the weighted cost for each DRG.

From this information, each hospital's DRG-weighted expected cost per case can be calculated. Calculation of the DRG-weighted expected cost per case for hospital A is shown in Table 6.4. The calculation takes the various percentages of Medicare discharges accounted for by the DRGs, and multiplies each one by the corresponding DRG average cost to give the figures in column 3 of Table 6.4. When the figures in column 3 are summed, the total is the DRG-weighted expected cost per case for hospital A: $1,660.40. The DRG-weighted expected cost per case for each of the five hospitals is shown in column 7 of Table 6.3. The average DRG-weighted ex-

Table 6.3.   Calculation of Medicare case-mix index: Proportion of Medicare discharges by DRG

Hospital	Percent of all cases by DRG						DRG-weighted expected cost per case	Case-mix index
	DRG 1	DRG 2	DRG 3	DRG 4	DRG 5	Total		
A	2.5	27.3	10.5	41.5	18.2	100	$1,660.40	0.890
B	21.0	0.9	30.1	2.0	46.0	100	$2,401.30	1.287
C	40.6	5.0	2.3	47.2	4.9	100	$1,346.30	0.722
D	5.1	18.4	62.5	10.0	4.0	100	$2,990.70	1.603
E	30.4	65.0	1.0	1.6	2.0	100	$929.00	0.498
Average proportion for all hospitals (A–E)	19.92	23.32	21.28	20.46	15.02	100	$1,865.54	—
DRG cost average	$1,000	$800	$4,100	$1,500	$2,000	—	—	—

Table 6.4.   Computation of DRG-weighted costs

	Percent of cases		Average DRG cost		DRG-weighted expected cost/ case
Hospital A					
DRG 1	2.5	×	$1,000	=	$25.00
DRG 2	27.3	×	$800	=	$418.40
DRG 3	10.5	×	$4,100	=	$430.50
DRG 4	41.5	×	$1,500	=	$622.50
DRG 5	18.2	×	$2,000	=	$364.00
	100.0				$1,660.40
Five-hospital average					
DRG 1	19.92	×	$1,000	=	$199.20
DRG 2	23.32	×	$800	=	$186.56
DRG 3	21.28	×	$4,100	=	$872.48
DRG 4	20.46	×	$1,500	=	$306.90
DRG 5	15.02	×	$2,000	=	$300.40
	100.0				$1,865.54

Hospital A case-mix index

$$\frac{\$1,660.40}{\$1,865.54} = .8900$$

pected cost per case for all five hospitals is calculated in the same way, as shown in Table 6.4. The average percentage of Medicare discharges over the five hospitals accounted for by each DRG is multiplied by the corresponding DRG cost weight. This gives the figures in column 3. When these figures are summed, they total $1,865.54, which is the average DRG-weighted expected cost per case.

From the calculations performed above, it is now possible to calculate a case-mix index for each of the five hospitals. One simply takes the DRG-weighted expected cost per case for a particular hospital and divides it by the average DRG-weighted expected cost per case. For example, as shown in Table 6.4, to calculate the case mix for hospital A, one would take the DRG-weighted expected cost per case ($1,660.40) for hospital A, and divide it by the average DRG-weighted expected cost per case ($1,865.54). This gives a case-mix index of .8900; that is, hospital A has, on average, a case complexity that is .89 that of the average hospital.

Table 6.5 lists the top 20 national DRGs as ranked by the total number of cases: The rightmost column shows the cost weight of each DRG. For example, DRG 132 (arteriosclerosis) ranks first in number of total cases and has a cost weight of .9451 (i.e., an arteriosclerosis case, on average, has a cost that is .9451 of the average DRG cost).

Severity of Illness Index   The Severity of Illness Index was developed under the leadership of Susan Horn. Her argument for its development is that hospital cost comparisons have meaning only if costs are adjusted to account for differences in the severity of illness. These adjustments must be based on case-mix groupings that are homogeneous with respect to resource consumption; Horn argues that DRGs are not (Horn, Sharkey, & Bertram, 1983). The Severity of Illness Index has seven variables, with each variable defined at four levels of increasing severity (Horn et al., 1983):

1.   The stage of principal diagnosis
2.   Other interacting diseases affecting the patient
3.   The rate of response to therapy
4.   Residual impairment following therapy

5. Complications resulting from the principal diagnosis
6. Patient's dependency on the nursing staff
7. Extent of non–operating room procedures

These seven scores can guide the rater in assigning a patient's severity of illness score. The Severity of Illness Index applies to almost all hospitalized patients; the information required is all available on the patient's chart. Because the Severity of Illness Index is retrospective, classifying variables that are defined more precisely than those in other case-mix measures, it is a more reliable method and easier to use. In fact, the Severity of Illness Index outperformed other case-mix measures in establishing homogeneous groups according to total charges, length of stay, laboratory charges, and routine charges (Horn et al., 1983).

The Severity of Illness Index can be used in the following ways (Plomann, 1982):

To analyze differences in severity of patient illness among departments or among hospitals
To analyze differences in charges and costs among hospitals
To compare mortality rates among hospitals by controlling for severity of illness
To monitor severity of illness over time
To analyze differences in physician practice while controlling for severity of illness
To predict hospital charges on the basis of severity of illness

The two major disadvantages of the Severity of Illness Index are: 1) the rater must collect information from medical records about the seven variables used in the index; and 2) the overall severity rating is a judgment by the rater. The advantage of the Severity of Illness Index is that it produces patient groups that are homogeneous with respect to resource use (Plomann, 1982).

Risk-Adjusted Outcome Measures The likelihood of death or disability is affected by patient characteristics. Thus the values of clinical interventions must be assessed apart from

Table 6.5. Top national DRGs ranked by total number of cases

Rank	DRG #	Name	Total cases	Cost weight
1	132	Atherosclerosis	73,848	0.9451
2	182	Esophagitis, gastroenteritis, and miscellaneous digestive disorders	70,232	0.6250
3	127	Heart failure and shock	66,510	1.0633
4	39	Lens procedures	54,520	0.5110
5	14	Specific cerebrovascular disorders except transient ischemic attacks	47,531	1.3326
6	88	Chronic obstructive pulmonary disease	46,613	1.0713
7	89	Simple pneumonia and pleurisy	40,874	1.0919
8	294	Diabetes	38,630	0.8229
9	122	Circulatory disorders without acute myocardial infarction	355,203	1.5252
10	243	Medical back problems	32,001	0.7869
11	140	Angina pectoris	30,536	0.7643
12	96	Bronchitis and asthma	24,205	0.8076
13	134	Hypertension	24,142	0.7185
14	138	Cardiac arrhythmia and conduction disorders	24,004	0.9664
15	15	Transient ischemic attack	22,275	0.6880
16	82	Respiratory neoplasms	21,089	1.2069
17	130	Peripheral vascular disorders	20,975	0.9886
18	320	Kidney and urinary tract infections	20,305	0.8108
19	467	Other factors influencing health status	18,784	0.9970
20	296	Nutritional and miscellaneous metabolic disorders	17,458	0.8966

the effects of social, economic, and personal (physiological and health) differences among patients. In other words, the investigator should evaluate the program's effect when the influences of patient characteristics are controlled simultaneously. Several risk-adjusted measures of clinical outcome are presented in Table 6.6.

EVALUATING PERFORMANCE OF HOSPITALS AND PHYSICIANS

DRGs and Their Applications

A diagnosis-related grouping is a homogeneous grouping of patients who, in the opinion of physicians, require roughly equivalent regimens of care and hence consume similar amounts of hospital resources. DRGs were developed at Yale University, beginning in the late 1960s, as a tool for utilization review; the measure of resource utilization is average length of stay (ALOS). Based on the application of DRGs in health care management, this demonstrates the utility of managerial epidemiology.

In developing DRGs, several objectives were followed:

1. DRGs must be medically interpretable, meaning that physicians should be able to relate patients to the various patient classes and be able to identify particular patient management processes for those patients.
2. DRGs should be based on variables commonly available in existing hospital patient abstracts and should be relevant to service utilization.
3. DRGs should be limited in number so that there are a manageable number of classes. DRGs also must cover the entire range of possible disease conditions without overlap.
4. Within a DRG, there should be limited variation in the length of stay.
5. DRGs should be based on explicit rules about how to subdivide a major diagnostic category.
6. DRG classes should be sufficiently large to permit comparative analysis across hospitals.
7. DRGs should represent the entire range of hospital patients.

For DRGs, the characteristics that explain ALOS are: 1) principal diagnosis, 2) principal procedure, 3) presence of substantial complications or comorbidity, 4) age, and 5) discharge status.

The *principal diagnosis* is the condition identified after patient examination that is mainly responsible for a patient's admission. The principal diagnosis is *not* always: 1) the first item listed by the physician on the medical record, 2) the most clinically serious item treated during hospitalization, 3) the most resource-intensive item treated during hospitalization, or 4) the diagnosis listed at the time of the patient's admission.

The *principal procedure* is "that procedure performed for definitive treatment rather than for diagnostic purposes." Substantial comorbidity and complications exist when there are conditions present that are likely to increase the patient's ALOS by at least 1 day in at least 75% of the cases (Office of Technology Assessment, 1983).

DRGs actually were formulated by collapsing the International Classification of Diseases (9th edition) (ICD-9) diagnosis classification system into mutually exclusive and exhaustive categories called major diagnostic categories (MDCs). Originally there were 23 MDCs, related to each major body system. To develop more homogeneous groups, each MDC was subdivided further using clinical judgment and statistical analysis, according to the variables that cause differences in length of stay. When one of the following conditions was fulfilled, the subdivision was stopped: 1) the group was not large enough to warrant another classification (less than 100 observations); or 2) none of the variables reduced unexplained variation by at least 1% (Plomann, 1982). To date, 494 DRGs have been developed; (see Appendix B); they are classified into 25 MDCs (Table 6.7).

Table 6.6. Clinically based risk-adjusted outcome measures

Outcome measure	Related studies	Definition of severity or risk	Data source
Acute Physiology and Chronic Health Evaluation (APACHE II)	Knaus, Draper, Wagner, and Zimmerman (1985); Knaus, Wagner, Draper, and Zimmerman (1981); Knaus and Wagner (1989); Knaus et al. (1993); Zimmerman (1989)	Risk of imminent death, primarily in intensive care	Medical record
Charleson Chronic Disease Index	Charlson, Pompei, Ales, and MacKenzie (1987)	Risk of death within 1 year of medical hospitalization	Medical record (adapted for discharge abstract)
Clinical Risk Index for Babies	Richardson and Tarnow-Mordi (1994)	Five major categories of neonatal severity: obstetrical risk, general-use pediatric scores, predictors of developmental outcome, bronchopulmonary dysplasia risk, acute mortality index	Medical record
Complication Screening Program	Iezzoni et al. (1994)	27 complications indicative of quality problems	Discharge abstract
Computerized Severity Index (CSI)	Averill et al. (1989); Horn and Horn (1986); Iezzoni, Ash, Coffman, and Moskowitz (1992); Thomas and Ashcraft (1989)	Treatment difficulty as reflected by length of stay	Medical record
Disease Staging Clinical Criteria	Gonnella and Louis (1987); Gonnella, Hornbrook, and Louis (1984); Louis and Gonnella (1986)	Complexity and extent of organ system involvement	Medical record
Disease Staging Q-Scale	Conklin and Houchens (1987)	Relative resource needs	Discharge abstract
Disease Staging Q-Stage	Gonnella and Louis (1987); Conklin, Lieberman, Barnes, and Louis (1984)	Complexity and extent of organ system involvement	Discharge abstract
Medicare Mortality Predictor System (MMPS)	Daley et al. (1988)	Risk of death within 30 days of admission for Medicare beneficiaries in four conditions	Medical record
MedisGroups	Blumberg (1991); Brewster et al. (1985); Iezzoni and Moskowitz (1988); Iezzoni et al. (1988); Iezzoni, Foley et al. (1992)	Clinical instability	Medical record
Patient Management Categories (PMCs)	Young (1984); Young, Swinkola, and Zorn (1982)	Relative cost of services required for effective management	Discharge abstract
Pediatric Risk of Mortality (PRISM) Score	Pollock, Ruttimann, Getson et al. (1987)	Risk of in-hospital death for patients hospitalized in pediatric intensive care units	Medical record
Rand Measure of "Sickness on Admission"	Keeler et al. (1992)	Risk of death at 30 and 180 days following admission in five conditions	Medical record
Uniform Clinical Data Set (UCDS)	Audet and Scott (1993)	Risk for various outcomes potentially related to effectiveness and quality of care	Medical record
Yale Refinement of Diagnosis-Related Groups (Refined DRGs)	Fetter, Freeman, Park, Schneider, Lichtenstein et al. (1989)	Relative hospitalization charges, considering complications and comorbidities	Discharge abstract

Table 6.7.   Major diagnostic conditions and diagnosis-related groupings

MDC codes	Conditions	DRG codes
1	Diseases of the nervous system	1–35
2	Diseases of the eye	36–48
3	Diseases of the ear, nose, and throat	49–74
4	Diseases of the respiratory system	75–102
5	Diseases of the circulatory system	103–145
6	Diseases of the digestive system	146–190
7	Diseases of the hepatobiliary system and pancreas	191–208
8	Diseases of the musculoskeletal system and connective tissue	209–256
9	Diseases of the skin, subcutaneous tissue, and breast	257–284
10	Endocrine, nutritional, and metabolic diseases	285–301
11	Diseases of the kidney and urinary tract	302–333
12	Diseases of the male reproductive system	334–352
13	Diseases of the female reproductive system	353–369
14	Pregnancy, childbirth, and puerperium	370–384
15	Normal newborns and other neonates with certain conditions originating in the perinatal period	385–391
16	Diseases of the blood and blood-forming organs and immunity	392–399
17	Myeloproliferative disorders and poorly differentiated malignancy and other neoplasms	400–414
18	Infectious and parasitic diseases	415–423
19	Mental disorders	424–432
20	Substance abuse disorders	433–438
21	Injury, poisoning, and toxic effect of drugs	439–455
22	Burns	456–460
23	Selected factors influencing health status and contact with health services	461–470
24	Multiple significant trauma	484–487
25	Human immunodeficiency virus infections	488–490

Note: DRGs 471–483 and 491–494 are not associated with a MDC at this time.

Applications of DRGs

Setting Prospective Reimbursement Rates   A principal application of DRGs is in setting prospective reimbursement rates. Under a DRG-based, prospective per-case payment system, hospitals are paid a specific predetermined amount for each patient treated, regardless of the number or types of services provided. The DRG in which the patient is classified determines the amount the hospital receives. DRG-based reimbursement assumes that patients with similar diseases need similar services that consume similar resources, and so hospitals should receive similar payments for treating the same diagnosis. Any prospective payment system (PPS) must incorporate an acceptable measure of a hospital's case mix. DRGs are just one accepted method for doing so; a recent study, however, found DRGs to be the best case-mix measure for prospective reimbursement (Office of Technology Assessment, 1983).

Under such a PPS, the hospital is rewarded for reducing the total cost of treating a patient. Per-case payment thus removes the incentive to provide more resources than are necessary. It is this characteristic of encouraging hospitals to "do less" for the patient that makes the use of DRGs controversial. Physicians argue that the incentive to do less for a patient is not good.

As of October 1, 1983, Medicare began a PPS for all hospitals participating in Medicare except psychiatric hospitals, rehabilitation hospitals, long-term care facilities, and children's hospitals. This program was phased in over 3 years, so that by 1987 hospitals were being reimbursed according to a national DRG system. During the 3-year phase-in, hospitals were reimbursed at rates based partly on actual hospital costs and partly on average national and regional DRG rates. With the national DRG system in place, there are only national rates for urban and for rural areas, adjusted to reflect area differences in hospital wages as well as inflation, advances in technology, and changes in hospital productivity.

The MPPS also allows payments above the DRG rates for atypical cases, termed *outlier cases*. An outlier case meets one of the following criteria: l) the length of stay exceeds the ALOS for a patient's DRG by some fixed number of days or by a certain number of standard deviations, or 2) the case is extraordinarily costly. The MPPS requires that hospitals receiving Medicare payments contract with a peer review organization (PRO) to review admission and discharge patterns of the hospital and evaluate its quality of care.

The states of New Jersey and Maryland have been exempted from participating in the MPPS because both states have implemented their own DRG-based prospective reimbursement systems. The New Jersey program, implemented in 1978, applies to *all* patients (not just Medicare patients) at *all* hospitals. A study by Davies, Westfal, Haskins, and Sells (1983) evaluated the New Jersey program. One of its problems was poor quality of medical records in most hospitals. Medical records were plagued with coding errors, missing information, and even missing patient bills and missing patient abstracts. In addition, many hospitals did not use current technology for billing payers or providers; instead, they still used manual DRG coding and manual billing. For coding discharge abstracts into DRGs and for billing, computers are a necessity.

Davies et al.'s study also criticized the DRG system for its intensive requirements of data and processing: reporting, editing, validation, and processing of hundreds of data elements and millions of patient records annually. In addition, computer programs running into the tens of thousands of lines had to be maintained. Davies et al. (1983) suggested that the amount of data required from hospitals be reduced, the data be presented in simplified forms, and the number of data manipulations be reduced.

Davies et al. (1983) also concluded that the reimbursement system in New Jersey was too complex and expensive. The system had been designed carefully to avoid potential inequities, but because this led to many detailed refinements in the system's methodology, Davies et al. suggested that the system be simplified. Although the New Jersey program and the MPPS differ, the lessons learned from the New Jersey program may apply to the Medicare program.

Cost Finding and Analysis   A second application of DRGs is in cost finding and cost analysis. By linking cost data with case-mix information, DRGs allow hospital administrators to define, monitor, and compare costs so that cost control programs can be designed and implemented. A basic problem of using DRGs in cost finding and cost analysis is that costs are assumed to correlate with length of stay. Length of stay, however, may not always correlate well with the amount of resources used (Burik & Nackel, 1981).

Management Planning   A third use of DRGs is as a case-mix measure, providing a framework within which to measure community health needs and distribute treatment facilities accordingly. Because DRGs measure resource use, they can identify excess beds, evaluate Certificate-of-Need applications, prepare for health systems plans (Burik & Nackel, 1981), and evaluate health care outcomes. DRGs also aid in management planning because they make better cost projections possible.

Case-Mix Comparisons Between Hospitals   A fourth application of DRGs is in comparing case mix between hospitals, because DRGs are one measure of case mix. Case-mix measures allow a hospital to compare its case mix with that of a comparable hospital. A teaching hospital, for example, would be expected to have a higher case-mix complexity than a nonprofit community hospital. If the hospital's case-mix complexity is abnormally above that of comparable hospitals, further investigation is indicated.

Quality of Care Evaluation   PROs use DRGs as retrospective review mechanisms to complement the PROs' concurrent review process. Outlier cases, those with abnormal lengths of stay or costs, can be pulled for further review by clinicians. In addition, within a DRG, comparisons of institutional and individual performance can evaluate quality of care (Burik & Nackel, 1981; Daley, Gutman & Delbanco, 1988; Iezzoni, 1992).

Utilization Management   DRGs are used in utilization management to assess the appropriateness of hospital admissions, continued stay, and the use of ancillary services. Hospital administrators use DRGs to develop a resource consumption profile that identifies some physicians as using too few resources and some as using too many (Burik & Nackel, 1981); severe problems warrant investigation. Through utilization management, health care organizations both manage costs and ensure quality.

Example of the Calculation of a DRG Reimbursement Rate   Under the New

Jersey system, measures of resource use (MRUs) serve as proxies for actual resource consumption; for example, nursing costs are estimated by patient days. The assumption is that equal amounts of nursing resources are consumed daily regardless of diagnosis, age, or any other patient factor (Wasserman, 1982).

MRUs are used to indicate the costs of the services supplied by hospital cost centers for a DRG, and ultimately to set DRG rates per case. This is done by first computing the ratio of MRUs consumed by all patients within a given DRG to the total number of MRUs supplied by a particular cost center. That ratio then is multiplied by the total cost of operating the cost center. This result gives the total cost of care for patients in that DRG. This result then is divided by the number of patients in the DRG to arrive at the cost per case (Wasserman, 1982).

For example, suppose we want to calculate the nursing costs per case for a given DRG. Suppose 300 patients are assigned to DRG 100, and that these 300 patients use a total of 1,500 of the 150,000 days of care provided annually by the hospital. If the total nursing cost of the center is $1 million, then the total costs of nursing care for DRG 100 and the nursing cost per case may be calculated as follows:

$$\text{Total nursing cost for DRG 100} = \frac{1,500}{150,000} \times \$1,000,000 = \$10,000$$

$$\text{Nursing cost per case} = \frac{\$10,000}{300} = \$33/\text{case}$$

Under the New Jersey system, the nursing cost per case figure would be added to the cost per case of providing ancillary services, to produce the hospital's direct-patient-care cost per case (Wasserman, 1982).

Once the hospital's direct-patient-care cost per case has been calculated, direct care reimbursement rates then are calculated by adding together the hospital's direct-patient-care cost per case, the hospital-based physician services costs, and a standard nonphysician-direct-care cost (Wasserman, 1982).

Advantages and Disadvantages of DRGs
Advantages

1. DRGs are a measure of resource utilization that is a meaningful way to assess resource need.
2. Data are obtained easily from a common hospital data source, the patient abstract.
3. The number of diagnostic categories is manageable.
4. DRGs are organized in a hierarchy, so the diagnostic groups can be collapsed into a few categories. Although more heterogeneous, these are still useful.
5. DRGs form relatively homogeneous groups for comparing case mix between hospitals.
6. DRGs can be used to set prospective reimbursement rates for hospitals (Plomann, 1982).

Disadvantages

1. DRGs lack clinical specificity (e.g., therapeutic philosophies and treatment regimens vary, and staging and readmission data are lacking).
2. Small hospitals may not be able to use DRGs because in some categories they may not have enough patients to make DRG data meaningful.
3. DRGs rely on discharge abstracts, but those often contain classification and coding errors.
4. The external validity of DRGs has not been assessed.
5. The predictive validity of DRGs has not been ascertained.
6. DRGs group patients into homogeneous categories on the basis of ALOS data. Thus, a DRG is not a standard for what should be done, nor is it a measure of quality of care.
7. DRGs group and classify only inpatients.
8. Because a surgical procedure often moves a patient into a more complex DRG, surgical procedures may be encouraged to obtain higher reimbursement.
9. DRGs reflect the state of medical technology and practice at the time of their development, so they must be reformulated often to reflect advances in diagnostic procedures and medical technology.
10. In the attempt to keep the number of patient classes manageable, some clinical homogeneity within groups was lost (Plomann, 1982). DRGs should take into account the differences in severity of illness (Horn et al., 1983).

Cost–Benefit Criticisms of DRGs   The economic feasibility of a DRG-based prospective reimbursement system has been questioned. A significant investment in information systems is necessary to develop a uniform reporting system and also to improve discharge data by training personnel, routinizing hospital procedures, and instructing physicians. There are also costs in keeping DRGs current with technological advances, as well as in establishing DRG-based review mechanisms, updating resource consumption profiles for DRGs, and accumulating individual hospital case cost profiles (Burik & Nackel, 1981). All these costs must be weighed against the significant benefits that accrue in hospital planning as a result of improved information systems.

Impact of DRGs on Hospital Utilization and Cost   The change from a retrospective cost-based reimbursement system to a PPS by Medicare occurred because there were wide variations between hospitals and between regions of the country in the cost of treating similar diagnoses, with no difference in the quality of care provided (Lutjens, 1993). Rather than continuing to encourage cost increases by reimbursing hospitals for costs incurred, Medicare adopted the PPS. The MPPS allows Medicare to purchase a known and defined product—the hospital stay—at a fixed price, with price varying by case classification in specific DRGs. This system is designed to change hospital behavior by changing the economic incentives of providers (Guterman, Eggers, Riley, Greene, & Terrell, 1988; Prospective Payment Assessment Commission, 1992).

The MPPS has had many effects on the health care system since its implementation, particularly on the hospital industry. There has been a decline in inpatient admissions for both Medicare and non-Medicare patients (Guterman et al., 1988). This decline, combined with a decrease in ALOS for Medicare patients (Figure 6.2), has resulted in overall declining inpatient volumes, mostly in small hospitals. The financial pressure imposed by the MPPS and the resulting declines in ALOS indicate that the MPPS has been encouraging hospitals to change the way they provide inpatient care. Even follow-up visits for Medicare surgical patients decreased after implementation of the MPPS (Kominiski & Biddle, 1993). Occupancy rates are at an all-time low and competition between hospitals for inpatients has increased dramatically. There is evidence, however, that the dramatic declines in ALOS following the implementation of the MPPS may be leveling off. This may be because there were strong initial responses to the MPPS or, because utilization review has diverted less severely ill patients to ambulatory care facilities. There

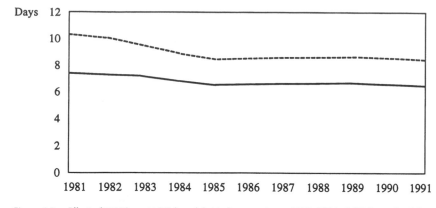

Figure 6.2.   Effect of MPPS on ALOS for adult Medicare patients, 1981–1991. Solid line, all adults; dashed line, adults 65 and over.

has been an increase in the average severity of illness among Medicare patients admitted to the hospital (Guterman et al., 1988).

There also have been changes in the utilization of post–acute care services by elderly, chronically disabled Medicare patients as a result of the implementation of the MPPS (Manton, Woodbury, Vertrees, & Stallard, 1993). In an effort to reduce inpatient stays, it seems that more and more hospitals have been discharging patients to home health agencies and that even home health users have been discharged earlier, increasing the number of users and the number of visits per year. In fact, outlays for home health services have increased by an estimated 25% as of 1991 (Kenney, 1991). The MPPS has even had an effect on nursing home utilization. Because hospitals have the incentive to discharge Medicare patients as quickly as possible, many hospitals attempt to substitute nursing home days for hospital inpatient days. The utilization of skilled nursing facilities increased following the implementation of the MPPS; however, in those areas with low nursing home bed supply, nursing home transfers were fewer and there were longer ALOSs in hospitals (Guterman et al., 1988; Kenney & Holahan, 1991).

The MPPS also has had impacts on the operating costs of hospitals and their subsequent margins (see Figure 6.3). Data on hospitals' financial performance after the implementation of the MPPS indicate that overall they did well in the first few years. It seems, however, that the gap between those hospitals doing well and those doing poorly as a result of the MPPS is increasing. The case-mix index may be rewarding some hospitals in excess of the actual cost per

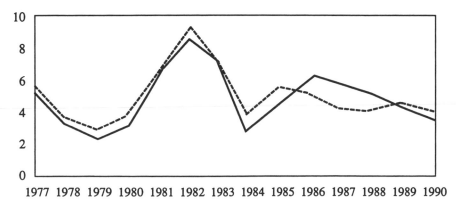

Figure 6.3.   Percentage of change in real hospital expenses and revenues per admission, 1977–1990. Solid line, expenses; dashed line, revenues.

case, while rewarding others less than the actual cost per case (Williams, Hadley, & Pettengill, 1992). Those hospitals that seem to be faring well include urban hospitals, large hospitals, and teaching hospitals. Those that seem to be faring worse include rural and community hospitals, smaller hospitals, and nonteaching hospitals. Although the overall profits rose among hospitals in the early years of the MPPS, as can be seen in Figure 6.3, this increase was not distributed uniformly among hospitals.

Hospital administrators are undertaking many initiatives in attempting to control costs and increase the long-run viability of their institutions as a response to the PPS system. Some of these methods include structural changes, such as eliminating or converting beds to more efficient uses, changes in the use of both labor and nonlabor inputs, such as staffing reductions and skill-mix reconfigurations, and organizational changes, such as hiring more business-oriented managers and the establishment of intrafacility cost sharing arrangements (Guterman et al., 1988). Currently, the Health Care Financing Administration's Bureau of Program Operations is working with insurance carriers to conduct area-wide utilization reviews that can profile the variations in medical practice (Physician Payment Review Commission, 1994). Thus, the examination of practice patterns will help direct the effort in reducing inappropriate use of hospital and physician services.

Resource-Based Relative Value Scale

Historically, the difference between payments to surgeons and those to nonsurgeons has been significant, mostly because surgeons' outputs are tangible (something is removed or corrected in most cases), whereas the products of nonsurgeons are not. The benefits of nonsurgical services, being often intangible, lend themselves less plausibility to remunerative beneficence.

Over the years, this difference in reimbursement had widened until, by 1965, "the disparity between remuneration for surgical, procedural services and evaluative, managerial services was evident" (Grossman, 1990, p. 42). Congress reacted by forming the Physician Payment Review Commission to design a rational framework for Medicare reimbursement. The Commission recommended that the work of Hsiao, Braun, Dunn, Becker, Yntema, Verrilli, Stamenovic, and Chen (1992) and the resource-based relative value system (RBRVS) be used to establish the Medicare fee schedule for physicians.

RBRVS Method   The RBRVS system matches physicians' fees to the cost of the resources used in producing their services, without allowing the play of scarcity and demand to raise fees. RBRVS bases reimbursement on factors in the *supply* of services. Grossman (1990) states that under the new payment schedule for medical professional fees, RBRVS reallocates the payments to decrease fees for surgical and technological services and increase fees for evaluative and consultative services.

RBRVS systems do not set dollar values for physicians' services. Instead, the system assigns a number of nonmonetary work units to each procedure. The formula is as follows:

$$RBRV = TW + PC + AST$$

where TW = *t*otal *w*ork input by the physician, PC = *p*ractice *c*osts of the physician, and AST = *a*mortized value of the opportunity cost of *s*pecialized *t*raining. Total work in this equation is broken down into three component periods: preservice, intraservice, and postservice. During the intraservice period, the physician sees the patient and performs the service; the pre- and postservice periods account for activities with the patient other than treatment. Practice costs, such as liability (malpractice) insurance, "consume approximately 45% of physicians' gross practice revenues" (Hsiao et al., 1992, p. NS6). Each specialty requires a different length of training time; for example, cardiovascular surgeons train significantly longer than do general practitioners. The opportunity costs of extended specialized training are calculated as lost income-earning opportunities or salary differences. RBRVS systems calculate the income forgone for a given residency period and amortize it over the working lifetime of the physician. The opportunity cost for each specialty then is derived by multiplying estimates of physician work by the ratio of annual opportunity cost to net income for that specialty (Hsiao et al., 1992, p. NS7).

Effects of RBRVS   The system of usual, customary, and reasonable fee-for-service reimbursement of physicians historically has been associated with the rise in the number of specialists and the relatively smaller number of general practitioners. The high concentration of specialists has drawn patient care toward costly specialist services that correct problems *after* they have developed, and diminished preventive primary care services. A primary goal of the RBRVS system is to create disincentives for the use of specialized invasive procedures and to promote the use of less costly yet more effective primary care.

If the Physician Payment Review Commission holds a budget-neutral position—that is, readjusts Medicare professional fees using the same total amount of funds currently allocated—family practitioners, for example, will see an increase of 60%–70% in revenues while ophthamologists will have revenue decline by 40%–50% (Grossman, 1990, p. 45). The changes are designed to encourage physicians to become general practitioners rather than specialists and thus to shift the focus of care from corrective medicine as practiced by specialists toward preventive medicine. Increased use of preventive services will reduce the overall fees paid for physician services, and will reduce the risk and suffering of patients as well.

ANALYZING VARIATIONS IN MEDICAL CARE: SMALL AREA ANALYSIS

Methods and Uses

Small area analysis, or social area analysis, measures and compares the use of medical care services by defined populations. Using statistical techniques such as adjustments for age and random variation, the method compares one group's use of medical care with another's. Such comparisons can help identify issues of access, volume, cost, and quality of medical care.

Small area analysis views aggregated health care encounters of all members of a specific group or residents of a specific area regardless of where they received the services. "Health service" or "medical market" areas are defined in several ways. For example, the market area can be defined by the place where most residents receive medical care; in that case, the pattern of use observed for a service tends to be influenced by the practice style of local physicians.

Small area analysis reveals differences between similar populations in per capita rates of hospitalization for medical treatments and surgical procedures (Einstadter, Kent, Fihn, & Deyo, 1993; Greenfield et al., 1992; Wennberg, 1984; Wennberg & Gittelsohn, 1982). Some of the variation is due to differences in illness levels and other patient characteristics, and some to differences in community resource capacity—the level and variety of outpatient services that might replace inpatient care or reduce hospitalization through earlier intervention and treatment. Much of the variation, however, seems to stem from two other factors: physician styles of practice, and the supply of beds and physicians and surgeons in the health care industry in a particular community.

Small area analysis explores the relationships among different components of use, fees, and outcomes. The examination of resource availability and use patterns provides the data from which providers, payers, and consumers can reach consensus on programs to ensure access to high-quality care while containing costs. Such analysis also contributes to improving the quality of medical care by revealing which areas are *underserved*, and also by identifying areas where very high rates of use suggest that services are used unnecessarily, raising the risks for patients as well as costs.

Einstadter et al. (1993) retrospectively identified cervical spine surgery cases from a statewide hospital discharge registry in Washington and found that cervical spine surgery for neck pain was an increasingly common procedure with wide geographic variability. The results of this study demonstrate the need to understand the causes of geographic variation in treatment of neck pain. Information from this study can be disseminated to surgeons and other health care providers so that educational efforts can help reduce the variation in physician "practice style."

Small area analysis most commonly examines patterns of medical and surgical care for the population of a certain area (e.g., a state) or for subsets of a defined population (e.g., all Medicare beneficiaries or all Medicaid recipients). If the number of medical encounters in a given year is too small to calculate statistically significant rates, small area analysis can use aggregate data from several aggregating years, or group major diagnostic categories into broader categories.

Defining Geographic Areas or Units

The unit of small area analysis is the population of a given geographic area or group, not the physicians or hospitals. The first step in an analysis is to define the boundaries of the components or "small areas" within the larger area or group. For instance, in Wan and Ozcan's (1991) study on psychiatric rehospitalization in Virginia, the unit of analysis was the area of the community service board, a designated geographic area within the Commonwealth of Virginia. Similarly, medical market areas in Quebec, Canada, were used as the unit of analysis in a study of the variations in service use and population health by Wan and Broida (1983, 1986).

A statewide study of hospital utilization, for example, generally begins with a zip code–based review of records of where patients receive health care services. "Hospital market areas" then are formed by aggregating the contiguous zip codes in which a plurality, and often a strong majority, of the residents have received their medical care from providers within the same area. Sometimes the market area contains only a single hospital; in other cases, two or more hospitals and their associated physicians and surgeons jointly influence the area's practice style.

Example of Calculating Utilization Rates

In calculating utilization rates, the most important thing to keep in mind in interpreting a population-based rate is that it takes into account all the hospitalization experiences of an area's residents, whether they went to local or distant hospitals (community or referral). We can calculate a rate of major joint surgery, for example, for a hypothetical hospital market area (HMA) we will call New Kent. There are 271,340 Medicare beneficiaries in the New Kent area (Table 6.8).

Table 6.8. Population and major joint surgery utilization of the New Kent HMA

Zip code area	Population	Number of major joint operations[a]
A	26,906	26
B	25,000	40
C	15,000	15
D	30,000	60
E[b]	77,526	114
F	58,145	145
G	38,763	45
Total	271,340	445

[a]Admissions of all New Kent residents, whether to New Kent Memorial Hospital or to hospitals outside the New Kent HMA.

[b]Contains New Kent Memorial Hospital.

Records of hospitalization reveal that 75% of the admissions of residents of the seven zip codes that make up the New Kent Hospital Market Area are to New Kent Memorial Hospital. Thus, the total population of each of these zip codes is assigned to the New Kent HMA, and the rates of hospitalization we calculate will reflect the practice style of physicians and surgeons in that area more than any other single group of providers.

To construct a utilization rate, we first count the admissions of Medicare beneficiaries in the New Kent HMA for major joint surgery at Memorial Hospital in a given year. Then we count admissions of New Kent HMA Medicare residents to hospitals outside the area for such surgery in that year. The total number is 445. We do not count admissions to Memorial Hospital of non–New Kent residents, but we do count the admissions of New Kent residents to hospitals elsewhere.

Now we need a denominator for the rate, which is 271,340, the total Medicare-eligible population living in the New Kent HMA. Dividing the number of major joint operations by the population gives a rate for the operation of 0.00164/person. This is often expressed by multiplying by 1,000, giving a rate of 1.64 admissions per 1,000 population at risk.

$$\text{Utilization rate} = \frac{\text{Major joint operations}}{\text{HMA population}}$$

$$= \frac{445}{271,340}$$

$$= 0.00164 \text{ person}$$

$$= 1.64/1,000 \text{ persons}$$

The utilization rate also can be expressed as a likelihood of 1.64 in 1,000 that a Medicare beneficiary living in the New Kent HMA will have a major joint operation in a given year. This rate can be adjusted further for the differences of age, gender, race, or socioeconomic status when it is compared to the rates of other medical market areas.

Example of Small Area Analysis

Statement of Problem   To effect any beneficial change, clear understanding of the problem is needed first; this involves quantifying the elements of the situation to develop baseline information for planning a course of action, and later evaluating its performance. One can use small area analysis in this effort to quantify various measures of health care resources and utilization and then analyze their variations and possible associations.

This example of a hypothetical case demonstrates methods of measuring the relevant concept and shows how analysis of descriptive statistics can illustrate their variability and interrelationships. The purpose of this example is:

1. To use information on education level, the rates of knee replacement and hip replacement, and bed/population and doctor/population ratios to investigate the variation (if any) in the number of replacement procedures done.
2. To assess the degree of association that the rate for each procedure has with socioeconomic and health resource indicators such as education level, bed/population ratio, and doctor/population ratio.

This example illustrates a measure of the variation in utilization rates and resource availability, and illuminates the associations between them. A study such as this assists managers as they allocate resources and provides further analysis of factors affecting health services utilization.

Methodology

Data Sources The data in this study are compiled from 10 HMAs. Information on education level, knee replacement rates, hip replacement rates, bed/population ratios, and doctor/population ratios for each area appears in Table 6.9.

Measurement of the Variables The education level, which is a general indicator of the socioeconomic status of the market area, is measured by the percentage of persons completing a high school education. Total knee and hip replacement rates give the number of knee and hip replacement procedures, respectively, per 1,000 persons per HMA; these measurements indicate the utilization rates of each HMA. The bed/population and doctor/population ratios give the number of hospital beds and doctors, respectively, per 1,000 persons in the HMA; these data indicate the level of health resources available for each HMA.

Analytical Techniques Descriptive statistics include average and standard deviation for each of the five variables. A higher standard deviation shows more variation in the measured data. Outlier measurements for each measured variable are defined as those outside the range comprising the mean ±2 standard deviations. The two standard deviations include 95% of the total area under the curve; thus an individual measurement classified as an outlier is suspicious because it falls in the 5% area under the curve. Scatterplots are included in this example to help identify outliers.

The coefficient of variation also was calculated for each of the five variables; it adjusts for the differences in numerical range of the information, producing a standardized measure of variation for each of the variables. Because a high level of standardized variation indicates the sample lacks cohesiveness and is likely not to provide accurate information, the information drawn from such a sample is considered to be of lower quality.

This example also includes correlation coefficients to provide a rough picture of the association between pairs of different variables. These associations, however, should not be interpreted as causal relationships. The scatterplots used to aid in the identification of outliers also help to illustrate graphically possible correlations between variables.

Results The results of the calculations for the descriptive statistics are shown in Table 6.10. Also included are the outliers identified through the use of scatterplots: market J for knee replacement rate, hip replacement rate, and doctor/population ratio. The correlation coefficient

Table 6.9. Measured data by HMA

HMA	Education level[a]	Knee replacement rate[b]	Hip replacement rate[b]	Bed/population ratio[c]	Doctor/population ratio[d]
A	50	5	4	10	5
B	55	7	5	12	6
C	61	8	6	12	5
D	65	9	8	13	6
E	60	9	7	12	6
F	65	10	9	13	8
G	58	12	10	15	10
H	68	14	11	16	9
I	80	18	15	18	12
J	85	25	20	20	15

[a]Education level refers to percentage of persons completing high school education.
[b]Rate refers to number of replacements per 1,000 population.
[c]Bed/population ratio refers to number of hospital beds/1,000 persons.
[d]Doctor/population ratio refers to number of physicians/1,000 persons.

Table 6.10.   Descriptive statistics calculated by HMA

Variable	Average	Standard deviation	Coefficient of variation	Identified outliers
Education level	64.7	10.7915	0.1668	None
Knee replacement rate	11.7	5.9638	0.5097	HMA J
Hip replacement rate	9.5	4.8819	0.5139	HMA J
Bed/population ratio	14.1	3.1073	0.2204	None
Doctor/population ratio	8.2	3.3267	0.4057	HMA J

matrix shown in Figure 6.4 illustrates the correlation coefficient resulting from each pair of variables.

An analysis of the values computed for the coefficient of variation suggests a ranking of the variation in the measurements taken. The higher coefficients of variation were found for knee replacement rates, hip replacement rates, and doctor/population ratios. This indicates that investigation into the specific measuring devices and/or the sample size may be warranted. The sample was small—10 HMAs—and a larger sample size would lend greater credibility to the analysis.

Results of the correlation analysis indicated high levels of correlation between two of the resource indicators, educational level and knee replacement rates, and between the two measures of utilization, bed/population ratio and doctor/population ratio. This outcome is not surprising, because the resource and utilization measurements each try to measure the same things. The correlation coefficients from the pairing of resource factors (educational level, bed/population ratio, doctor/population ratio) and utilization factors (knee replacement rates and hip replacement rates) indicate a high degree of association, with values ranging from .856 to .979. Scatterplots of some of these correlations are illustrated in Figures 6.5 through 6.9; they show a significant positive correlation, suggesting further study of whether a causal relationship exists between the resource factors and utilization rates. Information provided by an analysis such as this is used to support further sampling in the defined area, or an investigation into the possibility of a causal relationship between health resource factors and utilization rates.

	Education level	Knee replacement rate	Hip replacement rate	Bed/population ratio	Doctor/population ratio
Education level	1				
Knee replacement rate	0.934	1			
Hip replacement rate	0.944	0.994	1		
Bed/population ratio	0.919	0.979	0.978	1	
Doctor/population ratio	0.856	0.967	0.972	0.965	1

Figure 6.4.   Correlation coefficient matrix.

CONCLUSION

Managerial epidemiology plays an important role in health care management as competition in the health care industry increases, and health care managers attempt to maximize their use of health resources and increase the effectiveness of their programs to prevent disease and promote health. Among other purposes, managerial epidemiology may be used to: 1) assess the health status of the community, 2) identify health problems, 3) establish priorities, 4) plan for services, 5) analyze utilization patterns, and 6) evaluate program performance and outcomes.

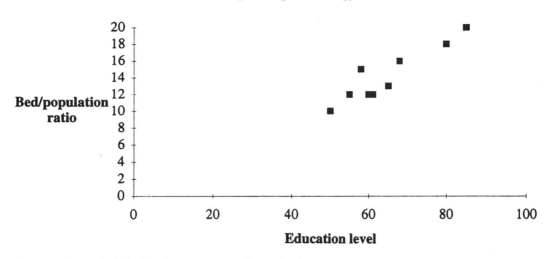

Figure 6.5.   Scatterplot for bed/population ratio versus education level.

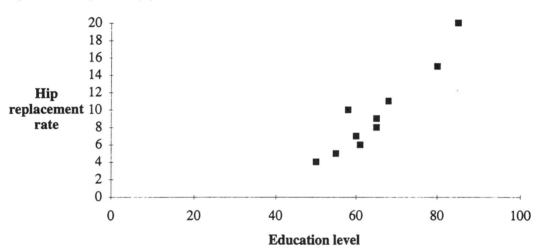

Figure 6.6.   Scatterplot for hip replacement rate versus education level.

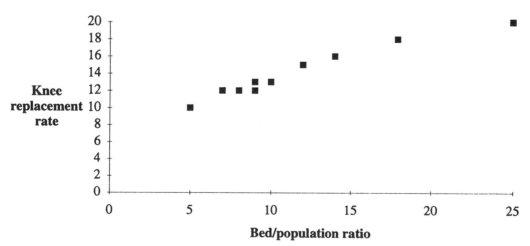

Figure 6.7.   Scatterplot for knee replacement rate versus bed/population ratio.

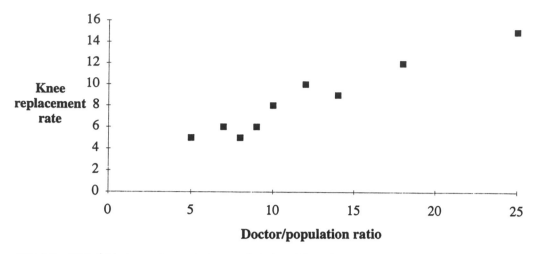

Figure 6.8.   Scatterplot for knee replacement rate versus doctor/population ratio.

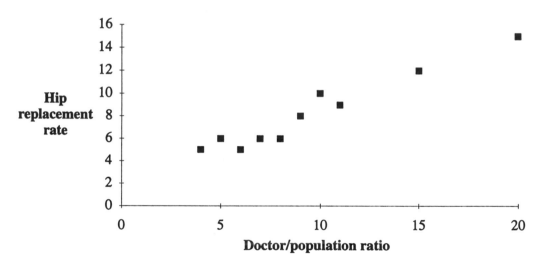

Figure 6.9.   Scatterplot for hip replacement rate versus doctor/population ratio.

REFERENCES

Audet, A.M., & Scott, H.D. (1993). The uniform clinical data set: An evaluation of the proposed national database for Medicare's Quality Review Program. *Annals of Internal Medicine, 119,* 1209–1213.

Averill, R.F., McGuire, T.E., Manning, B.E., Fowler, S.D., Horn, P.S., Dickson, P.S., Coye, M.J., Knowlton, D.L., & Bender, J.A. (1989). *A study of the relationship between severity of illness and hospital cost in New Jersey.* New Haven, CT: Health Systems International.

Barker, D.J., & Rose, G. (1990). *Epidemiology in medical practice* (4th ed.). New York: Churchill Livingstone.

Becker, E.R., & Sloan, F.A. (1983). Utilization of hospital services: The roles of teaching, case-mix, and reimbursement. *Inquiry, 20,* 248–257.

Becker, E.R., & Steinwald, B. (1981). Determinants of hospital case-mix complexity. *Health Services Research, 16,* 439–458.

Benenson, S.A. (1990). *Control of communicable diseases in men.* Washington, DC: American Public Health Association.

Blumberg, M.S. (1991). Biased estimates of expected acute myocardial infarction mortality using Medis-Groups admission severity groups. *Journal of the American Medical Association, 265,* 2965–2970.

Brewster, A.C., Karlin, L.A., Hyde, L.A., Jacobs, C.M., Bradbury, R.C., & Chae, Y.M. (1985). Medis-Groups: A clinically based approach to classifying hospital patients at admission. *Inquiry, 22,* 377–387.

Burik, D., & Nackel, J.G. (1981, Winter). Diagnosis-related groups: Tool for management. *Hospital and Health Services Administration*, pp. 25–40.

Burstin, H.R., Lipsitz, S.R., & Brennan, T.A. (1992). Socioeconomic status and risk for substandard medical care. *Journal of the American Medical Association, 268*, 2383–2387.

Caper, P. (1987). The epidemiologic surveillance of medical care. *American Journal of Public Health, 77*, 669–670.

Carson, C.A., & Zucconi, S.L. (1993). Epidemiologic indicators of health status to guide health care management decision-making. *Journal of Health Administration Education, 11*, 551–562.

Charlson, M.E., Pompei, P., Ales, K.L., & MacKenzie, C.R. (1987). A new method of classifying prognostic comorbidity in longitudinal studies: Development and validation. *Journal of Chronic Diseases, 40*, 373–383.

Conklin, J.E., & Houchens, R.L. (1987). *DRG refinement using measures of disease severity.* Santa Barbara, CA: SyseMetrics, Inc.

Conklin, J.E., Lieberman, J.V., Barnes, C.A., & Louis, D.Z. (1984). Disease staging: Implications for hospital reimbursement and management. *Health Care Financing Review, Annual Supplement*, 13–22.

Daley, J., Gertman, P.M., & Delbanco, T.L. (1988). Looking for quality in primary care physicians. *Health Affairs, 7*, 107–113.

Daley, J., Jencks, S., Draper, D., Lenhart, G., Thomas, N., & Walker, J. (1988). Predicting hospital-associated mortality for Medicare patients. *Journal of the American Medical Association, 260*, 3617–3624.

Davies, R.H., Westfal, G., & Sells, D.H. (1983). Reimbursement under DRGs: Implementation in New Jersey. *Health Services Research, 18*, 233–244.

Dever, G.E.A. (1991). *Community health analysis: Global awareness at the local level* (2nd ed.). Gaithersburg, MD: Aspen Publishers.

Einstadter, D., Kent, D.L., Fihn, S.D., & Deyo, R.A. (1993). Variation in the rate of cervical spine surgery in Washington state. *Medical Care, 31*, 711–718.

Elwood, J.M. (1982). The importance of epidemiology in the training of health planners. In A. Crichton & D. Neuhauser (Eds.), *The new epidemiology: A challenge to health administration* (pp. 51–60). Arlington, VA: Association of University Programs in Health Administration.

Fetter, R.B., Freeman, J.L., Park, H., Schneider, K., Lichtenstein, J., & Health Systems Management Group. (1989). *DRG refinement with diagnostic specific commodities and complications: A synthesis of current approaches to patient classification.* (Final report). New Haven, CT: Health Systems Management Group, School of Management. (Health Care Financing Administration under Cooperative Agreement No. 15-C-8930/1-01 and 17-C-98930/1-0251)

Filerman, G.L. (1982). The need for creative managerial epidemiology. In A. Crichton & D. Neuhauser (Eds.), *The new epidemiology: A challenge to health administration* (pp. 3–14). Arlington, VA: Association of University Programs in Health Administration.

Gable, C.B. (1990). A compendium of public health data sources. *American Journal of Epidemiology, 131*, 381–394.

Gertman, P.M., & Restuccia, J.O. (1981). The appropriateness evaluation protocol: A technique for assessing unnecessary days of hospital care. *Medical Care, 19*, 855–871.

Goldberg, K.C., Hartz A.J., Jacobsen, S.J., Krakauer, H., & Rimm, A.A. (1992). Racial and community factors influencing coronary artery bypass graft surgery rates for all 1986 Medicare patients. *Journal of the American Medical Association, 267*, 1473–1477.

Gonnella, J.S., Hornbrook, M., & Louis, D.Z. (1984). Staging of disease: A case-mix measurement. *Journal of the American Medical Association, 251*, 637–644.

Gonnella, J.S., & Louis, D.Z. (1987). Disease staging classification system. *Medical Care, 25*, 360.

Greenfield, S., Nelson, E.C., Zubkoff, M., Manning, W., Rogers, W., Kravitz, R.L., Keller, A., Tarlov, A.R., & Ware, J.E., Jr. (1992). Variations in resource utilization among medical specialties and systems of care: Results from the Medical Outcomes Study. *Journal of the American Medical Association, 267*, 1624–1630.

Grossman, J. (1990). Physician reimbursement and the Resource-Based Relative-Value Scale. *Quality Assurance and Utilization Review, 5*, 42–46.

Guterman, S., Eggers, P., Riley, G., Greene, T., & Terrell, S. (1988). The first three years of Medicare prospective payment: An overview. *Health Care Financing Review, 9*, 67–77.

Henderson, M.M., & MacStravic, R.E.S. (1982). The growing role of epidemiology in health administration. In A. Crichton & D. Neuhauser (Eds.), *The new epidemiology: A challenge to health administration* (pp. 15–24). Arlington, VA: Association of University Programs in Health Administration.

Horn, S.D., & Horn, R.A. (1986). The Computerized Severity Index: A new tool for case-mix management. *Journal of Medical Systems, 10*, 73–78.

Horn, S.D., Sharkey, P.D., & Bertram, D.A. (1983). Measuring severity of illness: Homogeneous case mix groups. *Medical Care, 21*, 14–30.

Hsiao, W.C., Braun, P., Dunn, D.L., Becker, E.R., Yntema, D., Verrilli, D., & Stamenovic, E. (1992). An overview of the development and refinement of the Resource-Based Relative Value Scale. *Medical Care, 30*, NS1–NS11.

Hulka, B.S. (1976, October 20). *Epidemiologic basis of health services research.* Paper presented to the American Public Health Association Meeting, Miami, FL.

Ibrahim, M.A. (1983). Epidemiology: Applications to health services. *The Journal of Health Administration Education, 1*, 1.

Iezzoni, L.I. (1992). Risk adjustment for medical outcome studies. In M.L. Grady & H.A. Schwartz (Eds.), *Medical effectiveness research: Data and methods* (pp. 83–97). Rockville, MD: Agency for Health Care Policy and Research.

Iezzoni, L.I., Ash, A.S., Coffman, G.A., & Moskowitz, M.A. (1992). Predicting in-hospital mortality: A comparison of severity measurement approaches. *Medical Care, 30*, 347–359.

Iezzoni, L.I., Burnside, S., Sickles, L., Moskowitz, M.A., Sawitz, E., & Levine, P.A. (1988). Coding of acute myocardial infarction: Clinical and policy implications. *Annals of Internal Medicine, 109*, 745–751.

Iezzoni, L.I., Daley, J., Heeren, T., Foley, S.M., Hughes, J.S., Fisher, E.S., Duncan, C.C., & Coffman, G.A. (1994). Using administrative data to screen hospitals for high complication rates. *Inquiry, 31*, 40–55.

Iezzoni, L.I., Foley, S.M., Daley, J., Hughes, J., Fisher, E.S., & Heeren, T. (1992). Comorbidities, complications, and coding bias: Does the number of diagnosis codes matter in predicting in-hospital mortality? *Journal of the American Medical Association, 267*, 2197–2203.

Iezzoni, L.I., & Moskowitz, M.A. (1988). A clinical assessment of MedisGroups. *Journal of the American Medical Association, 260*, 31–59.

Keeler, E.B., Rubenstein, L.V., Kahn, K.K., Draper, D., Harrison, E.R., McGinty, M.J., Rogers, W.H., & Brook, R.H. (1992). Hospital characteristics and quality of care. *Journal of the American Medical Association, 268*, 1709–1714.

Kenney, G. (1991). Understanding the effects of PPS on Medicare home health use. *Inquiry, 28*, 129–139.

Kenney, G., & Holahan, J. (1991). Nursing home transfers and mean length of stay in the prospective payment era. *Medical Care, 29*, 589–609.

Knaus, W.A., Draper, E.A., Wagner, D.P., & Zimmerman, J.E. (1985). APACHEII: A severity of disease classification system. *Critical Care Medicine, 13*, 818–829.

Knaus, W.A., Wagner, D.P., Draper, E.A., & Zimmerman, J.E. (1981). APACHE—acute physiology and chronic health evaluation: A physiologically based classification system. *Critical Care Medicine, 9*, 591–597.

Knaus, W.A., & Wagner, D.P. (1989). APACHE: A nonproprietary measure of severity of illness. *Annals of Internal Medicine, 110*(4), 327–328.

Knaus, W.A., Wagner, D.P., Zimmerman, J.E., & Draper, E.A. (1993). Variations in mortality and length of stay in intensive care units. *Annals of Internal Medicine, 118*(10), 753–761.

Kominiski, G., & Biddle, A. (1993). Changes in follow-up care for Medicare surgical patients under the prospective payment system. *Medical Care, 31*, 230–246.

Lilienfeld, A.M. (1976). *Foundations of epidemiology.* New York: Oxford University Press.

Lion, J. (1981). Case-mix differences among ambulatory patients seen by internists in various settings. *Health Services Research, 16*, 407–413.

Louis, D.Z., & Gonnella, J.S. (1986). Disease staging: Application for utilization review and quality assurance. *Quality Assurance and Utilization Review, 1*, 13–18.

Lutjens, L. (1993). Determinants of hospital length of stay. *Journal of Nursing Administration, 23*(4), 14–18.

MacDowell, N.M., & Lutz, J. (1993). Applications of epidemiologic and managed care plans. *Journal of Health Administration Education, 11*, 541–550.

Malcolm, L.A. (1993). Service management: An epidemiological model of health services. *Journal of Health Administration Education, 11*, 563–574.

Manton, K., Woodbury, M., Vertrees, J., & Stallard, E. (1993). Use of Medicare services before and after introduction of the prospective payment system. *Health Services Research, 28*, 269–292.

Mausner, J.S., & Bahn, A.K. (1974). *Epidemiology: An introductory text.* Philadelphia: W.B. Saunders.

MediQual Systems, Inc. (1993). *MEDISGROUPS scoring algorithm, January 1993 version: A technical description.* Westborough, MA: MediQual Systems.

Office of Technology Assessment. (1983). *Diagnosis related groups (DRGs) and the Medicare program: Implications for technology: A technical memorandum.* Washington, DC: Author.

Okada, L.M., & Wan, T.T.H. (1980). Impact of community health centers and Medicaid on the use of health services. *Public Health Reports, 95*, 520–534.

Oleske, D.M. (1993). Linking the delivery of health care to service population needs: The role of the epidemiologist on the health care management team. *Journal of Health Administration Education, 11*, 531–540.

Physician Payment Review Commission. (1994). *Annual Report to Congress.* Washington, DC: Author.

Plomann, M.P. (1982). *Case-mix classification systems: Development, description, and testing.* Chicago: The Hospital Research and Educational Trust.

Pollock, M.M., Ruttimann, U.E., Getson, P.R., and members of the Multi-Institutional study group. (1987). Accurate prediction of the outcome of pediatric intensive care: A new quantitative method. *New England Journal of Medicine, 316*, 134–139.

Prospective Payment Assessment Commission. (1992). *Medicare and the American health care system: Report to Congress.* Washington, DC: Author.

Richardson, D.K., & Tarnow-Mordi, W.O. (1994). Measuring illness severity in newborn intensive care. *Journal of Intensive Care Medicine, 9*, 20–33.

Safran, C. (1991). Using routinely collected data for clinical research. *Statistics in Medicine, 10*, 559–564.

Shapiro, S. (1991). Epidemiology and public policy. *American Journal of Epidemiology, 134*, 1057–1061.

Steen, P.M., Brewster, A.C., Bradbury, R.C., Estabrook, E., & Young, J.A. (1993). Predicted probabilities of hospital death as a measure of admission severity of illness. *Inquiry, 30*(2), 128–141.

Thomas, J.W., & Ashcraft, M.C. (1989). Measuring severity of illness: A comparison of inter-rater reliability and severity methodologies. *Inquiry, 26*, 483–492.

Wan, T.T.H., & Broida, J.H. (1983). Indicators for planning of health services: Assessing impacts of social and health care factors on population health in Quebec, Canada. *Socio-Economic Planning Sciences, 17*, 225–234.

Wan, T.T.H., & Broida, J.H. (1986). Socio-medical determinants of hospital utilization in Quebec, Canada, 1920–1975. *International Journal of Health Services, 16*, 43–55.

Wan, T.T.H., & Ozcan, Y. (1991). Determinants of psychiatric rehospitalization: A social area analysis. *Community Mental Health Journal, 27*, 3–15.

Wasserman, J. (1982). *DRG evaluation, Vol. I: Introduction and overview.* Princeton, NJ: Health Research and Educational Trust of New Jersey.

Wennberg, J.E. (1984). Dealing with medical practice variations: A proposal for action. *Health Affairs, 3*(2), 6–32.

Wennberg, J.E., Freeman, J.L., Shelton, R.M., & Bubolz, T.A. (1989). Hospital use and mortality among Medicare beneficiaries in Boston and New Haven. *New England Journal of Medicine, 321*, 1168–1173.

Wennberg, J.E., & Gittelsohn, A. (1982). Variations in medical care among small areas. *Scientific American, 246*, 120–134.

Williams, D., Hadley, J., & Pettengill, J. (1992). Profits, community role, and hospital closure: An urban and rural analysis. *Medical Care, 30*, 174–187.

Young, W.W. (1984). Incorporating severity of illness and comorbidity in case-mix measurement. *Health Care Financing Review, Annual Supplement*, 23–31.

Young, W.W., Swinkola, R.B., & Zorn, D.M. (1982). The measurement of hospital case mix. *Medical Care, 20*, 501–513.

Zimmerman, J.E. (Ed.). (1989). The APACHE III study design: Analytic plan for evaluation of severity and outcome. *Critical Care Medicine, 17*, S169–S221.

7

Forecasting and Strategic Planning Methods for Hospital Services

Strategy is the art of making use of time and space.

Napoleon

In planning hospital services, the first step is to understand the demand for care. Measures of demand include daily census of hospital bed utilization, inpatient admissions to the hospital, total inpatient days, occupancy rates, hours of nursing care, number of surgical procedures performed, and the like. Data on the demand for hospital care can be used: 1) to study the actual use of hospital services, 2) to understand factors affecting the actual use of services, 3) to forecast the demand for care, 4) to identify the needed levels of both short- and long-term care, and 5) to make critical decisions about program development, facility planning and construction, and the purchase of new equipment.

The central importance to hospital managers of examining demand in their research and subsequent decision making is illustrated in this chapter by the following example. A community hospital has a severe shortage of beds to meet the requests of its medical staff. An especially acute aspect of the problem is the delays it causes in scheduling elective surgery; in many cases, patients wait 5–6 weeks. Consequently, the managerial staff have raised a critical question: Would an increase in bed size be appropriate to meet the requests for more beds and have fewer delays for patients? The decision to increase bed capacity will be justified only if an empirical assessment of bed need supports it as rational.

Taking into consideration the market structure in the community the hospital serves, the board of directors should evaluate several strategies before increasing bed size. Questions about the actual and the potential demand for hospital beds should be answered:

1. Is it possible to identify a trend in bed demand at the hospital?
2. What is the most reliable and valid forecasting method to assess the bed need?
3. Do the demands for specific services vary?
4. What dynamic forces in the community affect demand?
5. How can qualitative information be obtained from the medical staff and included in deliberations about increasing resources or size?
6. What marketing strategies should be used to improve the hospital's market share and provide all the health care needed by the community?

It is the responsibility primarily of the management staff to develop strategies that respond to a hospital's critical operational problems; therefore, it is they who must lead in obtaining answers to such questions.

A research project to solve this problem would have four objectives: 1) to examine trends in the demand for hospital care and project the bed size needed for the various services provided by this hospital; 2) to identify the requirements of the medical staff for bed capacity, quality of care, and meeting potential demand for care; 3) to analyze the hospital's market share in the primary service area; and, finally, 4) to recommend managerial strategies for promoting the hospital's financial welfare.

METHODS FOR EMPIRICAL ASSESSMENT OF BED NEED

Methods to measure the need for general hospital beds first were developed in the 1920s. For several more decades, many reports made only crude assumptions about the demand for care. More recently, however, several investigators have employed statistical techniques (Cleary & Levenbach, 1982; Feldstein & German, 1965; Griffith & Wellman, 1979; Kao & Pokladnik, 1978; Laporte, 1994; Lederman, 1993; McGuires, 1992; Milner, 1988; VanVliet and Van de Ven, 1993; Walsh & Bicknell, 1977), operations research methods (Bithell, 1969; Kolesar, 1970; McClain, 1976; Nelson, 1982), and advanced simulation models (Daskin, 1982; Hancock, Magerling, Storer, & Martin, 1978; Wilson & Schuiling, 1992; Yett, Drabek, Intriligator, & Kimbell, 1979). A complete assessment of techniques for estimating bed need, in terms of their validity, reliability, and applicability, can be found in reports by Brown, Condia, and Gavin (1974), Farmer and Emami (1991), and Weiss, Ashton, and Wray (1993).

In general, estimation techniques can be classified into four groups: 1) regression methods, 2) formula models, 3) stochastic methods, and 4) simulation methods. *Regression methods* assume that the demand for hospital services can be determined analytically by using a series of independent variables as surrogate measures of demand. If surrogate measures are lacking, one can use time elements (month and/or year) as the independent variable(s) to forecast future demand; this is usually called a time series approach.

A common example of a *formula model* to estimate bed need is:

$$\text{Patient days} \atop (\text{per year}) = \frac{\text{Current patient population}}{\text{Current population}} \times \frac{\text{Average}}{\text{length}} \times \frac{\text{Projected}}{\text{population}}$$

A *stochastic model* incorporates probabilistic elements in estimating bed demand. For example, the use of the Poisson distribution in the study of patient admissions assumes that admissions, although random, have a certain expected average rate. A *simulation model* approach develops a dynamic (interactive) model to handle complex situations in which actually changing components of the real situation is not feasible. A simulation is useful only if an experimental design of an intervention in the hospital has been formulated—for example, to determine the possible impact of changes in admission criteria or other procedures on hospital utilization.

In the research project outlined earlier, we are not interested in using stochastic or simulation models. Instead, we propose to combine the regression and formula methods described above. The detailed analyses and estimation procedures are presented in the next section.

STATISTICAL ANALYSIS OF THE DEMAND FOR HOSPITAL BEDS

A forecasting model can help the hospital match resources to demand, and thus offer high-quality services at a minimum cost. This section presents an example of such a model, which uses data on previous patient days, both monthly and yearly, to forecast the demand for 12 hospital services in the years 1995–1996. Two major sources—the medical records department and the fiscal department—provide the historical data for long-range (beyond 1 year) and intermediate forecasting models. The forecasts assume that demand in previous years shows some measurable trend that will continue in the future. However, if in a given service area no trend is apparent, a single exponential smoothing model is applied; this procedure takes weighted sums of data to estimate changes for the time series. In practical terms, the plot of a smoothed time series of hospital bed demand can reveal the financial status of the hospital.

Analysis of Historical Trend

The historical trend of hospital utilization is found by examining data from medical records. The utilization data can be prepared and analyzed separately in terms of either 1) services offered, 2) nursing units, or 3) diagnostic categories of patients.

For this example, we organized the data on the basis of services or medical practices, because we plan to estimate bed need for the separate hospital services. Similarly, our survey of the medical staff will identify the potential bed demand for each physician practice.

Analysis of three kinds of utilization data from the department of medical records (Tables 7.1–7.3) shows important trends in hospital utilization.

Patient Discharge

1. General medicine services accounted for over one fifth of the total discharges, followed by the general surgery, obstetrics, and neonatology services. In the past 7 years, the use of general medicine services has increased steadily.
2. There was a small increase in the number of patients discharged from the general surgery service during 1989–1992. After 1992, the rate gradually declined. Less use of the general surgery service may be related to two changes in the environment: a) the availability of beds in other local hospitals, and b) the reimbursement policy of Blue Cross and Blue Shield, which now favors outpatient surgery.
3. A distinct decline in use of the neonatology service has occurred. This can be explained by the declining birth rate over the past decade in the United States. The number of patients

Table 7.1.   Percentages and numbers of patients discharged, 1988–1994, by type of service

Service	1988	1989	1990	1991	1992	1993	1994
General medicine	20.0	20.2	21.1	25.8	27.4	24.6	29.3
General surgery	15.3	13.6	13.8	16.0	16.7	14.6	13.9
Psychiatry	3.0	3.0	3.9	4.5	4.0	5.8	4.7
Neurology	1.1	1.1	.9	1.6	1.9	2.5	2.4
Neurosurgery	2.4	2.4	1.5	2.2	2.4	1.5	2.2
Ophthalmology	0.0	0.2	0.4	0.5	0.6	0.7	1.1
Orthopedics	8.7	8.1	7.4	8.3	7.9	8.9	8.0
Thoracic surgery	0.9	0.6	0.8	0.6	0.6	0.5	0.5
Urology	4.8	4.8	4.8	5.1	5.8	5.6	5.4
Pediatrics[a]	—	—	—	—	—	5.0	2.7
Gynecology	8.1	7.3	7.1	6.9	6.1	5.0	6.1
Obstetrics	19.2	20.8	20.6	15.5	14.5	13.6	13.1
Neonatology	16.5	17.8	17.8	12.9	12.3	11.7	10.7
Total							
Percentage	100.0	100.0	100.0	100.0	100.0	100.0	100.0
Number	18,109	17,706	18,706	16,720	16,750	17,346	17,018

[a]Before 1993, this category of service was not specifically identified in the medical records.

Table 7.2.   Percentages and numbers of patient days, 1988–1994, by type of service

Service	1988	1989	1990	1991	1992	1993	1994
General medicine	27.1	28.4	29.5	34.7	35.3	34.0	37.2
General surgery	13.7	13.4	14.1	15.5	16.3	15.7	14.2
Psychiatry	7.6	6.9	7.5	7.5	7.4	8.5	8.3
Neurology	1.4	1.2	1.2	1.7	2.0	2.7	2.8
Neurosurgery	3.4	3.1	2.3	2.8	3.9	2.4	3.1
Ophthalmology	0.0	0.1	0.3	0.3	0.3	0.3	0.4
Orthopedics	13.3	12.3	11.1	11.2	9.8	9.9	9.3
Thoracic surgery	1.2	1.1	0.9	0.9	0.8	0.8	0.6
Urology	3.9	4.6	4.0	3.8	4.7	4.7	3.9
Pediatrics[a]	—	—	—	—	—	2.8	1.5
Gynecology	5.5	5.0	5.0	4.4	4.1	3.1	4.0
Obstetrics	11.9	12.7	12.6	9.1	8.5	8.1	8.1
Neonatology	10.9	11.4	11.4	7.9	7.2	7.0	6.5
Total							
Percentage	100.0	100.0	100.0	100.0	100.0	100.0	100.0
Number	127,482	127,435	131,877	123,125	125,468	129,469	126,519

[a]Before 1993, this category of service was not specifically identified in the medical records.

discharged from the obstetrics service similarly declined, from 19.2% of the total discharges in 1988 to 13.1% in 1994.

Patient Days

1. The total number of patient days fluctuated over the past 7 years. In 1994, the total patient days dropped slightly.
2. Patients receiving general medicine services accounted for the largest proportion of total hospital days, ranging from 27.1% in 1988 to 37.2% in 1994.
3. The number of patient days in the general surgery service remained stable, although it declined slightly for 1994.
4. A moderate increase occurred in the use of specialized services such as psychiatry and neurology.

Table 7.3.   Annual average lengths of stay, 1988–1994, by type of service

Service	1988	1989	1990	1991	1992	1993	1994
General medicine	9.5	10.1	9.8	9.9	9.6	10.4	9.4
General surgery	6.3	7.1	7.2	7.1	7.3	8.1	7.6
Psychiatry	17.9	16.6	13.6	12.2	13.8	11.9	13.2
Neurology	8.8	7.6	9.9	8.1	7.7	8.3	8.6
Neurosurgery	10.1	9.9	10.9	9.5	12.2	12.1	10.7
Ophthalmology	5.0	4.4	4.7	4.5	4.1	3.4	2.9
Orthopedics	10.8	10.9	10.7	9.9	9.2	8.4	8.6
Thoracic surgery	9.5	12.5	8.8	10.9	10.2	11.8	10.5
Urology	5.7	6.9	5.9	5.5	5.8	6.3	5.4
Pediatrics[a]	—	—	—	—	—	4.3	4.2
Gynecology	4.8	4.9	5.0	4.7	5.1	4.7	4.9
Obstetrics	4.4	4.4	4.3	4.3	4.4	4.9	4.6
Neonatology	4.6	4.6	4.5	4.5	4.4	4.6	4.5
Total	8.1	8.3	7.8	7.6	7.8	7.5	7.3

[a]Before 1993, this category of service was not specifically identified in the medical records.

Annual Average Length of Stay This is computed by dividing the total number of patient days into the number of patients discharged in a given year.

1. The average length of stay has been relatively stable for the past 7 years but has declined slightly. The trend may be explained by the impacts of: a) utilization review and professional review organizations and b) the federal cost-containment policy on reimbursement by Medicare and Medicaid.
2. The average length of stay in the general surgery service fluctuated slightly. This fluctuation may be due to the variations in case mix.
3. Psychiatric patients had much longer stays than did those in other categories; so did patients who received the specialized surgical services of neurosurgery and thoracic surgery.

Long-Term Forecasting

Description of Forecasting Techniques

Linear Regression It is hypothesized that there is a time (t) effect (yearly trend) on the distribution of a measure of hospital demand (i.e., annual hospital days, annual admission, or average length of stay). The time is an independent variable, and the demand measure is a dependent variable. The estimation equation is represented by the following formula:

$$\hat{Y}_t = a + bt$$

where $\hat{Y}$ = the estimated value of the dependent variable, a = an intercept of the point where the regression line crosses the y axis, b = the regression coefficient or the slope of the regression line, and t = the year.

The regression line is derived by minimizing the sum of the squared deviations from the actual data points to the hypothesized value imputed by the line $\hat{Y}_t$. The parameters (a and b) are estimated by the following formulas:

$$b = \frac{n\sum(tY_t) - \left(\sum t\right)\left(\sum Y_t\right)}{n\left(\sum t^2\right) - \left(\sum t\right)^2}$$

$$a = \bar{Y} - b(\bar{t}), \text{ where } \bar{Y} = \frac{\sum Y_t}{n} \text{ and } \bar{t} = \frac{\sum t}{n}$$

From the estimation equation, we easily can compute the projected demand for future years. A graphical illustration of the regression line and how it relates to the X-Y data set is presented in Figure 7.1.

Simple regression also involves the following null hypothesis:

$H_0: b = 0$
$H_0: b \neq 0$

In order to examine whether there is a trend effect of the independent variable on the dependent variable, an analysis of variance (ANOVA) is performed. The formulas and data array format used for the ANOVA are shown in Table 7.4. To determine if a trend exists in the data points, the F statistic calculated in the ANOVA is compared to the value obtained from an appropriate statistical table. If the calculated F value is greater than the number provided in the table, then it can be concluded there exists a linear trend in the information, and that a forecast of the Y

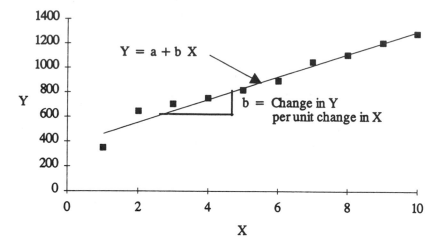

Figure 7.1. Scatterplot of hospital demand (*y*) versus time (*x*) showing regression line.

value may be made properly. Alternative formulas for calculating the error sum of squares (SS$_E$) and mean error sum of squares (MS$_E$) are provided here for convenience as well:

$$MS_E = \frac{SS_E}{n-2} = \frac{\sum(y_i - \hat{y}_i)^2}{n-2} = \frac{\sum(y_i - b_0 - b_1 X_i)^2}{n-2} = \frac{\sum e_i^2}{n-2}$$

$$SS_E = \sum y_i^2 = b_0 \sum y_i - b_1 \sum x_i y_i$$

$$SS_E = \sum(Y_i - \bar{Y})^2 - \frac{\left[\sum(X_i - \bar{X})(Y_i - \bar{Y})\right]^2}{\sum(X_i - \bar{X})^2}$$

$$SS_E = \left[\sum Y_i^2 - \frac{(\sum Y_i)^2}{n}\right] - \frac{\left(\sum X_i Y_i - \frac{\sum X_i Y_i}{n}\right)^2}{\sum X_i^2 - \frac{(\sum X_i)^2}{n}}$$

Table 7.4. ANOVA data array format for simple linear regression

Source of variation	SS	df	MS	F statistic
Regression	$SS_R = \sum(\hat{Y}_i - \bar{Y})^2$	1	$MS_R = \frac{SS_R}{1}$	$F = \frac{MS_R}{MS_E}$
Error	$SS_E = \sum(Y_i - \hat{Y}_i)^2$	$n-2$	$MS_E = \frac{SS_E}{n-2}$	
Total	$SS_T = \sum(Y_i - \bar{Y})^2$	$n-1$		

Note: SS, sum of squares; MS, mean sum of squares; SS$_R$, regression sum of squares; SS$_E$, error sum of squares; SS$_T$, total sum of squares; MS$_R$, mean regression sum of squares; MS$_E$, mean error sum of squares.

Confidence intervals are used as part of regression analysis to help compensate for the high degree of variability involved in making forecasts on a period-by-period basis. Using the t distribution, a range is determined for the prediction of the dependent variable with a given level of confidence. This level of confidence equals $1 - \alpha$, where α is the level of significance for the t distribution. The use of confidence intervals increases the practicality of forecasting through regression analysis; often, confidence levels of 95% and 99% are seen. Formulas for estimating the confidence intervals for forecasting estimates are as follows:

$$\hat{y}_i - t_{\frac{a}{2}} \cdot S_{y_i} \leq \text{Estimate} \leq \hat{y}_i + t_{\frac{a}{2}} \cdot S_{y_i}$$

where

$\hat{y}_i$ = estimated total number of patient days in a given service

$df = n - 2$

$t_{\frac{\alpha}{2}}$ = determined from the t statistical table (for α level of confidence)

$$S_{y_i} = \sqrt{(MS_E) \cdot \left[\frac{n + 1}{n} + \frac{(x_p - \bar{x})^2}{\sum x_i^2 - n\bar{x}^2} \right]}$$

where x_p is the ith year of projection (e.g., $x_p = i$th year) and x = average of years.

Nonlinear Regression When the test of linear effect of time (year) on the dependent variable shows a weak relationship between time and the demand measure, we perform nonlinear regression analyses, such as exponential regression or polynomial regression. If none of these estimation procedures can provide a good fit of the data, the investigator should search for a new independent variable or several independent variables to use in the regression.

Exponential Smoothing Model Many forecasting techniques use exponential smoothing (Farnum & Stanton, 1989; Gardner & Dannenbring, 1980; Levenbach & Cleary, 1981; Makridakis, Wheelwright, & McGee, 1983; Pindyck & Rubinfeld, 1981). Smoothing data refers to adjusting for the effects of trend, seasonal, and random fluctuation. In this analysis, we select a technique called nonadaptive, trend-adjusted linear modeling to forecast the demand for hospital beds, because this technique is a robust forecaster under a variety of conditions. A computer program contained in SAS computing packages is used to forecast demand; because the program generates monthly estimates for a given year, we sum 12 months in order to obtain the yearly bed projection. As long as the data are stationary, this method is considered a very accurate forecasting procedure.

Forecasting Results Three forecasting models are applied, first to estimate (i.e., past demand for hospital beds) and then to project (i.e., future demand) the number of hospital admissions and the number of patient days. The forecasting results are compared in terms of the goodness of fit of the models and the proportion of errors in estimating the demand. Then we perform a two-way ANOVA for each of the 12 categories of services, to determine the seasonal and yearly effects. No significant seasonal effect of the admission data is found for 6 service categories (general medicine, neurology, ophthalmology, orthopedics, thoracic surgery, and gynecology). The most accurate forecasting technique is used to forecast the number of patient admissions and patient days for 1995, 1996, and 1997.

Forecasting Patient Admission (Patient Discharge) The linear model, which examines the effect of time (year) on the number of patients discharged, shows a significant effect, by the past trend on admission discharges, for 8 out of the 12 categories of services in the years 1988–1994 (Table 7.5). (Pediatrics is not included in these analyses because the available data are insufficient for accurate statistical analysis.) The R^2 value indicates the proportion of variance in the number of patient admissions (discharges) that is accounted for by the past utilization trend. This value ranges from 14.7% for the general surgery service to 93.4% for the ophthalmology service.

We use the polynomial model, a nonlinear regression approach that includes time elements (t, t^2, and t^3) as independent variables in the equation, to estimate hospital admission. The results show that this model estimates only four categories of service adequately: the neurology, ophthalmology, gynecology, and general surgery (Table 7.5).

The single exponential smoothing technique is also applied to determine the effects of yearly trend and seasonal fluctuation on patient admission (discharge). Data in Table 7.5 show that for most of the services this model fits the data better than do the other models; the exceptions were the general medicine and ophthalmology services. Overall, the data support the use of the linear regression model, because this model outperforms the nonlinear (polynomial) regression model in estimating the number of patient admissions (discharges). Furthermore, this model is practical in that its power to forecast increases if additional independent variables (e.g., case-mix measures, patient attributes, market share measures) are included.

After assessing the models, we forecast the number of patients who would be admitted/discharged for 1995, 1996, and 1997. Table 7.6 summarizes the results for each of the 12 services except pediatrics.

Forecasting Patient Days (1995–1996)   A procedure similar to that just described for forecasting patient admissions (discharges) is used to examine the models for forecasting patient days. Table 7.7 presents the summary results of each model. Both linear and polynomial regression models show comparable results, but the linear regression appears to outperform the polynomial regression in four service categories—the general medicine, gynecology, obstetrics, and neonatology. Data in Table 7.7 also show no apparent yearly effects in four categories: general

Table 7.5. Comparison of three forecasting models using trend data to estimate annual number of patients discharged, 1988–1994, by type of service

| Service | Forecasting model[a] | | | | | |
| | Linear | | Polynomial | | Single exponential smoothing[b] | |
	R^2	F value	R^2	F value	R^2	F value
General medicine	82.6	23.7*	82.8	4.8	*68.5*	*8.1**
General surgery	4.7	0.3	91.9	11.4*	*45.4*	*3.7**
Psychiatry	61.9	8.1*	66.5	2.2	*80.9*	*15.7**
Neurology	82.0	22.8*	95.5	21.0*	*75.0*	*10.8**
Neurosurgery	20.9	1.3	32.1	0.5	*53.7*	*4.3**
Ophthalmology	93.4	70.5*	99.7	381.1*	*48.7*	*2.7**
Orthopedics	16.8	1.1	61.5	1.6	*49.0*	*2.7**
Thoracic surgery	77.7	17.4*	78.9	3.8	*44.7*	*3.0**
Urology	43.4	3.8	68.7	2.2	*34.3*	*2.0**
Gynecology	81.8	22.4*	91.6	10.9*	*77.6*	*9.4**
Obstetrics	75.0	15.0*	88.9	8.0	*90.6*	*35.9**
Neonatology	75.5	15.4*	86.6	6.5	*90.1*	*34.0**

*Significant at 0.05 or lower level.

[a]The goodness of fit of the model is determined by the magnitude of R^2 as well as the F ratio for the overall model applied to a specific type of service.

[b]Italics denote that model indicates both seasonal and yearly effects; it is necessary to adjust for these effects when forecasting.

Table 7.6. Forecasted number of patient discharges (admissions) for 1995, 1996, and 1997, by type of service

Service	1995	1996	1997
General medicine[a]	5,097	5,254	5,468
General surgery[b]	2,441	2,454	2,453
Psychiatry[b]	903	1,010	1,013
Neurology[b]	442	489	533
Neurosurgery[b]	316	296	282
Ophthalmology[b]	186	209	232
Orthopedics[b]	1,326	1,326	1,306
Thoracic surgery[a]	60	47	35
Urology[b]	970	968	984
Pediatrics[c]	657	657	657
Gynecology[b]	832	739	653
Obstetrics[b]	1,884	1,578	1,302
Neonatology[b]	1,564	1,286	1,043
Total	16,678	16,313	15,961

[a]Projected figures using a linear regression model.

[b]Projected figures using a single exponential smoothing technique when both yearly and seasonal effects were observed.

[c]Data were not available in this category before 1993; therefore, an average of 1993 and 1994 data was used as an estimate for future years.

surgery, psychiatry, neurosurgery, and urology services. A further comparison of the linear and polynomial models shows that the differences between past actual and estimated patient days are negligible (for the years 1993 and 1994), regardless of the type of regression model used.

When neither the linear nor the polynomial model can identify the yearly effect on patient days, forecasts use smoothed average estimates. In addition, if a seasonal effect is detected in the analysis of patient days, the smoothing model is used to forecast the data. Table 7.8 presents the hospital days forecasted for 1995, 1996, and 1997.

Table 7.7. Comparison of three forecasting models using trend data for estimating annual number of patient days, 1988–1994, by type of service

Service	Forecasting model[a]					
	Linear		Polynomial		Single exponential smoothing[b]	
	R^2	F value	R^2	F value	R^2	F value
General medicine	95.0	94.9*	96.5	27.8*	68.9	8.3*
General surgery	32.5	2.4	96.3	25.8*	49.3	3.6*
Psychiatry	35.1	2.7	54.0	1.2	34.9	2.0*
Neurology	83.3	24.9*	96.9	30.9*	60.4	5.7*
Neurosurgery	1.9	0.1	19.2	0.2	39.2	2.4*
Ophthalmology	87.4	34.6*	99.2	115.9*	33.0	1.4
Orthopedics	93.7	74.6*	96.9	31.2*	60.6	5.7*
Thoracic surgery	96.7	146.8*	97.8	43.7*	28.8	1.5
Urology	.7	0.0	.4	0.1	23.6	1.2
Gynecology	81.8	22.5*	91.6	10.9*	67.8	7.8*
Obstetrics	73.8	14.1*	88.5	7.7	88.2	27.9*
Neonatology	76.8	16.6*	87.3	6.9	87.0	24.8*

*Significant at 0.005 or lower level.

[a]The goodness of fit of the model is determined by the magnitude of R^2 as well as the F ratio for the overall model applied to a specific type of service.

[b]Italics denote that model indicates both seasonal and yearly effects; it is necessary to adjust for these effects when forecasting.

Intermediate Forecasting   Long-term forecasting yields an aggregate yearly measure of demand. An accurate forecast, however, must examine the seasonal or monthly fluctuations so that adjustments can be made for future observations. An intermediate forecasting method, such as the monthly indices technique, distributes a yearly forecast across the months of the year according to observed seasonal patterns of demand.

A two-way ANOVA examines the yearly and seasonal effects on two measures of hospital demand, patient admissions and patient days. Table 7.9 presents a summary of the analysis. First, the proportion of variance in hospital demand explained by the yearly and seasonal effects is computed. The residual, unexplained variance, is calculated by taking the difference between the total variance and the explained variance (yearly and seasonal factors). The data in Table 7.9 indicate that, with the exception of the urology service, the yearly effect on both demand measures, patient admissions (discharges) and patient days, is much stronger than the seasonal effect. In some cases, the seasonal fluctuation is statistically insignificant or negligible for four service categories: general medicine, neurology, orthopedics, and thoracic surgery. However, in several categories of services—urology, general surgery, neurosurgery, and neonatology—the seasonal effect is strong and statistically significant; therefore, it is necessary to adjust for seasonal fluctuations when the forecasting model is applied.

Short-Term Forecasting: Multiple Months Involved   The variability of utilization within the year is an unavoidable and significant fact of life for all providers of health care. In order to meet service needs, the planning of health services should take not only long-term trends, but also short-term fluctuations into account.

A seasonal fluctuation in demand may manifest itself as an increase in the incidence of cold and flu cases in the winter, or ski injuries and drowning in resort areas by season. To the extent that such fluctuations may be consistent, and linked to known factors in the environment, they may be predictable. If they can be forecast accurately, short-term fluctuations can enable management to make appropriate short-term planning decisions. In practice, short-term fluctuations in utilization often can be predicted with greater accuracy than long-term trend (Mac-Stravic, 1984).

Table 7.8.   Forecast number of patient days for 1995, 1996, and 1997, by type of service

Service	1995	1996	1997
General medicine[a]	49,376	51,449	53,921
General surgery[b]	21,752	19,900	20,172
Psychiatry[b]	10,520	10,713	10,905
Neurology[a]	3,842	4,209	4,578
Neurosurgery[b]	3,535	3,557	3,504
Ophthalmology[b]	639	716	794
Orthopedics[a]	10,616	9,769	8,922
Thoracic surgery[a]	687	571	456
Urology[b]	5,410	5,429	5,448
Pediatrics[c]	2,796	2,796	2,796
Gynecology[b]	3,931	3,714	3,272
Obstetrics[b]	8,737	7,272	6,236
Neonatology[b]	7,302	5,699	4,457
Total (projected)	129,143	125,794	125,061

[a]Projected figures using a linear regression model.

[b]Projected figures using a single exponential smoothing technique when both seasonal and yearly effects were observed.

[c]Data were not available in this category before 1993; therefore, an average of 1993 and 1994 data was used as an estimate for future years.

Table 7.9. Percentages of variance in hospital demand explained by yearly, monthly, and residual factors for 12 services studied

Service and effect	Percent of variance explained	
	Patient admissions	Patient days
General medicine		
Yearly effect	60.3*	58.3*
Monthly effect	8.2	10.7*
Residual	31.5	31.0
(Total)	(100.0)	(100.0)
General surgery		
Yearly effect	19.1*	33.0*
Monthly effect	27.5*	21.9*
Residual	63.4*	45.1
(Total)	(100.0)	(100.0)
Psychiatry		
Yearly effect	73.0	20.8
Monthly effect	7.9*	14.0
Residual	19.1	65.2
(Total)	(100.0)	(100.0)
Neurology		
Yearly effect	67.7*	49.7*
Monthly effect	6.9	10.8
Residual	25.4	39.5
(Total)	(100.0)	(100.0)
Neurosurgery		
Yearly effect	36.7*	25.0*
Monthly effect	16.9*	14.3
Residual	46.4	60.7
(Total)	(100.0)	(100.0)
Ophthalmology		
Yearly effect	34.1*	17.5
Monthly effect	14.9	15.0
Residual	51.0	66.9
(Total)	(100.0)	(100.0)
Orthopedics		
Yearly effect	28.4*	53.4*
Monthly effect	15.9	7.0
Residual	55.7	39.6
(Total)	(100.0)	(100.0)
Thoracic surgery		
Yearly effect	34.8*	18.7*
Monthly effect	9.9	10.1
Residual	55.3	71.2
(Total)	(100.0)	(100.0)
Urology		
Yearly effect	11.9	15.0
Monthly effect	22.5*	8.6
Residual	65.6	76.4
(Total)	(100.0)	(100.0)
Gynecology		
Yearly effect	63.1*	56.0*
Monthly effect	8.5	11.8*
Residual	28.4	32.2
(Total)	(100.0)	(100.0)

(*continued*)

Table 7.9.   (*continued*)

Service and effect	Percent of variance explained	
	Patient admissions	Patient days
Obstetrics		
Yearly effect	85.2*	82.8*
Monthly effect	5.7*	5.5
Residual	9.1	11.7
(Total)	(100.0)	(100.0)
Neonatology		
Yearly effect	84.1*	83.7*
Monthly effect	6.0*	5.1*
Residual	9.9	11.2*
(Total)	(100.0)	(100.0)

Note: The detailed ANOVA results can be obtained from the author.

*Indicates the effect is statistically significant at 0.005 or lower level.

Detecting Seasonal Trends in Demand: An Example   There are two possible temporal effects on the demand for intensive care unit (ICU) and coronary care unit (CCU) services: 1) a seasonal trend (month by month), and 2) a cyclical pattern. To detect the presence of seasonal changes or trends in the demand for ICU/CCU beds in the community hospital described in this chapter, seasonal fluctuation patterns are expressed as functions of consistent mathematical relationships. Monthly indexes are calculated between the underlying mean or trend in overall utilization and the use of services in specific months (Table 7.10), where

T_m = total number of patient days in ICU and CCU for that month over 4 years (e.g., for January: $98 + 100 + 98 + 121 = 417$).

$\overline{Y}_m$ = monthly average patient days: total number of patient days divided by number of years (e.g., for January: $417/4 = 104.3$).

I_m = monthly (seasonal) index: monthly average patient days divided by mean monthly average ($\overline{Y}_m/\overline{Y}_t$) (e.g., for January: $104.3/96.4 = 1.08$).

$\overline{T}$ = average total monthly demand: sum of the monthly totals (T_m) divided by the 12 months ($4625/12 = 385.4$).

$\overline{Y}_t$ = mean monthly average: the sum of the monthly averages divided by the 12 months ($1156.5/12 = 96.4$).

If the monthly index (I_m) = 1, there is no monthly or seasonal trend.

To determine if there is a monthly or seasonal trend in the demand for ICU/CCU beds, we calculate χ^2 for the following null hypothesis:

H_0: There is no seasonal trend ($I_m = 1$ for all months)
H_a: There is a seasonal trend ($I_m = 1$ for at least 1 month)

$$\chi^2 = \sum \left[(T_m - \overline{T})^2 / \overline{T} \right]$$

$$= \frac{(417 - 385.4)^2}{385.4} + \frac{(414 - 385.4)^2}{385.4} + \cdots + \frac{(425 - 385.4)^2}{385.4}$$

$$= 224.7$$

The chi-square statistic in this example has a degree of freedom of 11 (number of months minus 1 [$m - 1$]). If we let $\alpha = .001$, then the appropriate critical value is 31.3. Because our χ^2 value in this example ($\chi^2 = 224.7$) is greater than 31.3, we may reject H_0 and conclude that there is a seasonal trend in the demand for ICU/CCU beds.

Table 7.10. ICU/CCU patient days by month (January–December)

Year	J	F	M	A	M	J	J	A	S	O	N	D	Total
7	98	106	101	90	75	70	78	72	82	100	125	48	1045
8	100	94	96	82	70	61	66	72	88	84	144	143	1100
9	98	94	90	82	70	60	56	70	80	184	196	120	1200
10	121	120	98	110	100	96	88	92	102	114	125	114	1280
T_m	417	414	385	364	315	287	288	306	352	482	590	425	385.4[a]
$\bar{Y}_m$	104.3	103.5	96.3	91.0	78.8	71.8	72.0	76.5	88.0	120.5	147.5	160.3	96.4[b]
I_m	1.08	1.07	1.00	.94	.82	.74	.75	.79	.91	1.25	1.53	1.10	

[a]Average total monthly demand ($\bar{T}$).
[b]Mean monthly average ($\bar{Y}_t$).

To make monthly forecasts for a given year (i), we calculate $\hat{Y}_i$, the estimated annual demand for ICU/CCU beds in the ith year, based on the regression equation estimation from the following formula:

$$\hat{Y}_i = 371 + 92.2\, X_i$$

Therefore, if $I_m = \overline{Y}_m / \overline{Y}_t$, as calculated above, we can calculate $\hat{Y}_{I_m}$, the estimated demand in the ith year for the mth month:

$$\hat{Y}_{I_m} = I_m \cdot Y_i/12$$

Therefore, if we are interested in calculating the January demand for ICU/CCU beds in the 12th year: $\hat{Y}_{12} = 1.08 \times (1{,}477/12) = 133$. Table 7.11 presents projected ICU/CCU bed demand for each month in the 12th year.

ASSESSING THE POTENTIAL DEMAND FOR HOSPITAL BEDS: INCORPORATING PHYSICIANS' VIEWS

The study of physicians' practices can help to identify potential marketing strategies. Although data on bed use provide valuable information about the trend in bed demand, additional data from surveys or interviews of physicians can indicate needed adjustments to projections of hospital patient days.

Research that encompasses only objective data produces inaccurate forecasts when the data are imperfect. Straight trend analyses, although valuable, are not trustworthy if data are incomplete, unavailable, or inaccurate. Furthermore, even with adequate data, a straight trend analysis examines only past use patterns and neglects potential changes. For example, an analysis may show a hospital does not really need to add beds. However, it may be that physicians in the community find it so hard to admit their patients at the hospital that they do not use it as much as they could. It is just this kind of information on possibilities that should be built into a statistical forecast.

Sampling

Because both specialty and staff status affect physician productivity and contact with the hospital, the physicians with privileges at the hospital should be stratified by specialty and by privilege. This produces a list of the physicians in each specialty who have a given staff status. A stratified profile of the physician population makes it possible to draw a representative sam-

Table 7.11.   Projected ICU/CCU bed demand, year 12

Month	I_m	$\times$	$\hat{Y}_i/12$	$=$	$\hat{Y}_{I_m}$ [a]
January	1.08		123		133
February	1.07		123		132
March	1.00		123		123
April	0.94		123		116
May	0.82		123		101
June	0.74		123		91
July	0.75		123		92
August	0.79		123		97
September	0.91		123		112
October	1.25		123		154
November	1.53		123		188
December	1.10		123		135

[a]Projected monthly patient days by month in year 12.

ple. In our sample community hospital, the specialty categories are: general medicine, general surgery, psychiatry, neurology, neurosurgery, ophthalmology, orthopedics, urology, thoracic surgery, pediatrics, obstetrics, gynecology, and neonatology. Privilege statuses are: attending or active, associate, consulting, and courtesy.

Survey Instrument

A survey questionnaire of 20 items is used to elicit information about the size and location of the physician's practice as well as physicians' perceptions of the bed space and services needed at the study hospital (Table 7.12). The first 10 questions deal with the location (counties) of the physician's practice, number of hours worked per week, number of patient visits handled in the office each month, and number of in- and outpatient hospital admissions made each month (both to the study hospital and to all area hospitals in general). The last half of the survey asks about the perceived need for expanded beds and services at the study hospital and also solicits opinions about that hospital's operations.

Sampled staff members are notified by a formal letter and then contacted by phone or, if unavailable, by mail. Of the 204 physicians sampled, 46% responded by telephone and 16% by mail, giving a usable sample of 126 respondents.

Measurement of Variables

The perceived need and potential demand derived from the survey data are calculated as follows:

Potential demand = (number of patients admitted monthly to all the hospitals) − (number of patients admitted monthly to the study hospital)

Unmet need = (number of possible monthly admissions to the study hospital if space were available) − (number of actual monthly admissions to the study hospital)

Findings

Profile of Physicians   Table 7.13 shows the distribution of the total physician population in each status and specialty, including the number of physicians in each subgroup (e.g., the number of attending, associate, courtesy, and consulting surgeons). Of the total number of physicians, attending physicians account for 43%. Among the 11 specialties, physicians in internal medicine or surgery have the largest proportion.

A sample is drawn preserving the indicated population proportions. Table 7.14 presents a detailed profile of the sample population, giving average age, productivity, and number of hospital privileges held for the physicians in each specialty and status. (The specialties of pathology and radiology are not included in the sample because these specialists do not admit patients to the hospital.)

Potential Demand, Actual Use of, and Demand for Beds   An analysis is performed to determine the potential demand for hospital services, the actual perception of needed beds, and the actual use of the study hospital (see Table 7.15).

The following three variables of hospital use are correlated with physician characteristics to discover the relationships between physicians' characteristics and their perceptions of need:

1. *Potential demand* is calculated as the total number of hospital admissions less the total number of admissions at the study hospital. These figures represent the total number of admissions that the study hospital could capture if circumstances permitted.

2. The perceived *unmet need* for beds is calculated by subtracting actual admissions to the study hospital from the number of admissions possible if beds were available, to find the number of additional admissions each physician supposedly would generate if additional beds were available.

Table 7.12.   Physician survey questionnaire

1. How many hours do you practice in an average week? _____

2. Do you practice in any of the following geographic areas?

	Yes	No
County A?	_____	_____
County B?	_____	_____
County C?	_____	_____
County D?	_____	_____
County E?	_____	_____
Any other area?	If yes, where?_____

3. Please indicate, yes or no, whether your practice usually includes any of the following:

	Yes	No
Internal medicine?	_____	_____
Pediatrics?	_____	_____
Obstetrics/gynecology?	_____	_____
Emergency care?	_____	_____
Minor surgery?	_____	_____
Major surgery?	_____	_____
Other (please specify): _____

4. Of the above:
    a. Which one occupies most of your time? _____
    b. Which occupies the second largest amount of your time? _____

5. In your average monthly practice:
    a. How many *patient visits* occur in your office? _____
    b. How many patient admissions do you make for hospital INPATIENT care? _____
    c. How many patient referrals do you make for hospital OUTPATIENT care? _____

6. Do you have an office arrangement in which major laboratory and radiology services are provided to you?
    yes _____ no _____

7. Do you have any other clinical ancillary services in your office?   yes _____   no _____
    If yes, please describe: _____

8. Do you consider hospital X your primary place for admitting patients?   yes _____   no _____

9. In your last *complete* working month, how many of your patients were admitted to hospital X? _____

10. In your last complete month, *not including* emergency patients, how many patients *could* you have admitted to hospital X if there had been enough hospital beds available? _____

The following statements relate to your feelings about hospital X. For each statement, please indicate whether you strongly agree, agree, disagree, or strongly disagree. If you disagree or strongly disagree, please specify reason(s).

11. Hospital X has enough beds to meet my patient needs.
    Strongly agree? _____ Agree? _____ *Disagree? _____ *Strongly disagree? _____
    *Reason(s) _____

12. Hospital X provides adequate patient care.
    Strongly agree? _____ Agree? _____ *Disagree? _____ *Strongly disagree? _____
    *Reason(s) _____

13. Hospital X provides sufficient clinical ancillary services.
    Strongly agree? _____ Agree? _____ *Disagree? _____ *Strongly disagree? _____
    *Reason(s) _____

14. Hospital X provides adequate nursing.
    Strongly agree? _____ Agree? _____ *Disagree? _____ *Strongly disagree? _____
    *Reason(s) _____

(continued)

Table 7.12. (*continued*)

To better facilitate your relationship with hospital X, we would like to know how important the following areas are to you. On a scale of 1 (least important) to 5 (most important), how do you feel about:

15. The purchase of additional modern equipment.

    1   2   3   4   5

    Note: if response is 4 or 5, please specify: _____

16. Special ways to recognize and reward outstanding physician contributions.

    1   2   3   4   5

    Note: if response is 4 or 5, please specify: _____

17. The provision of more clinical ancillary services.

    1   2   3   4   5

    Note: if response is 4 or 5, please specify: _____

18. The development of innovative management strategies that include physician participation.

    1   2   3   4   5

    Note: if response is 4 or 5, please specify: _____

19. Fringe benefits for physicians.

    1   2   3   4   5

    Note: if response is 4 or 5, please specify: _____

20. The development of computerized scheduling procedures for areas such as surgery and admitting.

    1   2   3   4   5

    Note: if response is 4 or 5, please specify: _____

21. IF YOU ARE A SURGEON, which do you find more difficult:

    a. Getting beds for your patients?

    b. Getting time on the surgery schedule?

    THANK YOU VERY MUCH FOR YOUR TIME AND CONSIDERATION.

Table 7.13. Number and percentage distribution of medical staff at study hospital, by specialty and status

Specialty	Staff status (%)			
	Attending	Associate	Consulting	Courtesy
Family practice	6.4	6.6	1.3	5.1
Internal medicine	23.0	21.1	47.4	39.5
Obstetrics/gynecology	9.4	5.3	2.6	3.1
Orthopedics	9.4	10.5	1.3	3.6
Pediatrics	17.7	18.4	23.1	5.6
Psychiatry	3.0	10.5	3.9	11.8
Surgery	22.6	26.3	19.2	27.2
Anesthesia[a]	2.6	1.3	—	2.6
Emergency medicine[a]	1.5	—	—	1.5
Pathology[a]	1.1	—	—	—
Radiology[a]	3.0	—	—	—
Total				
Percentage	43.2	12.4	12.7	31.8
Number	265	76	78	195

[a]Dashes indicate that no physician is available with that specialty at that level.

3. A third variable is whether or not the *study hospital* is considered the primary place for admitting patients.

All three variables first are tested against the physician characteristics of specialty and status to see which traits bear heavily on the nature of the responses. The results, presented in Table 7.15,

Table 7.14. Mean age, admissions, days, inpatient, outpatient, and net incomes and hospital privileges by specialty and status for survey respondents

Specialty	Number of respondents	Mean age	Mean admissions	Patient days	Mean inpatient $	Mean outpatient $	Mean net $	Mean number of privileges
Family practice	2	41	39	401	146,587	14,654	149,387	3.5
Internal medicine	10	46	46	478	140,752	16,440	155,600	2.9
Obstetrics/gynecology	6	44	107	1648	284,987	11,645	358,374	1.5
Orthopedics	5	49	44	523	122,890	3,172	119,330	2.4
Pediatrics	11	45	65	304	53,736	3,285	53,915	2.8
Psychiatry	1	35	79	1425	266,963	−18	224,571	1.0
Surgery	13	46	58	389	132,923	12,024	141,212	3.3
Emergency medicine	1	50	1	5	927	476,325	400,725	0.0
Total	49							
Status								
Attending	49	46	60	569	134,940	156,241	156,241	2.7
Associate	19	34	74	286	102,349	16,780	66,713	2.1
Consulting	12	51	0	0	122	549	646	2.7
Courtesy	46	48	17	24	19,688	2,287	5,955	3.2
Total	126							

Table 7.15.   Potential demand, perceived bed need, and hospital viewed as primary hospital by physician, by status and specialty

Specialty	Potential demand[a]	Unmet need[b]	Hospital[c]
Family practice	23.7	5.0	42.9
Internal medicine	12.2	2.1	24.3
Obstetrics/gynecology	16.2	6.8	40.0
Orthopedics	21.9	11.6	37.5
Pediatrics	5.8	0.4	66.7
Psychiatry	2.9	0.5	33.3
Surgery	20.3	4.0	29.4
Anesthesiology[d]	0.0	0.0	0.0
Emergency medicine[e]	0.0	0.0	100.0
Status			
Attending	15	4.3	61.2
Associate	11.6	3.9	42.1
Consulting	7.6	0.6	25.0
Courtesy	15	2.9	10.9

[a]Average number of patients sent to hospitals other than hospital X.

[b]Average number of additional beds that would be used if available.

[c]Percentage of physicians in each category who say that hospital X is their primary hospital.

[d]There was only one respondent.

[e]Two respondents only.

show that, as expected, staff status affects whether the study hospital is considered the doctor's primary hospital, and specialty affects potential demand. Neither status nor specialty explains the responses to perceived unmet need for beds.

In a second procedure, the average responses for each demand variable are tabulated, then broken down by status and specialty. (The specialties of anesthesiology and emergency medicine are not included in this analysis because data for these specialties are insufficient for accurate statistical analysis.) Table 7.16 shows: 1) the average number of patients each month not being sent to the study hospital, but who could be (column 4), for each status and specialty category; 2) the average number of admissions perceived as needed (column 5), by physician status and specialty; and 3) the percentage of doctors in each category who consider the study hospital their primary place for admitting patients (column 2).

Data in Tables 7.15 and 7.16 reveal the following important findings:

1. More than 20 beds every month could be used by physicians in each of three specialties—family practice, orthopedics, and surgery—if they were to admit their patients to the study hospital (Table 7.16).
2. The potential for hospital beds for psychiatric patients is very small, averaging three patients per month (Table 7.16).
3. The most unmet need for hospital beds was perceived among physicians in orthopedics (12 beds), followed by obstetrics and gynecology (7 beds) and family practice (5 beds) (Table 7.16).
4. More than half of the pediatricians (66.7%) considered the study hospital their primary hospital for admitting their patients, while a relatively small proportion of physicians in internal medicine (24.3%) and in surgery (29.4%) did so (Table 7.16).
5. Only 61.2% of physicians with an attending status reported that they use the study hospital as a primary hospital for their patients (Table 7.15).

Table 7.16.   Estimation procedures for potential demand and unmet patient need at hospital for an average month

Specialty	(1) Number of medical staff	(2) % Doctors using hospital X	(3)[a] Estimated number of doctors	(4) Average potential demand (patients)	(5) Average unmet need (patients)	(6)[a] Estimated potential demand (patients)	(7)[a] Estimated unmet need (patients)
Family practice	33	42.9	14	23.7	5.0	331.8	70
Internal medicine	191	24.3	46	12.2	2.1	561.2	96.6
Obstetrics/gynecology	37	40.0	15	16.2	6.8	243	102
Orthopedics	41	37.5	15	21.9	11.6	328.5	174
Pediatrics	90	66.7	60	5.8	.4	348	24
Psychiatry	42	33.3	14	2.9	.5	40.6	7
Surgery	148	29.4	44	20.3	4.0	893.2	176
Total (monthly estimate)						2,746.3	649.6

[a]Column 3 = (1) × (2); column 6 = (3) × (4); column 7 = (3) × (5).

From the data presented in Table 7.16, we can estimate monthly figures for the hospital's potential bed demand and unmet need for beds. The estimates are shown in columns 6 and 7, respectively. It is important to note that our estimates for beds should be interpreted with caution, because differing assumptions underlie their computations. The figure for potential demand is derived by assuming all the medical staff at the study hospital would admit their patients there. The figure for unmet need is a more realistic estimate, because it takes into account physicians' perception of unmet bed needs. This figure also estimates the number of additional patient admissions that could be expected if additional beds were available.

When the average demand figures are multiplied by the total number of doctors in each category, quite high figures for potential demand and bed need emerge. It is estimated that a total of 2,746 patients are being sent *monthly* to hospitals other than the study hospital. The total perceived unmet need for beds is estimated to be about 650 admissions per month.

These figures are very large, and indicate potential demand; moreover they also reveal which physicians feel the greatest demand for additional beds. Even if only those physicians with attending and associate status are considered, the potential demand is 1,467 admissions and the perceived number of patient admissions that could be generated is 348 per month.

Thus there is apparently an unmet demand for beds at the study hospital. These analyses can help managers decide where the greatest demand lies. In addition, coupled with productivity analyses, they can help managers choose the most cost-effective strategies regarding bed capacity.

BED NEED ASSESSMENT: COMPLETE METHODOLOGY

In planning hospital services, understanding the extent of the demand for care is paramount. However, once we have analyzed the historical trends in demand, using hospital data and physician survey data, we should go on to consider how this information, together with market share information, can be used to develop marketing strategies.

This section incorporates the analysis of past use trends and demand projections from the previous two sections, together with other market share analysis, to describe a comprehensive methodology for assessing bed need in a local hospital. The assessment must answer three basic questions:

1.   What are the most pertinent data for estimating bed need at the study hospital?
2.   How many beds will be needed over a time span of at least 3 years?

3. Are there surplus beds in neighboring hospitals that may affect the expansion of bed capacity at the study hospital?

The assessment methodology is summarized in Table 7.17.

Initial Estimates of Bed Need

Defining the Population Served   The 1994 hospital census data, tabulated by the geographic origin of patients, characterizes the patient population at the study hospital as follows:

1. A large percentage (89%) of the patient population is white and residents of the area, with, on average, more education.
2. Over the past 3 years, characteristics of the patient population have shown little change.
3. The areas with a great potential for attracting more patient population are the zip-code areas in the county with a high concentration of whites.

Detailed population projections for small areas are needed to estimate the service population by geographic areas.

Understanding Past and Current Utilization   The analysis of data from the medical records and fiscal departments of the hospital, which is explained in the previous two sections, can be summarized as follows:

1. Patient discharges from the general medicine and surgery services show an increasing trend, and those from obstetrics and neonatology services a steady decline.

Table 7.17.   Step-by-step summary of methodology for determining need for hospital beds

Part A: Data analysis to estimate bed need at study hospital
    Step 1: Define the service population.
        a. Determine the primary service area.
        b. Identify major characteristics of the population served.
        c. Specify the change in size and distribution of the population in the primary service area.
    Step 2: Understand current and past utilization: trend analysis[a]
        a. Patient admission or discharge
        b. Patient days per year per service/unit
        c. Average length of stay
        d. Occupancy rate
        e. Comparison of budgeted patient days and actual patient days
Part B: Forecast of future demand for beds
    Step 1: Project future demand.
        a. Admissions and patient days
        b. Medical staff's perception of future bed need
    Step 2: Select normative standard for occupancy rate.
    Step 3: Calculate future bed need at the hospital.
Part C: Assessment of neighboring hospitals (adjusted factor)
    Step 1: Identify excess beds in the primary service area.
    Step 2: Determine the hospital's share of the surplus.
    Step 3: Estimate the hospital's assigned portion of future surplus.
Part D: Final calculation of bed need
    Step 1: Compute bed need as corrected for the minimum share of future excess beds.
    Step 2: Identify specific strategies for adding beds, and the issues associated with doing so.

[a]See "Assessing the Potential Demand for Hospital Beds: Incorporating Physicians' Views," p. 126.

2. For all the hospital services studied, yearly fluctuations are greater than monthly fluctuations, with the exception of neurosurgery and urology, for which the monthly fluctuation in demand for care is substantially larger than the yearly fluctuation. Forecasts of future demand must adjust for such seasonal variation.

3. Data from the physician survey show that surgery scheduling is a serious concern. Neurosurgeons and urologists reported more dissatisfaction with surgery scheduling in winter, which is probably due to the seasonal variation in admissions for these services.

4. The annual average length of stay at the study hospital ranged from 7.0 (1988) to 7.4 (1994) days. The patients for the psychiatry service appear to have relatively longer average stays than those for other service categories, ranging from 18 days in 1988 to 10.9 days in 1993.

The annual average occupancy rates (based on staffed beds) for the past 5 years are shown in Table 7.18.

Forecasting Future Demand in Beds

The estimate of bed need for the next 3 years at the study hospital, and the average for those years, is shown in Table 7.19.

Assessment of the Effect of Surplus Beds in Neighboring Hospitals

Surplus Beds in Other Community Hospitals   For the purpose of this study, hospital beds are only "staffed beds," not licensed beds; also, the Veterans Administration Medical Center and other local specialty hospitals are not considered relevant for computing the surplus beds in the surrounding community. Using a standard occupancy rate of 90%, we derive the number of surplus beds shown in Table 7.20.

Table 7.18.   Occupancy rate for 1990–1994

Year	Occupancy rate (= actual days/available days)[a]			
	Total	Medicine/surgery	Obstetrics	Pediatrics
1990	0.89	0.91	1.05	0.68
1991	0.87	0.91	0.80	0.66
1992	0.89	0.93	0.79	0.72
1993	0.91	0.93	0.78	0.89
1994	0.88	0.90	0.75	0.81

[a]The distribution of 369 beds for medicine/surgery, obstetrics, and pediatrics is 79%, 11%, and 10%, respectively.

Table 7.19.   Initial estimates of bed need for 1995, 1996, and 1997

		1995	1996	1997	Average
1.	Forecast patient days[a] (excluding neonatology service)	121,841	120,095	120,604	120,847
2.	Potential unmet patient demand[b] (= no. of patients × average length of stay)	4,810	4,810	4,810	4,810
3.	Total patient days (1 + 2)	126,651	124,905	125,414	125,658
4.	Estimate of beds required: [c]				
	At 90% occupancy	386	380	382	383
	At 85% occupancy	408	402	404	405

[a]The total number of patient days for all the service categories (from Table 7.8), excluding days of neonatology service.

[b]Total monthly estimated need from the physician survey (Table 7.16). Unmet patient demand can be computed as potential patient days that may be needed: expected patient admissions × 7.4 days (1994 value).

[c]The estimate of bed need is computed as total estimated patient days/(365 × occupancy).

Table 7.20.   Number of surplus beds in 11 community hospitals

Hospital	(1) Occupancy rate[a] (1993)	(2) Number of beds[a] (1993)	(3) Surplus beds[b]
A	.797	920	95
B	.872	454	11
C	.867	374	13
X (study hospital)	.892	369	3
D[c]	.710	292	56
E	.721	312	56
F	.799	224	23
G	.825	200	15
H	.744	180	28
I	.699	153	31
J	.859	99	4
Total surplus beds			335

[a]Adapted from American Hospital Association. (1993).

[b]Column 3 = 0.9 × (column 2) − (column 1) × (column 2).

[c]Data in 1994 are estimated, because 40 beds were not open for service in that year.

Assigned Portion of Surplus Beds in the Primary Service (Catchment) Area

The study hospital's minimum share of the surplus beds in each of the relevant hospitals is defined as the percentage overlap between the primary service area of the study hospital and those of the other relevant hospitals multiplied by the mean daily surplus beds in those hospitals. To compute this overlap in service areas, hospital-specific data on patient origin must be used to calculate the percentage of each other hospital's patients who come from the primary service area of the study hospital (see Table 7.21).

In Table 7.22, each hospital's mean daily surplus is multiplied by the percentage overlap of its primary service area with the primary service area of the study hospital. For example, hospital A has a surplus of 95 beds and draws 18.4% of its patients from the primary service area of the study hospital; thus the study hospital's share of hospital A's surplus beds is 17 beds (18.4% × 95 beds). As one can see in Table 7.21, the study hospital's total minimum share of surplus beds is 35 beds. The forecaster then adjusts the initial estimate of future bed need by assigning the minimum share of 35 beds to the study hospital.

Adjusted Estimate of Future Need for Beds   The initial estimates of future need, presented in Table 7.19, minus the surplus available in other relevant hospitals that is shared by the study hospital (35 beds of 335 estimated surplus beds), gives a crude estimate of beds needed. However, it is also necessary to adjust for the *future* share of surplus beds in the neigh-

Table 7.21.   Percentage overlap between primary service area of study hospital and service areas of other community hospitals

Primary service area of study hospital	Community hospitals									
	A	B	C	D	E	F	G	H	I	J
County A	12.9	5.2	7.1	2.9	2.3	3.3	1.5	3.5	1.7	0.7
County B	2.3	0.8	2.4	1.7	4.3	1.9	2.8	1.0	1.0	0.0
County C	1.9	8.9	0.8	0.9	1.4	1.1	0.5	0.6	0.7	0.0
County D	0.2	0.8	0.0	0.0	0.1	0.1	0.0	0.0	0.0	0.0
County E	0.3	0.0	0.0	0.0	0.2	0.0	0.2	0.0	0.0	0.0
County F	0.8	0.2	1.1	0.5	0.8	4.6	1.2	0.3	0.2	0.0
Total	18.4	15.9	11.4	6.0	9.1	11.0	6.2	5.4	3.6	0.7

Note: Figures represent percentages of total patient admissions of the 10 hospitals in each county. Data are compiled from patient origin survey.

Table 7.22. Study hospital's minimum share of surplus beds in other relevant hospitals

Hospital	(1) Percent overlap with hospital X's primary service area[a]	(2) Existing surplus[b]	(3) Hospital X's minimum share[c]
A	18.4	95	17
B	15.9	11	2
C	11.4	13	1
D	6.0	56	3
E	9.1	56	5
F	11.0	23	3
G	6.2	15	1
H	5.4	28	2
I	3.6	31	1
J	0.7	4	0
Total		335	35

[a]From Table 7.21.
[b]From Table 7.20.
[c]Column 3 = (column 1) × (column 2).

boring areas. Thus, a refined procedure is suggested for projecting the future share of surplus beds for the study hospital, using an inverse proportion of the ratio of current demand to future need. The detailed computation is shown in Table 7.23.

Final Calculation of Future Bed Need

The methodology presented above derives two sets of estimates for the future bed need at the study hospital. The first set indicates that, assuming the future occupancy rate at 90%, a total of 349 beds will be needed for the next 3 years. The second set, using an occupancy rate of 85%, estimates that 373 beds will be needed. Both figures are adjusted for the future share of the surplus beds in other community hospitals. Without this adjustment, the crude estimates would overestimate the study hospital's future demand.

Potential growth plus current demand for beds gives us a complete picture of the need for expansion. This thorough analysis, using both qualitative and quantitative data, derives an esti-

Table 7.23. Adjusted estimates of future need for beds at study hospital

	Number of beds	
	90% occupancy rate	85% occupancy rate
1. Current demand (existing beds)	369	369
2. Initial estimate of future need[a]	383	405
3. Surplus in other relevant hospitals		
a. Current surplus[b]	335	335
b. Study hospital's minimum share[c]	35	35
c. Future surplus[d]	323	305
d. Study hospital's assigned portion[e]	34	32
4. Adjusted estimate[f]: (2) − (3d)	349	373

[a]From Table 7.19 (at 90% occupancy rate).
[b]From Table 7.20.
[c]From Table 7.22.
[d](Current demand) × [(current surplus) × (future need)].
[e](Minimum share) × [(future surplus) × (current surplus)].
[f](Initial estimate) − (assigned portion of future surplus).

mate of bed capacity for the next 3 years ranging from 349 to 373. Thus, we can recommend that a maximum of four new beds be added annually. However, careful decisions remain to be made by the chief executive officer regarding 1) the cost–benefit of constructing the new beds, 2) the marketing strategies for attracting both patients and practitioners, 3) the occupancy level that is most desirable for the financial benefit of the hospital, and 4) the changing health care environment in the service area.

Conclusion

The study results show that the hospital should increase bed capacity if the occupancy rate remains 86% or lower. The decision to expand should depend as well on the availability of funds, the estimate of the future occupancy rate, the medical staff's needs, the managerial strategies for promoting the specialized services, and continued improvement of the various services. Strategic plans should consider the growth potential of certain specialized care services: orthopedic surgery, neurosurgery, and cardiology.

The views of the medical staff should be given greater weight in the development of a strategic plan. Necessary changes such as increasing bed capacity should improve physician satisfaction, so that those who previously perceived a severe hospital bed shortage then will be more willing to use the hospital. The hospital should continue to use the analytical approach illustrated in this study to update pertinent information and use it in planning. Although a variety of forecasting techniques are available for health planners, as MacStravic (1984) and Spiegel and Hyman (1991) stated, a good and valid forecast is dependent on both qualitative and quantitative assessment of multiple factors.

STRATEGIC PLANNING

In deciding on future programs, health administrators should 1) acquire relevant and accurate information about the population served by the hospital, 2) identify and interview key medical and administrative staff members, 3) assess managerial data and monitor necessary changes in the organization, 4) obtain data about the hospital's market share in the primary service (catchment) area, 5) document their decisions and periodically analyze how they affect the organization, and 6) evaluate strategic alternatives. These regular processes, focused on collecting, analyzing, and forecasting from managerial data and using them to develop strategic plans, constitute *strategic planning*.

The specific tasks an investigator should undertake are listed below:

1. Measure demand, using the daily census of hospital bed utilization, inpatient admissions to the hospital, total inpatient days, and occupancy rates for the study period.
2. Collect and analyze trend (monthly/yearly) data on the demand for each service specialty.
3. Design, conduct, and analyze a survey of the medical staff to document their perceptions of the potential demand for beds, and any related concerns.
4. Forecast the future demand for hospitalization, using a single exponential smoothing model and a linear regression model.
5. Compile census data for small geographic (medical market) areas and compute the hospital's share of inpatients.
6. Using patient origin and patient destination surveys, select marketing strategies based on a small area analysis of the data.
7. Use the empirical data described above to estimate bed needs.
8. Get feedback from the administrative staff before deciding on the final estimate of bed needs.

REFERENCES

American Hospital Association. (1993). *American hospital association guide to the health care field.* Chicago: American Hospital Association.

Bithell, J.F. (1969). The statistics of hospital admission systems. *Applied Statistics, 18,* 119–129.

Brown, G.D., Condia, G., & Gavin, G. (1974). *Methods for hospital service and bed need assessment.* University Park: The Pennsylvania State University.

Cleary, J.P., & Levenbach, H. (1982). *The professional forecaster: The forecasting process through data analysis.* Belmont, CA: Lifetime Learning Publications.

Daskin, M.S. (1982). Application of an expected covering model to emergency medical service system design. *Decision Sciences, 13,* 416–439.

Farmer, R.D., & Emami, J. (1991). Models for forecasting hospital bed requirements in the acute care setting. *Journal of Epidemiology and Community Health, 44,* 307–312.

Farnum, N.R., & Stanton, L.W. (1989). *Quantitative forecasting methods.* Boston: PWS-Kent Publishing Company.

Feldstein, P.J., & German, J. (1965). Predicting hospital utilization: An evaluation of three approaches. *Inquiry, 2,* 13–36.

Gardner, E.S., & Dannenbring, D.G. (1980). Forecasting with exponential smoothing: Some guidelines for model selection. *Decision Sciences, 11,* 370–383.

Griffith, J.R., & Wellman, B.T. (1979). Forecasting bed needs and recommending facilities plans for community hospitals. *Medical Care, 17,* 293–303.

Hancock, W.M., Magerlin, D.B., Storer, R.H., & Martin, J.B. (1978). Parameters affecting hospital occupancy and implications for facility size. *Health Services Research, 14,* 276–289.

Kao, E.P.C., & Pokladnik, F.M. (1978). Incorporating exogenous factors in adoptive forecasting of hospital census. *Management Science, 24,* 1677–1686.

Kolesar, P. (1970). A markovian model for hospital admission scheduling. *Management Science, 16,* B-381–B-396.

Laporte, R.E. (1994). How to improve monitoring and forecasting of disease patterns. *British Medical Journal, 307,* 1573–1574.

Lederman, R.P. (1993). Time series analysis. Part II: Forecasting. *American Journal of Maternal and Child Nursing, 18,* 283.

Levenbach, H., & Cleary, J.P. (1981). *The beginning forecaster.* Belmont, CA: Lifetime Learning Publications.

MacStravic, R.S. (1984). *Forecasting use of health services.* Rockville, MD: Aspen Systems Corporation.

Makridakis, S., Wheelwright, S.C., & McGee, V.E. (1983). *Forecasting: Methods and applications.* New York: John Wiley & Sons, Inc.

McClain, J.O. (1976). Bed planning using queuing theory models of hospital occupancy: A sensitivity analysis. *Inquiry, 13,* 167–176.

McGuires, S.M. (1992). A review of methods to forecast restorative treatment needs. *Journal of Public Health Dentistry, 52,* 292–298.

Milner, P.C. (1988). Forecasting the demand on accident and emergency departments in health districts in the Trent region. *Statistics in Medicine, 7,* 1061–1072.

Nelson, C.W. (1982). *Operations management in the health services.* New York: North-Holland.

Pindyck, R.S., & Rubinfeld, D.L. (1981). *Economic models and economic forecasts* (2nd ed.). New York: McGraw-Hill.

Spiegel, A.D., & Hyman, H.H. (1991). *Strategic health planning: Methods and techniques applied to marketing and management.* Norwood, NJ: Ablex Publishing Corporation.

VanVliet, R.C., & Van de Ven, W.P. (1993). Capitation payments based on prior hospitalization. *Health Economics, 2,* 177–188.

Virginia Hospital Association. (1978). *Virginia Hospital Association patient origin survey.* Richmond: Author.

Walsh, C., & Bicknell, W.J. (1977). Forecasting the need for hospital beds: A quantitavie methodology. *Public Health Reports, 92,* 199–210.

Weiss, T.W., Ashton, C.M., Wray, N.P. (1993). Forecasting areawide hospital utilization: A comparison of five univariate time series techniques. *Health Services Management Research, 6(3),* 178–190.

Wilson, J.H., Schuiling, S.J. (1992). Forecasting hospital laboratory procedures. *Journal of Medical Systems, 16,* 269–279.

Yett, D.E., Drabek, L., Intriligator, M.D., & Kimbell, L.J. (1979). *A forecasting and policy simulation model of the health care sector.* Lexington, MA: Lexington Books.

8

Concepts and Principles of Evaluation Research

The great tragedy of science:
The slaying of a beautiful hypothesis by an ugly fact.
Thomas Huxley, *Biogenesis and Abiogenesis*

DEFINITION OF EVALUATION

Evaluation is the process of finding out the value of something; evaluation research or evaluative research is the use of scientific methods to find out the value of a program by analyzing the cause-and-effect relationship. Program evaluation identifies and assesses the results of activities designed to accomplish a common organizational goal. It seeks logical explanations of why an intervention (program or treatment) has had certain expected or unexpected results. Proper data collection and analysis are the scientific bases for evaluating specific interventions. Program evaluation should be viewed as a means to improve decisions; the evaluation information is used to: 1) discontinue or continue the program, 2) improve its procedures, 3) add or drop specific strategies or techniques, 4) institute similar programs elsewhere, 5) allocate limited resources among competing programs, and 6) accept or reject a program's approach or theory.

TYPES OF EVALUATION

There are two types of evaluation. *Formative evaluation* produces information that is fed back during the development of a curriculum or program to help improve it. This helps the program developers. *Summative evaluation*, which is done after the program is finished, provides information about its effectiveness to the decision makers who are considering whether to implement it. Summative evaluation examines the effects or outcomes of a program. This kind of evaluation is not often done for two reasons. First, because of the time constraint, many programs must be assessed before they are complete. Second, the political implications of this type of scrutiny deter many administrators from conducting a full-fledged evaluation.

LEVELS OF EVALUATION

There are five levels at which evaluation can be done:

1. *Effort:* to assess the resources or capacities made available for the effort. How do the practices of the program/intervention compare with local or national standards?
2. *Performance:* to assess the output or outcome of the program.

3. *Adequacy of performance:* to assess the extent to which performance meets the program objectives, and the extent to which the program has alleviated the problem.
4. *Effectiveness:* to assess the amount of the intended outcome that has been attained. For example, in comparing program A to program B, we find:

Program	Cost	Outcome
A	Identical to program B	50% reduction of incidence
B	Identical to program A	90% reduction of incidence

Therefore, we conclude that program B is more effective than program A.
5. *Efficiency:* to assess the degree to which the program has achieved its result at the lowest possible cost. Could the same result be achieved at lower cost?

COMPONENTS OF EVALUATION

Donabedian (1980) proposed three aspects of program evaluation: *structure*, *process*, and *outcome*. He considered that these three aspects of evaluation are interrelated. The outcome is directly resulted from the use of structure and resources in performing activities or processes. If the structural aspects of the program were of high quality, and if the processes met certain standards, it might lead to good outcomes. The three components can be studied together to appraise the total quality of the program.

PRINCIPLES OF EVALUATION

Sydenstricker (1926) set forth the following basic principles of program evaluation:

1. Specific activities, rather than the program as a whole, should be assessed first.
2. The objectives and methods of a program effort should be defined clearly.
3. Principles of experimentation should be applied.
4. The use of "experimental" and "control" groups or areas should be followed.
5. A prospective, rather than retrospective, approach should be formulated.
6. The utility of evaluative results to program managers or administrators should be demonstrated.

DISTINCTIONS BETWEEN EVALUATION RESEARCH AND OTHER RESEARCH

Program evaluation assesses the end results of a program or, more frequently, assesses the adequacy, efficiency, and impact of an existing program. *Policy analysis*, in comparison, is stimulated by the perceived absence, inability, or abuse of an existing program. Its impetus also may be a legislative mandate, a delineation of new direction, or suggestions for correction and change. Finally, the purpose of *applied research* is to provide new knowledge and theory in an existing field of study.

ETHICS AND EVALUATION RESEARCH INVOLVING HUMAN SUBJECTS

Three basic principles provide ethical guidance for the structure and practice of studies involving human subjects. The principle of *democratic accountability* recognizes the responsibilities of those who serve on the behalf of others. The principle of *constitutional empowerment* refers to the capability of citizens to make informed decisions about political, economic, and social questions. Finally, the principle of *individual autonomy* refers to the capability of the members of society to function as individuals, uncoerced and with privacy. All three of these principles hold researchers accountable for two important functions in any study involving human subjects: 1) protecting the interests of data subjects through procedures that ensure appropriate standards of privacy and confidentiality, and 2) facilitating the responsible dissemination of data to the public (Panel on Confidentiality and Data Access, 1993). Congressional action has been recommended recently to establish penalties for those who abuse and misuse privileged information (U.S. Department of Health and Human Services, 1993).

Two key elements in any code of ethics applying to research involving human subjects are informed consent and confidentiality. The concept of *informed consent* simply refers to the right of the subjects of research to be informed that they are being researched and to be informed about the nature of the research. The assurance of *confidentiality* is the major safeguard against the invasion of the subjects' privacy. This sometimes involves assuring subjects that no harm or embarrassment will come to them as a result of participation in a study (Denzin & Lincoln, 1994). Recently, the National Committee on Vital and Health Statistics discussed the general issue of confidentiality and potential threats to data aspects of health care reform if ways are not found to assure the public that its privacy is being protected (U.S. National Committee on Vital and Health Statistics, 1993).

In the health care setting, to ensure that ethical guidelines are being followed in studies involving human subjects, researchers must submit a summary of the research project proposal to the institutional Human Research Committee for approval. All informed consent forms also must be submitted. The consent forms typically have two sections, one for the physician's informed consent and the other for the subject's informed consent. The study summary usually contains sections that explain the purpose of the study, the study design, the study settings, the study subjects, the duration of the study, the potential risks to participants of the study, the provisions for voluntary participation and confidentiality, the financial obligations of the study, the methods by which results will be collected, and the participating investigators. The informed consent form submitted to the Human Research Committee should include sections such as the introduction, the details of the study, the procedures of the study, the potential benefits of the study, the potential risks of the study, voluntary participation information, self-related injury information, confidentiality information, the financial cost of participation, and the consent to participate. An example of a consent form is given in Table 8.1.

Table 8.1. Sample informed consent form subject to Human Research Committee approval

Title: The treatment I am considering and the study in which I am considering participation is: [*the name of the proposed treatment and/or study*]

Purpose: [*the objectives of the proposed study*]

Statement of Physician Obtaining Informed Consent

I have fully explained this study to the patient, _____ . In my judgment and the patient's, there was sufficient access to information, including risks and benefits, to make an informed decision.

Date: _____

Physician's Signature: _____

Physician's Name: _____

Patient Statement

I have read the description of the clinical study or have had it translated into language I understand. I have also talked it over with the doctor to my satisfaction. I understand that my participation is voluntary. I know enough about the purpose, methods, risks, and benefits of the treatment and study to judge that I want to take part in it.

Patient: _____ Date: _____

Witness: _____ Date: _____

EVALUATION APPROACHES

Evaluation taxonomy by type and methodology is summarized in Figure 8.1.

PRINCIPAL EVALUATION METHODS

There are several principal evaluation methods employed in the evaluation of health services. These evaluation methods include experimental design, quasi-experimental design, preexperimental design, survey research, benefit–cost analysis, cost-effectiveness analysis, administrative audits, operations research techniques, and formal theory. A summary of these principal evaluation methods is presented in Table 8.2.

EVALUATION ASPECTS OF MEDICAL CARE

High-Priority Issues

The evaluation of health services plays an important role in improving the performance of our health care system. Its importance has increased as the health care industry has become more turbulent, with sharper competition. At the same time, the nation is challenged by the obligation to care for an increasingly aged population.

Health care expenditures in the United States now account for 13.2% of the gross domestic product, as reported in *Health United States, 1993* (National Center for Health Statistics, 1994). The federal government, recognizing that this growth must be contained, has established the Medicare Prospective Payment System (MPPS): Medicare reimburses hospitals according to prospective payment rates set by patients' diagnosis-related groups (DRGs). Operating under such a prospective payment system, hospitals and physicians must give serious attention to how they allocate resources. Program evaluation is thus an inescapable necessity for health services managers.

	Methodology								
Evaluation type	Experiment	Quasi-experiment	Preexperiment	Survey research	Benefit–cost analysis	Cost-effectiveness analysis	Administrative audit	Operations research	Formal theory
Strategic (etiology)	X	X		X	X	X	X	X	X
Compliance (monitoring)		X	X	X	X	X	X	X	
Program design (goal achievement)	X	X	X	X	X	X	X	X	X
Program management		X	X	X	X	X	X	X	
Intervention effect (outcome analysis)	X	X	X	X	X	X		X	
Program impact (legislated goals & program outcomes)	X	X	X	X	X	X	X	X	

Note: X = applicable.

Figure 8.1.   Evaluation type and methodology.

Table 8.2. Summary of principal evaluation methods

Method	Equivalent or related terms	Characteristics	Exemplar
Experimental design (Campbell & Stanley, 1966)	Randomized experiment	Full control over scheduling of experimental stimuli	Pretest-posttest control group: prior measurement of two randomly constituted groups, introduction of treatments to one group, and subsequent comparison of outcome measures between experimental groups (Wan, Weissert, & Livieratos, 1980)
Quasi-experimental design (Campbell & Stanley, 1966; Trochim, 1986)	Field experiment	Partial control over experimental stimuli	Time series: the periodic measurement of some variable, the introduction of an experimental event, and the identification of a discontinuity in the measurement pattern (McDowall, 1980)
Preexperimental design (Campbell & Stanley, 1966)	Naturalistic observation; case study	Relatively little control over rival explanations of hypothesized effect	Case study: the analysis of a single group, drawing inferences based on expectations of what might have occurred without experimental intervention (Shortell & Richardson, 1978)
Survey research (Aday, 1989; Rosenberg, 1968)	Sample survey	Cross-sectional studies, applying multivariate techniques to analyze data collected from large samples	Survey: assessing the impacts of neighborhood health centers on use of health services in low-income communities (Okada & Wan, 1980)
Benefit–cost analysis (Hellinger, 1980; Thompson, 1980; Warner & Bryan, 1980)	Systems analysis; program planning; budgeting system	Evaluation of the relative effectiveness of alternative programs in dollar terms, compared to dollar costs	Evaluation of health promotion programs (McKenzie & Jurs, 1993); methods for the economic evaluation of health care programs (Drummond, Stoddard, & Torrance, 1987)
Cost–effectiveness analysis (Thompson, 1980; Weinstein & Stason, 1976)	Systems analysis; cost–outcome analysis	Comparison of alternative programs on the basis of program costs, and results measured in equivalent units	Evaluation of cost-effectiveness of geriatric day care (Wan, Weissert, & Livieratos, 1980); assessment of hypertension programs (Weinstein & Stason, 1976)
Administrative audit (Dunland, 1987)	Utilization review; peer review; quality assurance; tracer approach	Evaluation of health program policies and practices in terms of compliance with internal and external standards	Assessment of impacts of second-opinion program on surgery (Rutgow, 1989; Finkel, McCarthy, & Miller, 1982); use of tracer approach to assess the performance of medical care system (Nutting, Shorr, & Burkholter, 1981)
Operations research technique (Churchman, 1979; Shuman, Wolf, & Speas, 1974; Stimson and Stimson, 1972; Swain, 1981)	Systems analysis/management science	Application of quantitative methods to find the best solutions to problems of program operation	Development of model for optimizing staffing through work sampling and targeted continuing education for nurses (Shukla, 1985)
Formal theory (Sutherland, 1989)	Reconstructed logic (Kaplan, 1964)	Construction of abstract models of behavior systems, performing logical manipulations to adduce new insights	Analysis of normative predicates of next-generation management support systems (Sutherland, 1989)

From a review of the recent literature, the following questions concerning evaluation stand out:

1. What aspects of the health care system should be evaluated?
2. Who should conduct evaluations of health care? How should evaluations be financed?
3. How can evaluation assure high-quality health care and accountability to the public for the use of its moneys?
4. What criteria should be used in evaluations, and who should develop the criteria?
5. What is the relationship between medical necessity and quality of care? Is medical necessity an aspect of quality of care, or a separate issue? (Consensus on this point is essential to evaluating care.)
6. Evaluation of a health care system examines three major aspects: the cost, the quality, and the accessibility of medical care; what is the appropriate balance among these?
7. Can DRGs be a basis for evaluations of health care? (This, too, is an essential question.)
8. In evaluating health care that uses experimental treatments, how can the strengths and integrity of the treatments themselves be evaluated in order to ensure construct validity in the evaluation of care?

Each of these issues is reviewed briefly in the following pages.

Aspects of Health Care to Evaluate

Seven major aspects of health care are evaluated: 1) the accessibility or availability of health resources, 2) the quality of care, 3) the continuity of care, 4) the efficacy of care, 5) the effectiveness of care, 6) the efficiency involved in providing the care given, and 7) the acceptability of the care by the physician or the quality of the physician's relationship with the patient. Each aspect may be evaluated on two levels: the individual level (i.e., the outcome for each patient) and the organizational level (i.e., the overall health of the population or community).

Access   Donabedian (1980) defined accessibility of care as the ease with which a person can begin care or continue to receive it. Davis and Rowland (1983) have deplored the lack of access for Americans, asserting that over 25 million Americans cannot obtain adequate health care. They suggested that this lack of either generous income or health insurance keeps people from seeking care for themselves or their children until the health problem becomes life threatening, and that then many obtain care only at crowded and understaffed public hospitals. Bashshur, Homan, and Smith (1994) reported that 17% of the population of Michigan had access problems resulting from financial, temporal, attitudinal, and geographical barriers.

Okada and Wan (1980), in their study of the impact of community health centers and Medicaid on the use of health services, found that community health centers in low-income areas improved the access to care for people with low incomes. They also documented that extensive Medicaid coverage among the study populations indicated better access to care. Using the same data, Wan (1984) pointed out that black males have the least access to private physicians. Wan suggested that differing attitudes toward seeking help may be one cause of the low rate at which black men get care from private physicians. In their study, Clement, Retchin, Brown, and Stegall (1994) found reduced utilization of services for those elderly patients with specific ambulatory conditions enrolled in health maintenance organizations (HMOs) with Medicare risk contracts. Wan (1989), in a study on the effect of managed care on health services used by the elderly population, found the managed care demonstration group to make more frequent visits to community health clinics and to have longer stays in the hospital. Wan found the relationship between ambulatory physician visits and hospitalization of the elderly complementary rather than substitutive. Aday, Begley, Lairson, and Slater (1993) strongly advocated the need to incorporate measures of equity in evaluating health care system performance.

Quality   To evaluate quality, that concept must be defined first. Donabedian (1980) stated that

> quality is a property of, and a judgment upon, some definable unit of care, and that care is divisible into at least two parts: technical and interpersonal . . . at the very least, the quality of technical care consists of the application of medical science and technology in a manner that maximizes its benefits to health without correspondingly increasing its risks. (p. 5)

The quality of the interpersonal process, according to Donabedian, is measured by how well the physician–patient interaction conforms to the socially defined norms for that relationship.

Williams and Torrens (1980) have shown how important it is to evaluate the quality of health care, given that Americans make over 1 billion physician visits each year. Brown, Clement, Hill, Retchin, & Bergeron (1993), in their study on HMOs and Medicare, found that HMOs provide care of comparable quality to that delivered by fee-for-service providers while using fewer health care resources. Enrollees experience reduced out-of-pocket costs and greater coverage in Medicare HMOs. Greenfield (1989) advocated the use of multiple outcome indicators to monitor and evaluate quality of care. Lohr, Yordy, and Their (1988) identified the need to understand the multidimensional nature of the concept of quality.

Continuity   Donabedian (1980) stated that continuity is concerned with interruptions in needed care, and "the maintenance of the relatedness between successive sequences of medical care" (p. 23). Donabedian stipulated that an important feature of continuity is that health care personnel keep records of past findings and decisions and use those findings in current care, in a way that demonstrates constancy in management objectives and methods.

Some studies have found no significant relationship between continuity and quality (Nassif, Garfink, & Greenfield, 1982; Roos, Roos, Gilbert, & Nicol, 1980). In contrast to these findings, Breslau (1982) concluded that a continuous doctor–patient relationship is paramount when a patient has a severe illness. Breslau suggested that severe illness often causes social isolation, and the physician becomes the source of information and emotional support for the patient.

Efficacy   In the words of Roper, Winkenwerder, Hackbarth, and Krakauer (1988), efficacy of care refers to the traditional meaning of medical effectiveness, or the efficacy of medical interventions in actual practice. Efficacy refers to how effective a particular treatment is on a specific condition in a controlled clinical trial. It is concerned with the therapeutic benefits achievable under ideal conditions (Aday et al., 1993).

Chan et al. (1994) tested the efficacy of calcitriol and dihydrotachysterol treatments on growth failure in children with chronic renal insufficiency and found that dihydrotachysterol, the less costly treatment, can be used with an efficacy equal to that of calcitriol. White, Russell, Green, & Whittle (1994) tested the efficacy of screening magnetic resonance angiography and Doppler ultrasonography in the evaluation of carotid artery stenosis in a controlled clinical trial. Szpalski and Hayez (1994) tested the efficacy of tenoxicam in the treatment of acute low back pain. The study found tenoxicam to be effective in a controlled clinical study. Limouzin-Lamothe, Mairon, Joyce, & Le-Gal (1994) tested the efficacy of hormonal replacement therapy on the quality of life after menopause and found that the therapy is superior to symptomatic treatment.

Effectiveness   Greenlick (1981) defined effectiveness as the degree to which the health care system (or practitioner) has met stated or accepted goals. Effectiveness refers to medical appropriateness, or the appropriate use of an intervention in a given situation (Kahan et al., 1994). Effectiveness of care refers to how effective a particular treatment is on a specific condition when applied to the general public.

Greenlick stressed that two types of evaluations must be conducted: technical effectiveness, and also the effectiveness of psychosocial care (i.e., the physician's relationship with the patient). Technical effectiveness is evaluated by the degree to which a physician achieves a positive patient outcome, whereas psychosocial effectiveness is how beneficially the physician—patient relationship affects the outcome of care. Zuckerman, Huntley, & Waterbrook (1980), in their study of patient care in a primary care clinic, found both deficiencies in technical effectiveness (failures to order necessary tests, inadequate diagnostic workups) and psychosocial deficiencies (patient dissatisfaction, poor communication between physician and patient).

Efficiency   Efficiency is the ratio of a product to the resources used to produce it. Greenlick (1981) has stressed the need to assess how physician behavior affects the use of limited health care resources, suggesting that evaluating physicians' efficiency would reduce the pressure to buy costly but not necessarily more effective medical technology.

Several recent studies have dealt with efficiency. For example, Gertman and Restuccia (1981) have developed the Appropriateness Evaluation Protocol (AEP), using 27 objective criteria to assess the appropriateness of admissions. Their study found that 10% of the reviewed admissions were inappropriate. Thus the AEP could improve the efficiency of hospital utilization significantly. In a similar study, Knaus, Draper, & Wagner (1983) reported on the successful use of the Acute Psychology and Chronic Health Evaluation (APACHE) to assess the appropriateness of intensive care for a patient. Their study found that over 50% of the monitored admissions at the study hospital were at less than 10% risk of needing intensive care unit (ICU) therapy, meaning that they could have been treated on a regular hospital unit. Scheffler, Clement, Sullivan, Hu, & Sung (1994) found, in their study on hospital response to the MPPS, that the implementation of the system was associated with a lower rate of hospital admissions, days, and deflated inpatient payments for Blue Cross and Blue Shield plan members under age 65. Other studies have suggested that understanding the underlying pathophysiology and precise treatment can predict outcomes for acute diseases (Wagner, Draper, & Knaus, 1989; Wagner, Knaus, & Draper, 1986).

Physician–Patient Relationship   Brook, Davis, & Kamberg (1980) have argued that factors other than the technical process are important for successful management of care and health care outcomes. They reviewed several studies showing that patient expectations are important determinants of how well patients follow regimens of care, and yet physicians are often ignorant of patient expectations. They suggested that physicians should discuss patients' expectations with them, because that could improve patient outcomes dramatically, at least in regard to compliance.

Waitzkin (1984, 1985) has shown that doctors' nonverbal communication abilities are associated with outcomes of medical care such as satisfaction and compliance.

Evaluators and Financing of Evaluations

Questions of increasing importance within our health care system are who should evaluate health care, and how these evaluations should be financed. The answer to the first question depends on which aspects of the health care system are being evaluated. The technical quality of care can be evaluated only by the medical profession, because only the medical profession has the knowledge required (Greenlick, 1981). Psychosocial effectiveness and efficiency are broader issues; therefore a range of nonmedical professions and lay persons with up-to-date competencies should participate in evaluating those aspects (Greenlick, 1981).

Frazier and Hiatt (1980) also stressed that evaluation is not simply a medical undertaking. They cited problems, however, in combining evaluations by physicians and those by other professionals. Frazier and Hiatt contended that most physicians are not trained in quantitative techniques used in the clinical skill of assessing quality of life, and, conversely, most nonmedical professionals lack confidence in dealing with medical problems. Thus the evaluation of health care has suffered (Frazier & Hiatt, 1980).

Sieverts (1982), of Blue Cross and Blue Shield, stressed the responsibility of third-party payers to evaluate health care. Sieverts stated that Blue Cross and Blue Shield has an obligation to its subscribers to evaluate the health care they receive and ensure that the care is proper and of acceptable quality. Blue Cross and Blue Shield, Sieverts commented, reviews each claim with this in mind. Blue Cross and Blue Shield standards for diagnostic and surgical procedures disallow obsolete, unsafe, or ineffective procedures. Sieverts expects that evaluation by third-party payers will increase.

The answer to the question of who should finance evaluations depends on whether one evaluates the health of the population in general or the health of the individual patient. For evaluations of the overall health care of the population, the public should pay, through the government. If the focus is an individual's health care, then a variety of sources, such as third-party payers or private foundations, should finance these evaluations. However, the group practice organizations should finance evaluations of the health care provided by them. Funding agencies for evaluation research are presented in Table 8.3.

Evaluation of health care should follow basic principles. First, objectives must be defined; this is the clinician's role. The clinician should not only specify the objectives of care, but also rank their priorities. Second, health care evaluations should use a prospective approach. The retrospective approach is inappropriate; one must identify how one intends to evaluate a program before implementing it entirely. Finally, a feedback system must be established that collects information about a program or a process, executes an evaluation, and then feeds that information back to program managers so deficiencies in the program can be corrected.

Roles of Evaluation

Evaluation plays two major roles in health care: 1) as a step in ensuring the delivery of high-quality health care, and 2) as an important tool for controlling health care expenditures and ensuring accountability for public program expenditures.

Fineberg and Hiatt (1979) concluded that systematic evaluation of medical practices is needed in order to improve the quality of care. They found it unacceptable that ineffective practices continue because systematic information on their outcomes has not been gathered, or because inappropriate incentives operate. Fineberg and Hiatt proposed that, at the minimum, systematically collected data should trace the natural history of a disease and assess the outcomes of interventions. Frazier and Hiatt (1980) concluded that new medical procedures should be used first only experimentally, so as to test their usefulness before their widespread application.

Beraud (1979) stated that evaluating medical practices could eliminate unnecessary interventions, reduce iatrogenic effects, and improve the quality of care by disseminating information on useful and efficient medical procedures. Beraud cites two medical procedures as examples of unnecessary and expensive interventions: chemotherapy for digestive system cancer and cholecystectomy for silent gallstones.

Besides improving the quality of care, evaluation also is essential to reduce health care costs. Evaluation using cost–benefit studies can assess the value of a procedure. For example, despite the publication of safe discharge criteria for low-birth-weight infants, many pediatricians continue to hospitalize premature infants until they reach a conventional weight, at a cost of thousands of hospital days (Fineberg & Hiatt, 1979).

The usefulness of evaluations in improving the quality of care and providing public accountability for public health program expenditures depends on feedback. Restuccia and Holloway (1982) concluded that the way to ensure high-quality health care is to inform practitioners systematically about the interaction of health services and their patients. Restuccia and Holloway recommended that feedback should be prompt, relevant to the situation, and not necessarily prescriptive, but rather, timely information about patient progress.

Table 8.3.　Funding agencies for health services evaluation and research

Agency name	Address	Telephone number
Public Agencies		
Agency for Health Care Policy and Research (AHCPR)	Executive Officer Center 2101 East Jefferson Street, 501/502 Rockville, Maryland 20852	301-594-1354
U.S. Department of Health and Human Services, Assistant Secretary for Planning and Evaluation	200 Independence Avenue, S.W. Room 405F Washington, D.C. 20201	202-690-7858
Centers for Disease Control and Prevention	1600 Clifton Road, NE Atlanta, Georgia 30333	404-842-6655
Center for Mental Health Service	5600 Fishers Lane Room 15C-04 Rockville, Maryland 20857	301-443-3343
Health Care Financing Administration	Office of Research and Demonstrations 2230 Oak Meadow Building 6325 Security Boulevard Baltimore, Maryland 20857	410-443-2216
National Institute of Mental Health	5600 Fishers Lane Park Lawn Building Room 1405 Rockville, Maryland 20857	301-443-3364
National Institute on Aging	7201 Wisconsin Avenue Gateway Building Room 2C-218 Bethesda, Maryland 20892	301-496-9322
National Institute on Drug Abuse	5600 Fishers Lane Room 10-42 Rockville, Maryland 20857	301-443-2755
National Cancer Institute	Executive Plaza North Room 636 Bethesda, Maryland 20892	301-496-3428
National Institute on Alcohol Abuse and Alcoholism	Willco Building Suite 402 6000 Executive Boulevard Rockville, Maryland 20892	301-443-2530 *or* 301-443-4730
National Institute on Disability and Rehabilitation Research	U.S. Department of Education 4000 Maryland Avenue, SW Washington, D.C. 20202	202-205-8134
Private Foundations		
Robert Wood Johnson Foundation	P.O. Box 2316 Princeton, New Jersey 08540	609-452-8701
Commonwealth Fund	1 East 75th Street New York, New York 10021	212-535-0400
Hartford Foundation	55 East 59th Street New York, New York 10022	212-832-7788
Kellogg Foundation	1 Michigan Avenue East Battle Creek, Michigan 49017	616-968-1611
AARP Andrus Foundation	601 E Street, NW Washington, D.C. 20049	202-434-6190
Pew Charitable Trusts	One Commerce Square 2005 Market Street Suite 1700 Philadelphia, Pennsylvania 19103	215-575-4780

Rosen and Feigin (1983) also have found that feedback can improve performance. They offer three principles. First, the group most likely to be influenced by the feedback must help select what is to be measured. Second, the feedback must be relevant to that group's goals. Third, the feedback should be used only in a positive way as support, and never in a negative or punitive way (Rosen & Feigin, 1983).

Evaluation Criteria

There are four major types of evaluation criteria for health care, which measure: 1) performance adequacy, 2) effectiveness, 3) acceptability of treatment, and 4) efficiency.

Performance Adequacy   Performance adequacy is the extent to which performance meets program objectives, and is measured more by qualitative factors than quantitative ones. The AEP study performed by Gertman and Restuccia (1981), which evaluated hospital days as necessary or not, is a good example of a performance adequacy study.

Effectiveness   Effectiveness is evaluated by the extent to which an intended attainment was reached. An example of an effectiveness evaluation is the study conducted by Zuckerman et al. (1980) using the "trajectory" method to assess the quality of care provided by a primary care clinic. The study found failures to order required tests and also inadequate diagnostic workups at the clinic. Effectiveness studies tend to use quantitative measures.

Acceptability   Acceptability of treatment is decided by a clinician, because only he or she has the ability to decide this question. Beraud (1979), as discussed earlier, questioned the use of several medical practices. Beraud's viewpoint is that of a gastroenterologist; he is qualified to argue that chemotherapy for digestive system cancer is of doubtful worth, or that cholecystectomy for silent gallstones is unnecessary and expensive. Another example of clinical acceptability as an issue is the usefulness of electronic fetal monitoring, which has not been demonstrated fully in controlled clinical trials (Banta, Burns, & Behney, 1983).

Efficiency   Efficiency is measured by whether the same result can be achieved at a lower cost. An example is the study by Ruchlin, Finkel, & McCarthy (1982) that evaluated the effects of a second-opinion consultation program. In this study, 16% of the recommended surgeries were nonconfirmed. The total program savings were estimated at $534,791, whereas the cost of the program was $203,300, yielding a cost–benefit ratio of 2.63:1.

The four types of evaluation criteria can be formulated as either process criteria or outcome criteria. The major advantages of using *process criteria* are: 1) it is relatively easy for practitioners to specify process criteria that reflect good medical practices; 2) information on the process of care can be found in the medical record, so it is accessible and timely and thus available for either preventive or interventive purposes; and 3) process criteria allow for responsibility to be specifically assigned, which in turn allows for specific corrective action to be taken (Donabedian, 1980). The disadvantages of process criteria are: 1) many of the medical practices accepted today lack a scientific basis; and 2) process criteria tend to overemphasize technical care at the expense of the interpersonal process, because practitioners tend not to be as concerned about interpersonal relations (Donabedian, 1980).

The major advantages of *outcome criteria* are: 1) outcome criteria allow a more flexible approach to management, and 2) outcome measures are integrative measures of the quality of care provided by all practitioners (Donabedian, 1980). The major disadvantages of outcome criteria are: 1) it is difficult to pinpoint the responsibility for an outcome to a certain segment of care, 2) data on outcomes are often not available in time for some types of monitoring, and 3) reliance on outcome measures overlooks the possibility of redundant or excessive costs of care (Donabedian, 1980).

Wan, Weissert, and Livieratos (1980), in their study of geriatric day care and homemaker services, used outcome measures (activities of daily living) in order to assess the influence of day care and homemaker services on patient status. They found that, among those subjects who used these experimental services, increased use of services was associated with improved outcomes of care.

Brook et al. (1980) argued that outcome measures should be used to assess quality of care. They contended that evaluations of the quality of care should include the contributions to care provided by all types of health professionals, and should focus on the patient rather than on the individual practitioner's process of care. If evaluations focus on the primary care provider, important services provided by other practitioners often are ignored, and thus not all important outcomes are assessed (Brook et al., 1980).

Donabedian (1980) concluded that the choice of an assessment approach, such as whether to use process or outcome criteria, depends on the individual situation. He added, however, that whenever possible both process and outcome criteria should be used simultaneously. Outcome measures may serve as indirect measures of process, because they may add to or confirm information obtained by process measures and screen out cases requiring more detailed assessment (Donabedian, 1980).

A final issue regarding evaluation criteria is whether to use explicit criteria (clearly defined and specific) or implicit criteria (implied but not directly expressed). The advantages of *explicit criteria* are: 1) they are simple and less expensive, 2) they are applicable on a large scale and allow more control, and 3) they are more reliable than implicit criteria (Donabedian, 1981). The disadvantages of explicit criteria are: 1) it is not practical to develop explicit criteria specific enough to meet the large variety of conditions characterizing medical practice; 2) explicit criteria may achieve high reliability at the expense of low validity; and 3) explicit criteria tend to ignore nontechnical factors, such as the interpersonal process, that are important in determining health status (Donabedian, 1981).

The major advantage of *implicit criteria* is that they can consider the wide variety of conditions that arise in medicine (Greenspan, 1980). The disadvantages of assessments using implicit criteria are: 1) they are time consuming, 2) they are costly, and 3) they tend to be unreliable unless applied by competent and motivated professionals (Greenspan, 1980).

Evaluation of Medical Necessity and Quality of Care

It is questionable whether medical necessity and quality of care are two separate issues, or whether medical necessity is intrinsic to the consideration of quality. The literature tends to agree with the latter position. Donabedian (1980) argued that unnecessary care may even be harmful. Unnecessary care is poor in quality, according to Donabedian, because: 1) it does not yield benefits, 2) it reduces individual and social welfare, and 3) it indicates carelessness, poor judgment, or ignorance on the part of the practitioner. Donabedian concluded that whenever a judgment is made about the necessity or suitability of the quantity of care a judgment of quality is implied.

The importance of evaluating medical necessity when evaluating the quality of health care is attested to by the overwhelming literature on unnecessary surgery, inappropriate hospital admissions, and inappropriate admissions to ICU beds. Gertman and Mitchell (1980) cited three types of evidence as indicating a rise in unnecessary surgery: 1) rapid growth in the number of operations performed, 2) wide variations in surgical rates across geographic areas, and 3) significant proportion of disagreement about elective surgery in second-opinion programs. Gertman and Mitchell criticized unnecessary surgery not only because of its waste of resources, but also because it endangers the health of the patient. Wagner, Kraus, Draper & Zimmerman (1983), in their study of the appropriateness of ICU admissions, found that roughly 13% of the ICU admissions at their study hospital were at less than 5% risk of needing ICU care (i.e., inappropriate). Gertman and Restuccia (1981), in their survey of the literature, found that inappropriate hospital patient days generally accounted for over 10% of all hospital patient days. Kahan et al. (1994), however, found that both performers and nonperformers of a specific medical procedure did not achieve a consensus on the necessity of the procedure. Additional research is necessary to define a method to promote consensus and further validate ratings of necessity.

Balancing Cost, Quality, and Access in Evaluating Medical Care

The critical issue involved in assessing cost, quality, and accessibility is finding the appropriate balance among these three criteria. Jirka (1984) and Brook et al. (1980) have stressed the necessity of reaching a balance, or trade-off, between cost and quality. Brook et al. (1980) noted that we need to identify where the trade-offs between cost and quality actually are now within our mix of services and facilities, and then decide how cost and quality should be traded off from that point; we should decide where to allocate more money, or where to allocate less, as appropriate. Jirka (1984), former president of the American Medical Association, argued that the medical profession must meet the economic demands of the marketplace. He encouraged physicians to be aware of the cost of the care they provide, to learn how to modify medical costs, and to learn to balance the demands for high-quality care with the demands for more reasonable costs. Donabedian (1983) treated this balancing of quality and cost as a conflict between an individualized definition of quality that takes into account the patient's wishes, expectations, valuations, and means, and a social definition of quality that balances the expected net benefits of care against its social and individual costs. The conflict places practitioners in a difficult position: Patient expectations, ethical precepts, and personal pride call on them to do the best possible for each patient, yet society asks them to consider social priorities (Donabedian, 1983). Donabedian concluded that, as our real or perceived ability to pay for health services diminishes, the conflict between individual and social priorities will be intensified and the practitioner's role will be more stressful.

Accessibility also must be balanced against cost. Donabedian (1980) cited the fact that, although more access usually is associated with better quality, more access also can lead to costly, redundant, unnecessary, or even harmful care. Donabedian also pointed out that more access by some population segments to care may lower quality, according to the social valuation given to equitable distribution of health benefits.

Diagnosis-Related Groups and Evaluation

Diagnosis-related groups, which are now the basis for calculating reimbursement rates for Medicare patients, also are a potential basis for evaluating health care. It is estimated that as many as 5% of all physicians are outliers (Brook et al., 1980). These physicians account for a large proportion of inappropriate and excessive medical care. If a physician orders unnecessary tests, or provides deficient care that leads to complications and longer hospitalization, he or she causes excessive costs of care. DRGs can be used to identify such physicians so that their practice can be changed. The role of DRGs in evaluation will be even greater if the federal government begins to reimburse physicians for Medicare patients according to a DRG system for ambulatory care.

Treatment Strength and Integrity, and Evaluation

Sechrest, West, Phillips, Redner, & Yeaton (1979) have outlined two critical issues in evaluation: 1) the planned strength of treatment, and 2) the integrity of the treatment (i.e., the fidelity with which the treatment is given). Both of these issues affect the construct validity of the evaluation.

Sechrest et al. contended that the strength of a treatment is important because, when one is evaluating the results of a treatment, it is relatively easy to assume that something has occurred when it has not. They stressed that one may conclude a treatment is effective only when one knows the strength of the treatment. Likewise, one cannot judge the effectiveness of a treatment unless one evaluates the integrity of the treatment. To maximize the integrity of a treatment, first the treatment must be well-defined so that standards can be formulated to judge its integrity (Sechrest et al., 1979). Sechrest et al. suggested that, in practice, programs should be tested in their strongest forms in order to assess their potential impacts, and later can be reduced in strength until one reaches the desired outcome at minimal cost. As a final note, Sechrest et al. (1979) pointed out how essential it is for evaluators to have insight about why treatments succeed or fail.

COST–BENEFIT VERSUS COST–EFFECTIVENESS ANALYSIS

Cost–effectiveness analysis is an essential tool for the health care manager. Not only does cost–effectiveness analysis allow for the identification of alternative solutions to problems and their consequent effectiveness, but it is useful when costs are not expressed in ordinary dollar terms. Cost–benefit analysis, in contrast, is used to compare projects with benefits and costs expressed in dollar terms. Cost–benefit analysis is becoming ever more important to health care managers in a time of cost–containment efforts, and cost–effectiveness analysis is becoming ever more important in a time of emphasis on outcomes measurement. Combinations of both approaches are beginning to be used in evaluation of health services.

Methodology of Cost–Benefit Analysis

Cost–benefit analysis is based on the following assumptions: 1) the problem can be identified, 2) the cost of its consequences can be measured within a permissible range of accuracy, 3) the problem can be eradicated or controlled at some predetermined level by a new program, and 4) the cost of the new program also can be determined. To illustrate this type of analysis, two examples are presented using a break-even analysis.

Example 1   Suppose the chief executive officer of a local hospital has reviewed the current demand for pathological laboratory tests in the facility and decided that the increased demand for these services should be met in one of the following two ways: 1) lease additional space and hire another pathologist and two technicians, or 2) contract, per test, with a local private pathological laboratory. The variable costs, respectively, are $10 per case for the lease plan and $20 per case for the contract plan. The fixed cost for the lease plan is estimated to be about $12,000 per month, including rental costs and wages, salaries, and fringe benefits for the new pathologist and two technicians. There are no fixed costs under the contract option. How do you decide which plan to select? What is your rationale for the selection?

The objective is to choose the plan (X) that minimizes the total cost (TC). The fixed cost–variable cost (FCVC) model can be used, where $TC(X) = FC(X) + VC(X)$. In this model, FC is the fixed cost—that is, the portion of the cost that does not depend on the amount of output involved; variable cost (VC) is the cost that varies directly with the level of output. There are two options: lease (M) and buy (B).

The output is 1,000 tests per month. For the lease option:

$$TC(M) = FC(M) + VC(M) = \$12,000 + (1,000)(\$10) = \$22,000$$

For the buy option:

$$TC(B) = FC(B) + VC(B) = \$0 + (1,000)(\$20) = \$20,000$$

A break-even point computation is used to determine the number of tests (Y) at which $TC(M) = TC(B)$ (i.e., total cost is minimized). If

$$\$12,000 + \$10Y = \$0 + \$20Y$$

then, solving for Y,

$$Y = \$12,000 = 1,200 \text{ (break-even point)}$$

The indifference level of output can be calculated by comparing the total costs of the lease and buy options at various output levels (Table 8.4). Thus, for levels of output higher than 1,200 tests (break-even point), the lease decision is preferred; and for levels below 1,200 tests, the buy decision is preferred.

Example 2 The Commissioner of the Department of Health and Mental Hygiene has hired a managerial firm to investigate the inappropriate placement of geriatric psychiatric patients in the state. Under the policy of deinstitutionalization, it was noted that patients should be discharged from state hospitals to community-based facilities. There are two possible options for programs to deal with the placement of elderly psychiatric patients (Table 8.5).

Assume that there are 1,000 patients. There are no fixed costs for option I; the annual fixed cost of option II is $500,000. The following computations are necessary to make a recommendation to the Commissioner:

1. Minimize $TC(X) = FC(X) + VC(X)$ for the two options.
2. Calculate the break-even point.
3. Calculate the indifference levels of output for 500, 1,000, and 1,500 patients.

Minimizing Total Costs

$$TC(I) = FC(I) + VC(I) = \$0 + (1,000)(\$200) = \$200,000$$

$$TC(II) = FC(II) + VC(II) = \$500,000/12 + (1,000)(\$150) = \$191,667$$

Break-Even Point Computation

$$0 + (Y)(\$200) = \$41,667 + (Y)(\$150)$$

$$Y = \$41,667/\$50 = 833 \text{ (break-even point)}$$

Calculation of Indifference Level of Output The indifference levels of output for 500, 1,000, and 1,500 patients are shown in Table 8.6. According to the table, for levels of output higher than 833 patients (break-even point), option II is preferred; for levels of output lower than 833 patients, option I is preferred.

Methodology of Cost–Effectiveness Analysis

The other major way to analyze the costs and benefits of health care is cost–effectiveness analysis, which is actually a form of cost–benefit analysis (Warner & Luce, 1982). In cost–

Table 8.4. Indifference level of output for lease and buy options

Output	TC (M)	TC (B)	Difference: TC (M) − TC (B)
0	$12,000	$0	$12,000
250	$14,500	$5,000	$9,500
500	$17,000	$10,000	$7,000
1,000	$22,000	$20,000	$2,000
1,200	$24,000	$24,000	$0
1,500	$27,000	$30,000	$-3,000
2,000	$32,000	$40,000	$-8,000

Table 8.5. Program options for placement of elderly psychiatric patients

Program option	Variable cost per month
I: To subcontract to a community health center/facility	$200 per patient
II: To retain the patients in a state hospital with no change in organization, but formulate new activities in the state hospital	$150 per patient

effectiveness analysis, costs are calculated and alternate means compared for achieving a specific outcome. The outcome normally is not expressed in dollar amounts, but rather in terms of years of life saved or days of illness avoided. Cost–effectiveness analysis identifies alternative solutions to a problem in terms of their costs and their effectiveness in attaining certain objectives. The following is an example of a cost–effectiveness analysis of a screening test that prolongs life in an individual who is tested and found to have a disease. The possible outcomes of testing versus not testing in the presence or absence of the disease are shown in Table 8.7.

A decision rule can be developed if we let

L = the value of additional and improved life beyond the time of the decision whether to test
C = the total cost of the test
M = the cost of the medical procedure used to cure the disease

A decision matrix can be constructed to represent the outcomes (Table 8.8). This information also can be represented in a decision tree (Figure 8.2), where P is the probability of the disease being present (D), and the probability of the disease being absent (D_0) is $1 - P$. The difference between the expected value of testing $(E[A])$ and the expected value of not testing $(E[A_0])$ is the cost criterion. The expected values are calculated as follows:

$$E(A) = (P)(\Delta L - C - M) + (1 - P)(\Delta L - C)$$

$$= (\Delta L - C) - MP$$

$$E(A_0) = (P)(0) + (1 - P)(\Delta L) = \Delta L - \Delta L P$$

Thus, the cost of not having the test is

$$E(A_0) - EA = (\Delta L - \Delta L P) - (\Delta L - C - MP) = C + (M - \Delta L)P$$

Cost–Effectiveness Analysis of Health Care Outcomes One of the major goals of health services research is to measure the efficacy of health and social services for a target population, in order to ensure the best possible physical, mental, and social functions for them. In evaluating the effects of the medical care delivery system on patients' health, Brook and Lohr

Table 8.6. Indifference levels of output for placement of elderly psychiatric patients

Output	TC (II)	TC (I)	Difference: TC (II) − TC (I)
0	41,667	0	41,667
500	116,667	100,000	16,667
1,000	191,667	200,000	−8,333
1,500	266,667	300,000	−33,333

Table 8.7. Outcomes of screening test use and nonuse

Presence of disease	Action	
	Test (A)	Not test (A_0)
D (present)	Full life remains	Premature death
D_0 (absent)	Full life remains	Full life remains

(1985) suggested that returns from health services research will come more from integrating efficacy, effectiveness, variations in population-based rate of use, and quality of care into an operational model for policy, planning, and evaluation needs than from continuing to treat them as separate evaluative subjects. Other researchers (Kane, Bell, Reigler, Wilson, & Keeler, 1983; Wan et al., 1980) have noted as well the importance of including prospective outcomes (i.e., prognosis) when analyzing the effect of medical care on a patient's functional status. Recent evaluation studies also include patient satisfaction (T.K. Greenfield & Attkisson, 1989; Nguyen, Attkisson, & Stegner, 1983; Strasser & Davis, 1991; Ware, 1993) and quality of life (Fowler et al., 1988; Hlatky et al., 1989; Wortman & Yeaton, 1985) as indicators of health care outcomes.

The following example illustrates how the cost–effectiveness of a geriatric day care program designed for elderly persons with severe disabilities was evaluated in a randomized trial (Wan et al., 1980; Weissert, Wan, Livieratos, & Katz, 1980). The day care demonstration programs were required to have a strong health care component and incorporate physical rehabilitation. They also were required to provide the following services: nursing, social services, personal care, nutritional services, transportation, patient activities, occupational therapy, speech therapy, and eye, hearing, and podiatric examinations.

The study followed a randomized experimental design in which 194 patients received the experimental service (the experimental group), and 190 received regular services without the day care services (the control group). Initial analysis of the experimental effect shows that the mortality rate was 20.5% in the control group and 12.9% in the experimental group. The difference in mortality rate between the two groups was 7.6% and statistically significant. To detect the net effect of experimental services, however, it is necessary to control for the differences in patient characteristics as well as the intensity of services received. Multiple classification analysis of the mortality risk was employed; the predictor variables included demographic factors, measures of previous physical–mental–social functioning, prognostic measures, and utilization of services. The study found that the effect of day care services on the reduction in mortality risk was statistically significant after controlling for the effect of 24 patient attributes. A similar analysis evaluated patient care outcomes such as physical functioning, contentment, mental functioning, and activity. The detailed results are presented in Table 8.9.

The cost analysis of geriatric day care in the demonstration project shows that cost per patient averaged $52 per day and $3,235 per year. When the day care costs were added to Medicare costs for other services, costs for day care patients averaged $2,692 more than costs for the control group ($3,809)—an increase of 71% for the experimental group compared to the control group. The cost–effectiveness analysis indicates that health-oriented day care may not be

Table 8.8. Decision matrix for testing outcomes

Presence of disease	Action	
	Test (A)	Not test (A_0)
D (present)	$\Delta L - C - M$	0
D_0 (absent)	$\Delta L - C$	ΔL

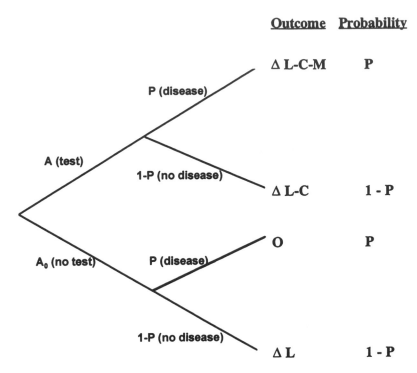

Figure 8.1.   Decision tree for the outcomes of the use or nonuse of a screening test for disease.

cheaper than nursing homes. Thus, the evaluation of the day care demonstration suggests that most patients used geriatric day care as a supplement to existing health care services rather than as a substitute for them (Weissert et al., 1980).

Advantages and Disadvantages of Cost–Effectiveness and Cost–Benefit Analysis

Cost–Benefit Analysis   Cost–benefit analysis is used to compare programs whose costs and benefits are expressible in monetary terms (Hellinger, 1980). All consequences in cost–benefit analysis are valued in monetary terms, and thus programs competing for scarce resources are compared to see which program yields the greatest benefits. The advantage of cost–benefit analysis is that, because the unit of measurement is the same (dollars), diverse as well as similar types of programs can be compared to select the program with the highest net benefit per dollar invested (Warner & Luce, 1982).

The disadvantage of cost–benefit analysis is that many elements of health care are intangible and either difficult to measure or possessing other than monetary value. Examples include the relief of pain and suffering, improved quality of life, and survival itself. Some such variables have been given dollar values, although doing so remains controversial. The "price" of homemakers, or the cost to society from a member's loss of productivity, calculated numerically from estimates and national averages in age and sex categories, may have little relevance to the essential values involved; the use of such terms in cost–benefit analysis remains questionable.

For example, the most common method for assigning a value to life is to use the present value of the future flow of income, which is often called the livelihood–savings approach (Hellinger, 1980). However, the accumulation of earning flows is not the primary objective of health care; moreover, the livelihood–savings approach assumes that an individual's worth is measured by that person's wealth (Hellinger, 1980). Another method used in determining a

Table 8.9. Multiple classification analysis of factors affecting outcomes of care among 384 participants in the day care study sample

Predictors	ADL physical functioning		Contentment level		Mental functioning		Activity level	
	Adjusted %	β^{2*}	Adjusted %	β^{2*}	Adjusted %	β^{2*}	Adjusted %	β^{2*}
Demographic Factors								
Age:		0.001		0.001		0.001		0.002
Under 75	61.6		68.2		70.8		72.3	
75 or older	60.9		66.0		70.1		68.6	
Sex:		0.002		0.000		0.011		0.003
Male	59.4		66.8		76.2		67.3	
Female	63.7		67.2		66.4		72.4	
Race:		0.001		0.000		0.002		0.006
White	62.1		67.2		69.5		72.0	
Nonwhite	57.5		66.2		74.4		63.3	
Living Arrangement:		0.005		0.005		0.001		0.000
Living alone	55.1		61.1		73.3		70.4	
Not living alone	63.2		69.0		69.5		70.3	
Marital Status:		0.001		0.002		0.020#		0.006
Married	58.5		63.8		60.6		75.4	
Not married	62.4		68.5		74.7		68.0	
Social and Psychological Functioning[†]								
Contentment Level:		0.005		0.063#		0.007		0.001
Low	63.9		85.2		78.1		70.1	
Medium	64.2		71.5		69.9		69.2	
High	56.8		53.9		67.6		71.6	
Activity Level:		0.009		0.004		0.001		0.113#
Low	64.7		67.4		72.0		90.4	
Medium	55.1		63.5		70.6		64.0	
High	64.9		71.2		68.4		53.3	
Mental Functioning Level:		0.079#		0.011		0.000		0.061#
Low	32.5		57.9		69.3		48.3	
Medium	54.9		64.0		71.0		63.7	
High	72.4		71.2		70.3		80.0	
Physical Functioning[†]								
Dependency Level:		0.005		0.004		0.012‖		0.014‖
Minimally dependent	56.1		71.7		78.0		78.9	
Moderately dependent	60.2		65.4		64.2		68.7	
Severely dependent	64.1		65.0		68.3		66.4	
No. of Chronic Conditions:		0.003		0.013		0.005		0.001
None	56.8		52.4		63.4		68.9	
One	59.0		69.4		72.8		69.8	
Two	64.0		69.0		72.2		72.5	
Three or more	62.9		68.7		68.6		69.2	
Bed Disability Days:		0.007		0.003		0.023#		0.003
Low (under 11 days)	57.1		64.4		69.2		68.6	
Medium (11–30 days)	65.8		69.7		62.9		69.7	
High (31 days or more)	64.8		69.6		82.4		75.0	

(continued)

Table 8.9. *(continued)*

Predictors	ADL physical functioning		Contentment level		Mental functioning		Activity level	
	Adjusted %	β^{2*}	Adjusted %	β^{2*}	Adjusted %	β^{2*}	Adjusted %	β^{2*}
Primary Diagnosis:		0.051‖		0.071‖		0.046‖		0.037‖
Neoplasms	64.2		22.4		47.3		52.1	
Metabolic system	47.7		43.7		49.6		74.3	
Mental disorder	58.0		68.0		64.5		77.9	
Nervous system	50.4		71.1		78.7		68.4	
Circulatory system	61.8		69.4		71.7		69.0	
Respiratory system	35.3		31.3		55.8		42.2	
Digestive system	86.6		58.9		74.1		57.7	
Genitourinary system	13.1		34.8		46.4		29.8	
Musculoskeletal system	65.1		59.2		68.7		52.4	
External injuries	78.8		87.3		87.4		83.0	
Other systems	62.6		64.9		64.0		72.6	
Prognostic Measure								
ADL Prognosis:		0.007		0.010		0.008		0.012
Decline	100.0		77.7		65.6		0.0	
Maintain	65.3		75.0		77.3		76.0	
Improve	59.6		64.0		68.0		68.6	
Psychological Functioning:		0.001		0.000		0.009		0.003
Decline[‡]	—		—		—		—	
Maintain	62.9		66.1		74.9		67.9	
Improve	59.6		67.8		66.4		72.5	
Social Functioning:		0.001		0.001		0.006		0.004
Decline[‡]	—		—		—		—	
Maintain	58.5		70.3		62.0		77.0	
Improve	61.7		66.4		72.0		69.1	
Impairment Prognosis:		0.018‖		0.026‖		0.023‖		0.018‖
Decline	0.0		0.0		1.7		1.0	
Maintain	62.3		68.2		74.2		71.7	
Improve	61.3		67.2		68.1		70.1	
Bed Disability Prognosis:		0.009		0.013		0.002		0.016‖
Decline	81.2		92.0		79.2		93.1	
Maintain	56.8		71.9		68.7		64.7	
Improve	65.5		61.8		72.1		75.8	
Institutionalized Prognosis:		0.003		0.001		0.019‖		0.001
Decline	74.1		69.2		88.2		69.3	
Maintain	61.1		65.8		65.4		71.2	
Improve	60.1		68.7		76.4		68.9	
Health Services Utilization								
Skilled Nursing Facilities:		0.002		0.006		0.006‖		0.007
None	61.9		68.6		70.9		71.6	
Low (1–10 days)	63.7		55.3		76.4		54.4	
Medium (11–29 days)	54.4		60.7		55.3		58.8	
High (30 days or more)	57.1		59.0		72.5		70.0	

(continued)

Table 8.9. *(continued)*

Predictors	ADL physical functioning Adjusted %	β²*	Contentment level Adjusted %	β²*	Mental functioning Adjusted %	β²*	Activity level Adjusted %	β²*
Inpatient Hospital Days:		0.076#		0.073#		0.139#		0.142#
None	71.5		77.4		85.4		83.1	
Low (1–8 days)	59.6		63.7		62.5		67.0	
Medium (9–23 days)	59.7		63.8		64.4		71.3	
High (24 days or more)	35.0		43.2		40.9		36.3	
Day Care Use:		0.014#		0.013#		0.004#		0.002#
None	56.4		65.8		70.2		68.7	
Low (1–25 days)	59.2		56.3		66.1		71.3	
Medium (26–77 days)	67.4		73.6		69.0		73.5	
High (78 days or more)	69.4		72.3		75.1		70.9	
Home Health Care Use:		0.001		0.005		0.005		0.007
None	61.7		65.0		72.2		72.7	
Low (1–9 visits)	61.6		68.0		63.3		63.5	
Medium (10–26 visits)	56.2		74.4		69.4		67.6	
High (27 visits)	62.3		73.7		67.4		63.3	
OPD Use: [§]		0.020#		0.017		0.034‖		0.063‖
None	53.4		60.5		59.5		55.8	
Low ($1–$281)	57.0		73.4		66.5		67.6	
Medium ($282–$859)	60.4		59.3		68.5		63.6	
High ($860 or more)	73.5		68.3		85.5		90.7	
Ambulatory Care Use:		0.030#		0.016		0.029		0.046#
None	64.8		62.1		58.7		64.0	
Low ($1–$272)	67.9		61.3		75.3		77.9	
Medium ($273–$802)	63.4		69.5		77.1		76.2	
High ($803 or more)	46.3		75.7		60.6		54.4	
Site:		0.018‖		0.062#		0.071#		0.010
1	65.9		69.6		84.3		73.2	
2	70.2		91.6		87.4		78.1	
3	49.4		64.8		53.9		64.0	
4	61.0		58.2		65.6		69.0	
Mean	61.2		67.0		70.4		70.3	
R^2		0.328		0.303		0.306		0.406

Adapted from Wan, Weissert, & Livieratos. (1980).

*β² is the proportion of variance explained by each predictor when other variables are controlled. The four outcome measures used as the dependent variables are binary variables; favorable outcome, either to improve or maintain, is coded as 1 and unfavorable outcome, to decline in the level of functioning, is coded as 0.

[†]Measures were based upon the first assessment made in the study period.

[‡]No cases in the subclass.

[§]OPD, outpatient department.

‖Significant at 0.05 level.

#Significant at 0.01 or lower level.

value for life is the willingness-to-pay method. This method assumes that the value of a health care program is the sum of the amounts persons are willing to pay for the reduction in risk attributable to the program (Hellinger, 1980). The disadvantages of this method are that it requires a survey, and thus is costly, and that in any case the reliability of the survey responses is questionable (Hellinger, 1980).

Another debatable point about cost–benefit analysis concerns inflation, or discounting future benefits into terms of current values. When looking at long-term programs, present values of future benefits must be taken into account: Future benefits yielded by a program almost certainly will vary from present values. Statistical forecasts of benefits may provide close estimates, but economists with varying theoretical positions argue over this as well as the aforementioned issues (Hellinger, 1980; Thompson, 1980; Warner & Hutton, 1980).

Cost–Effectiveness Analysis   In cost–effectiveness analysis, costs are calculated and alternate means for achieving a specific outcome are compared. Note that costs in this analysis usually are not expressed in dollar amounts, but may be expressed in terms of years of life saved or days of illness avoided. Cost–effectiveness analysis is most useful when it is impossible or undesirable to put a monetary value on the element being evaluated. For example, many economists are reluctant to place a dollar sign on the value of life. Pain and discomfort from an illness or injury are also qualitative rather than quantitative assessments. With the lack of congruence between qualitative and quantitative measures, however, only programs with similar objectives can be compared with one another. Note that the inherent worth of the programs themselves is not measured by cost–effectiveness analysis (Levin, 1975; Rubin et al., 1993; Thompson, 1980; Veney & Kaluzny, 1991; Warner & Hutton, 1980).

Cost–effectiveness analysis is advantageous when it is impossible or inappropriate to put a money value on the element being evaluated, such as a life. The disadvantages of cost–effectiveness analysis are: 1) only programs with similar objectives can be compared, and 2) cost–effectiveness analysis does not consider the inherent worth of a program.

Roles in Health Program Evaluation   With the increasing emphasis in the health care industry on cost containment, more effort will go toward ensuring that the benefits of health care outweigh their costs. Cost–benefit analysis can assess the desirability of programs if their costs and benefits are expressible in monetary terms, which allows for comparisons between programs (Warner & Luce, 1982). Cost–effectiveness analysis, in contrast, takes noneconomic values into account, and many administrators and politicians consider humanitarian values in their health care decisions. Thus combinations of the two methods are evolving as the methodology for evaluation of health services.

HEALTH CARE OUTCOMES AND EVALUATION

Outcomes research involves linking the type of care received by patients with a specific condition to positive and negative outcomes in order to identify what works best for which patients. More broadly defined, outcomes research includes the collection and reporting of data that can be used to compare quality of care delivered by various health care organizations. Assessment of health care outcomes consists of three major activities: 1) *outcome measurement*—quantification of observed outcome measures at a point in time; 2) *outcome monitoring*—repeated measurement over time of outcome indicators; and 3) *outcome management/improvement*—achievement of optimal patient care outcomes through appropriate medical interventions, improved medical decision making, and improvement of the service delivery system (Davies et al., 1994).

In recent years, interest in outcomes research has grown because of the variety of ways in which information from outcomes research can be used. The major uses of outcomes research information for public and private payers include: reducing health care costs based on effectiveness results, rationing care based on effectiveness results, establishing national guidelines based on effectiveness results, making reimbursement decisions based on quality assessment, and making purchasing decisions based on quality assessment. The major uses of outcomes research information for health care organizations include: using effectiveness results to establish local guidelines, using quality assessment data for marketing purposes, using quality assessment data to identify opportunities for improvement, and using quality assessment data for regulatory compliance. The major use of outcomes research information for individual providers is providing effectiveness information to patients to help make treatment decisions. For patients and the public, the major uses of outcomes research information include using effectiveness data in treatment decisions and using quality assessment data to make purchasing decisions (Guadagnoli & McNeil, 1994).

The national goal in the provision of personal and public health services is to achieve an optimal level of health of the population. Two of the public health services' objectives are 1) the Centers for Disease Control's Nation's Health: Measurable Goals and 2) the development of automated information systems for improving quality, access, and efficiency of services. Numerous efforts have been made to formulate measurable objectives that will improve not only personal health status but also community or population health. Several examples of these efforts are described here.

Under the Health Care Financing Administration's health care quality improvement initiative, the case-by-case peer review of clinical practice will be replaced by profiles of practice patterns (Audet & Scott, 1993). The focus will be placed on the patterns of care delivered by physicians at the aggregate level so that the variations in practice pattern by a specific condition can be detected and monitored.

In order to standardize the assessment of quality of care that Medicare beneficiaries receive, the Uniform Clinical Data Set (UCDS), an automated, computerized data set, was developed and is undergoing empirical validation for its validity, reliability, and applicability (Hartz, Gottlieb, Kuhn, & Rimm, 1993). The clinical assessment consists of a generic quality review (a random selection of a 5% sample of admissions for detecting the stability of patients discharged) and a disease-specific review (the management of patient care by specific conditions). The types of generic quality reviews include the adequacy of discharge planning, medical stability of the patient at the time of discharge, deaths, nosocomial infection, unscheduled return to surgery, and trauma suffered in the hospital. A total of 1,800 data elements or clinical variables can be abstracted from each review subject. The preliminary evaluation of the UCDS's generic quality screens shows that the lack of structured, explicit criteria in peer reviews has contributed to the low interrater and interitem reliability (Goldman, 1992; Sanazaro & Mills, 1991). However, if the validity of generic quality screens is improved further through reduction of the number of data elements, the reliability could be improved.

The disease-specific profiling approach is another way of conducting quality management. Through the analysis of patterns of care for a specific condition treated by groups of physicians, common causes and special causes of the variation can be identified. Data sources are based on claims data, medical records, and patient surveys.

The National Committee for Quality Assurance (NCQA) designed the Health Plan Employer Data and Information Set (HEDIS), a set of uniform performance indicators that will help employers and other health care purchasers assess health care performance at the plan level. Major areas of organizational (plan) performance include quality, access and patient satisfaction, membership and utilization, and financial stability. The quality measures for selected service areas are the percentages of childhood immunization, cholesterol screenings, mammography screenings, cervical cancer screenings, very-low-birth-weight infants (less than 1,500 grams), low-birth-weight infants (less than 2,500 grams), women receiving prenatal care in the first trimester, asthma inpatient admissions, diabetic retinal examinations, and ambulatory follow-ups after psychiatric hospitalization. Patient satisfaction is measured by a response of a good or high level of overall satisfaction with medical care, whereas accessibility is measured by the percentage of members who have visited a physician or provider within 3 years. Utilization measures serve to reveal membership stability or disenrollment, patterns of care, use of specific ambulatory and acute care services, mental health services, and frequency and average cost of five selected surgical procedures. About 15 financial indicators, such as measures of liquidity, efficiency, stability, and compliance with statutory requirements, also are utilized. Benchmarked performance standards can be derived from the data collected from multiple health plans so that the plan performance can be ranked to provide needed information for both employers and consumers (Corringan & Nielsen, 1993). By the end of 1993, the NCQA had conducted reviews on more than one third of the nation's 550 managed care organizations. The HEDIS 2.0 performance measures may be used to develop "report cards" on the quality of care rendered by health plans. (Detailed methodology for evaluation plan performance can be obtained by contacting the NCQA at 1350 New York Avenue, N.W., Washington, D.C. 20005.)

A similar private initiative on the development of systemwide measures of performance was developed jointly by 23 vertically integrated health care systems, using multiple data sources such as patient/member surveys, discharge data, and automated financial data (Nerenz, Zajac, & Rosman, 1994). The performance indicators consist of two tiers. The first tier includes the general health index (SF-36), prevention index, hospital readmission rate, proportion of system expenses devoted to charity care, hospital admissions per member per year, low-birth-weight incidence, number of services per episode, hospital days per 1,000 members, satisfaction with care, percentage of system expenses for administration, profitability, and debt–service coverage ratios. The second tier of performance measures, in the developmental phase, will include disease-specific outcomes of care, compliance with standard care patterns for selected conditions, redundancy of services provided within episodes, frequency of preventable acute episodes within chronic conditions, illness-based medical care episodes per member per year, and percentage of new breast cancer cases classified as "advanced."

In 1993, the Health Care Financing Administration led a number of efforts in developing a quality-of-care measurement instrument that will minimize the clinical case review and simplify the pattern-of-care analysis for the Medicare population. One of the Medicare peer review organizations, the Delmarva Foundation for Medical Care, located in Baltimore, Maryland, is leading the way to develop ambulatory review criteria for Medicare, to determine the minimal data requirements, and to formulate a valid methodology for assessing quality of managed care.

CONCLUSION

Evaluation will continue to be essential to our efforts to improve our health care system in an increasingly turbulent environment. The quality, accessibility, continuity, effectiveness, and efficiency of care all must be evaluated to ensure adequate performance. In particular, more effort must be directed toward assessing the physician–patient relationship and its effect on the quality of care. A growing body of research on patient satisfaction (Benson, 1992; Ho, Stegall, & Wan, 1993; Ross, Stewart, & Sinacore, 1993; Steiber & Krowinski, 1990) and on physician satisfaction (Matthews, Suchman, & Branch, 1993; Suchman, Roter, Green, Lipkin, & the Collaborative Study Group of the American Academy of Physician and Patient, 1993) is emerging in the changing health care environment. The effectiveness of evaluation depends on better cooperation among members of the medical profession, other health professionals, nonmedical professionals, and government agencies, all of whom have a role. If possible, evaluation should use both process and outcome measures (Clement et al., 1994). Because of the scarcity of health resources and the current effort to control health care costs, cost–benefit and cost–effectiveness calculations increasingly will dominate evaluation. The medical profession must come to consensus and perhaps develop standards for safe and effective medical practices. Finally, both treatment strength and treatment integrity must be considered in order to ensure the validity of the evaluation.

REFERENCES

Aday, L.A. (1989). *Designing and conducting health surveys: A comprehensive guide.* San Francisco: Jossey-Bass Publishers.

Aday, L.A., Begley, C.E., Lairson, D.R., & Slater, C.H. (1993). *Evaluating the medical care system: Effectiveness, efficiency, and equity.* Ann Arbor, MI: Health Administration Press.

Audet, A.M., & Scott, H.D. (1993). The uniform clinical data set: An evaluation of the proposed national database for Medicare's quality review program. *Annals of Internal Medicine, 119,* 1209–1213.

Banta, H.O., Burns, A.K., & Behney, C.J. (1983). Policy implications of the diffusion and control of medical technology. *Annals of the American Academy of Political and Social Science, 468,* 165–181.

Bashshur, R.L., Homan, R.K., & Smith, D.G. (1994). Beyond the uninsured: Problems in access to care. *Medical Care, 32*(5), 409–419.

Benson, D.S. (1992). *Measuring outcomes in ambulatory care.* Chicago: American Hospital Publishing, Inc.

Beraud, C. (1979). Quality of outcome, or efficacy of medical process: When criteria should be chosen. In A. Alperovitch, F.T. de Dombal, & F. Gremy (Eds.), *Evaluation of efficacy of medical action* (pp. 3–12). New York: North-Holland.

Breslau, N. (1982). Continuity reexamined: Differential impact on satisfaction with medical care for disabled and normal children. *Medical Care, 2C,* 347–359.

Brook, R.H., & Lohr, K.N. (1985). Efficacy, effectiveness, variations, and quality: Boundary-crossing research. *Medical Care, 23,* 710–722.

Brook, R.H., Davis, A.R., & Kamberg, C.J. (1980). Selected reflections on quality of medical care evaluation in the 1980s. *Nursing Research, 29*(2), 127–133.

Brown, R.S., Clement, D.G., Hill, J.W., Retchin, S.M., & Bergeron, J. (1993). Do health maintenance organizations work for Medicare? *Health Care Financing Review, 15*(1), 7–23.

Campbell, J.T., & Stanley, J.C. (1966). *Experimental and quasi-experimental designs for research.* Skokie, IL: Rand McNally.

Chan, J.C., McEnger, P.T., Churchill, V.M., Abitbol, C.L., Boineau, F.G., Friedman, A.L., Lum, G.M., Roy, S., 3rd, Ruley, E.J., & Strife, C.F. (1994). A prospective, double-blind study of growth failure in children with chronic renal insufficiency and the effectiveness of treatment with calcitriol versus dihydrotachysterol. *Journal of Pediatrics, 124,* 520–528.

Churchman, C.W. (1979). *The systems approach.* New York: Dell.

Clement, D.G., Retchin, S.M., Brown, R.S., & Stegall, M.H. (1994). Access and outcomes of elderly patients enrolled in managed care. *Journal of the American Medical Association, 271,* 1487–1492.

Corrigan, J.M., & Nielsen, D.M. (1993). Toward the development of uniform reporting standards for managed care organizations: The Health Plan Employer Data and Information Set (Version 2.0). *Journal on Quality Improvement, 19,* 566–575.

Davies, A.R., Doyle, M.A.T., Lansky, D., Rutt, W., Stevic, M.O., & Boyle, J.B. (1994). Outcomes assessment in clinical settings: A consensus statement on principles and best practice in project management. *Journal on Quality Improvement, 20,* 6–16.

Davis, K., & Rowland, D. (1983). *Securing access to health care: The ethical implications of differences in the availability of health services: Vol. 3. Uninsured and underserved: Inequities in health care in the U.S.* Washington, DC: U.S. Government Printing Office.

Denzin, N., & Lincoln, Y. (1994). *Handbook of qualitative research.* Thousand Oaks, CA: Sage Publications.

Donabedian, A. (1980). *Explorations in quality assessment and monitoring: Vol. I. The definition of quality and approaches to its assessment.* Ann Arbor, MI: Health Administration Press.

Donabedian, A. (1981). Advantages and limitations of explicit criteria for assessing the quality of health care. *Milbank Memorial Fund Quarterly/Health and Society, 59,* 99–106.

Donabedian, A. (1983). Quality, cost, and clinical decisions. *Annals of the American Academy of Political and Social Science, 468,* 196–204.

Drummond, M.F., Stoddard, G.L., & Torrance, G.T. (1987). *Methods for the economic evaluation of health care programs.* New York: Oxford University Press.

Dunland, E.N. (1987). Colorado's nursing home alternative progam: An evaluation designed to be used. *New England Journal of Human Science, 7*(1), 35–37.

Fineberg, H.V., & Hiatt, H.H. (1979). Evaluation of medical practice: The case for technology assessment. *New England Journal of Medicine, 301*(20), 1086–1091.

Finkel, M.L., McCarthy, E.G., & Miller, D. (1982). Podiatric surgery: The need for a second opinion. *Medical Care, 20*, 862–870.

Fowler, F.J., Wennberg, J.E., Timothy, R.P., Barry, M.J., Mulley, A.G., & Hanley, D. (1988). Symptom status and quality of life following prostatectomy. *Journal of the American Medical Association, 259*, 3018–3022.

Frazier, H.S., & Hiatt, H.H. (1980). Evaluation of medical practices. In S.J. Williams (Ed.), *Issues in health services* (pp. 363–371). New York: John Wiley and Sons.

Gertman, P.M., & Mitchell, J.B. (1980). Surgical care: A policy focus of the 1980s. *Medical Care, 18*, 881–882.

Gertman, P.M., & Restuccia, J.D. (1981). The Appropriateness of Evaluation Protocol: A technique for assessing unnecessary days of hospital care. *Medical Care, 19*, 855–871.

Goldman, R.L. (1992). The reliability of peer assessment of quality of care. *Journal of the American Medical Association, 267*, 958–960.

Greenfield, S. (1989). The state of outcome research: Are we on target? *New England Journal of Medicine, 320*, 1142–1143.

Greenfield, T.K., & Attkisson, C.C. (1989). Steps toward a multifactorial satisfaction scale for primary care and mental health services. *Evaluation and Program Planning, 12*, 271–278.

Greenlick, M.R. (1981). Assessing clinical competence: A society view. *Evaluation and the Health Professions, 4*(1), 3–12.

Greenspan, J. (1980). *Accountability and quality assurance in health care*. Bowie, MD: Charles Press Publishers.

Guadagnoli, E., & McNeil, B.J. (1994). Outcomes research: Hope for the future or the latest rage? *Inquiry, 31*, 14–24.

Hartz, A.J., Gottlieb, M.S., Kuhn, E.M., & Rimm, A.A. (1993). The relationship between adjusted hospital mortality and the results of peer review. *Health Service Research, 27*(6), 765–777.

Hellinger, F.J. (1980). Cost-benefit analysis of health care: Past applications and future prospects. *Inquiry, 17*, 204–215.

Hlatky, M.A., Boineau, R.E., Higginbotham, M.B., Lee, K.L., Mark, D.B., Califf, R.M., Cobb, F.R., & Pryor, D.B. (1989). A brief self-administered questionnaire to determine functional capacity. *American Journal of Cardiology, 64*, 651–654.

Ho, P.S., Stegall, M.B., & Wan, T.T.H. (1994). Modeling two dimensions of patient satisfaction: A panel study. *Health Services Management Research, 7*(1), 66–76.

Jirka, F.J., Jr. (1984). Three major challenges: Quality, cost, and balance. *Journal of the American Medical Association, 251*, 1867–1868.

Kahan, J.P., Bernstein, S.J., Leape, L.L., Hilborne, L.H., Park, R.E., Parker, L., Kamper, C.J., & Brook, R.H. (1994). Measuring the necessity of medical procedures. *Medical Care, 32*, 357–365.

Kane, R.L., Bell, R., Reigler, S., Wilson, A., & Keeler, E. (1983). Assessing the outcomes of nursing home patients. *Journal of Gerontology, 38*, 385–393.

Kaplan, A. (1964). *The conduct of inquiry*. New York: Harper & Row Publishers, Inc.

Knaus, W.A., Draper, E.A., & Wagner, D.P. (1983). Toward quality review in intensive care: The APACHE system. *Quality Review Bulletin, 9*(7), 196–204.

Levin, H.M. (1975). Cost effectiveness analysis in evaluation research. In M. Guttentag & E.L. Struening (Eds.), *Handbook of evaluation research* (Vol. 2, pp. 89–122). Beverly Hills, CA: Sage Publications.

Limouzin-Lamothe, M.A., Mairon, N., Joyce, C.R., & Le-Gal, M. (1994). Quality of life after menopause: Influence of hormonal replacement therapy. *American Journal of Obstetrics and Gynecology, 170*, 618–624.

Lohr, K.N., Yordy, K.D., & Their, S.O. (1988). Current issues in quality of care. *Health Affairs, 7*(1), 5–18.

Matthews, D.A., Suchman, A.L., & Branch, W.T. (1993). Making 'connexions': Enhancing the therapeutic potential of patient-clinician relationships. *Annals of Internal Medicine, 118*(12), 973–977.

McDowell, D., McCleary, R., Meidinger, E., & Hay, R. (1980). *Interrupted time series analysis*. Thousand Oaks, CA: Sage Publications.

McKenzie, J.F., & Jurs, J.L. (1993). *Planning, implementing, and evaluating health promotion programs*. New York: Macmillan.

Nassif, D., Garfink, C., & Greenfield, C. (1982). Does continuity equal quality in the assessment of well-child care? *Quality Review Bulletin, 8*(6), 11–18.

National Center for Health Statistics. (1994). *Health United States, 1993*. Hyattsville, MD: Author.

Nerenz, D.R., Zajac, B.M., & Rosman, H.S. (1994). Consortium research on indicators of system performance (CRISP). *Journal of Quality Indicators, 19*, 577–585.

Nguyen, T.D., Attkisson, C.C., & Stegner, B.L. (1983). Assessment of patient satisfaction: Development and refinement of a service evaluation questionnaire. *Evaluation and Program Planning, 6,* 299–314.

Nutting, P.A., Shorr, G.I., & Burkhalter, B.R. (1981). Assessing the performance of medical care systems: A method and its application. *Medical Care, 19*(3), 281–296.

Okada, L.M., & Wan, T.T.H. (1980). Impact of community health centers and Medicaid on the use of health services. *Public Health Reports, 95,* 520–534.

Panel on Confidentiality and Data Access. (1993). *Private lives and public policies.* Washington, DC: National Academy Press.

Restuccia, J.D., & Holloway, D.C. (1982). Methods of control for hospital quality assurance systems. *Health Services Research, 17,* 241–251.

Roos, L.L., Roos, N.P., Gilbert, P., & Nicol, J.P. (1980). Continuity of care: Does it contribute to quality of care? *Medical Care, 18,* 174–184.

Roper, W.L., Winkenwerder, W., Hackbarth, G.M., & Krakauer, H. (1988). Effectiveness in health care: An initiative to evaluate and improve medical practice. *New England Journal of Medicine, 319,* 1197–1202.

Rosen, H.M., & Feigin, W., Sr. (1983). Quality assurance and data feedback. *Health Care Management Review, 8*(1), 67–74.

Rosenberg, M. (1968). *The logic of survey analysis.* New York: Basic Books, Inc.

Ross, C.K., Stewart, C.A., & Sinacore, J.M. (1993). The importance of patient preferences in the measurement of health care satisfaction. *Medical Care, 31,* 1138–1149.

Rubin, H.R., Gandek, M.S., Rogers, W.H., Kosinske, M.A., McHorney, C.A., & Ware, J.E. (1993). Patients' ratings of outpatient visits in different practice settings. *Journal of the American Medical Association, 270,* 835–845.

Ruchlin, H.S., Finkel, M.L., & McCarthy, E.G. (1982). The efficacy of second-opinion consultation programs: A cost-benefit perspective. *Medical Care, 20,* 3–19.

Rutgow, I.M. (1989). *Socioeconomics of surgery.* St. Louis: C.V. Mosby.

Sanazaro, P.J., & Mills, D.H. (1991). A critique of the use of generic screening in quality assessment. *Journal of the American Medical Association, 265,* 1977–1981.

Scheffler, R.M., Cement, D.G., Sullivan, S.D., Hu, T.W., & Sung, H.Y. (1994). The hospital response to Medicare's prospective payment system: An econometric model of Blue Cross and Blue Shield plans. *Medical Care, 32,* 471–485.

Sechrest, L., West, S.G., Phillips, M.A., Redner, R., & Yeaton, W. (1979). Some neglected problems in evaluation research: Strength and integrity of treatments. *Evaluation Studies Review Annual, 4,* 15–35.

Shortell, S.M., & Richardson, W.C. (1978). *Health program evaluation.* St. Louis: Mosby.

Shukla, R. (1985). Admission monitoring and scheduling to improve work flow in hospitals. *Inquiry, 22,* 92–101.

Shuman, C.J., Wolf, H., & Speas, H.D. (1974). The role of operations research in regional health planning. *Operations Research, 22,* 234–248.

Sieverts, S. (1982). The assurance of appropriate medical care: The role of Blue Cross and Blue Shield. *Bulletin of the New York Academy of Medicine, 58,* 49–55.

Steiber, S.R., & Krowinski, W.J. (1990). *Measuring and managing patient satisfaction.* Chicago: American Hospital Publishing, Inc.

Stimson, D., & Stimson, R. (1972). *Operations research in hospitals: Diagnosis and prognosis.* Chicago: HRET.

Strasser, S., & Davis, R.M. (1991). *Measuring patient satisfaction for improved patient services.* Ann Arbor, MI: Health Administration Press.

Suchman, A.L., Roter, D., Green, M., Lipkin, M., & the Collaborative Study Group of the American Academy of Physician and Patient. (1993). Physician satisfaction with primary care office visits. *Medical Care, 31,* 1083–1092.

Sutherland, J.W. (1973). *A general systems philosophy for the social and behavioral sciences.* New York: George Braziller.

Sutherland, J.W. (1989). *Toward a strategic management and decision technology: Modern approaches to organizational planning and positioning.* Boston: Kluwer Academic Publishers.

Svarstad, B.L. (1979). Physician-patient communication and patient conformity with medical advice. In G.L. Albrecht & P.C. Higgins (Eds.), *Health, illness, and medicine: A reader in medical sociology* (pp. 243–259). Chicago: Rand McNally.

Swain, R. (1981). *Quantitative analysis of health care delivery systems.* Columbus, OH: Grid Publishing Co.

Sydenstricker, E. (1926). The measurement of results of public health work. In *Annual reports of the Milbank Memorial Fund* (pp. 1–35).

Szpalski, M., & Hayez, J.P. (1994). Objective functional assessment of the efficacy of tenoxicam in the treatment of acute low back pain. *British Journal of Rheumatology, 33,* 74–78.

Thompson, M.S. (1980). *Benefit-cost analysis for program evaluation.* Beverly Hills, CA: Sage Publications.

Trochim, M.K. (1986). *Advances in quasi-experimental design and analysis.* San Francisco: Jossey-Bass.

U.S. Department of Health and Human Services. (1993). *The National Committee on Vital and Health Statistics.* Hyattsville, MD: National Center for Health Statistics.

United States National Committee on Vital and Health Statistics. (1993). *The national committee on vital and health statistics: [Summary report].* Hyattsville, MD: U.S. Department of Health and Human Services, Public Health Service, Office of Health Research, Statistics, and Technology, National Center for Health Statistics.

Veney, J.E., & Kaluzny, A.D. (1991). *Evaluation and decision making for health services.* Ann Arbor, MI: Health Administration Press.

Wagner, D.P., Knaus, W.A., Draper, E.A., & Zimmerman, J.E. (1983). Identification of low-risk monitor patients within a medical-surgical intensive care unit. *Medical Care, 21,* 425–434.

Wagner, D.P., Draper, E.A., & Knaus, W.A. (1989). Analysis: Quality of care. In APACHE III Study Design: Analytic Plan for Evaluation of Severity and Outcome. *Critical Care Medicine, 17*(12, part 2), 5210–5212.

Wagner, D.P., Knaus, W.A., & Draper, E.A. (1986). Physiologic abnormalities and outcome from acute disease: Evidence for a predictive relationship. *Archives of Internal Medicine, 146,* 1389–1396.

Waitzkin, H. (1984). Doctor-patient communication: Clinical implications of social scientific research. *Journal of the American Medical Association, 252,* 2441–2446.

Waitzkin, H. (1985). Information giving in medical care. *Journal of Health and Social Behavior, 26,* 81–101.

Wan, T.T.H. (1984). Social differentials in the use of preventive and ambulatory care services. *Journal of Ambulatory Care Management, 7*(3), 57–64

Wan, T.T.H. (1989). The effect of managed care on health services use by dually eligible elders. *Medical Care, 27,* 983–1001.

Wan, T.T.H., Weissert, W.G., & Livieratos, B. (1980). Geriatric day care and homemaker services: An experimental study. *Journal of Gerontology, 35,* 256–274.

Ware, J.E. (1993). *SF-36 health survey: Manual and interpretation guide.* Boston: The New England Medical Center Health Institute.

Warner, K., & Luce, B.R. (1982). *Cost-benefit and cost-effectiveness analysis in health care: Principles, practice, and potential.* Ann Arbor, MI: Health Administration Press.

Warner, K.E., & Hutton, R.C. (1980). Cost-benefit and cost-effectiveness analysis in health care. Growth and composition of the literature. *Medical Care, 18*(11), 1069–1084.

Weinstein, M.C., & Stason, W.B. (1977). *Hypertension: A policy perspective.* Cambridge, MA: Harvard University Press.

Weissert, W.G., Wan, T.T.H., Livieratos, B., & Katz, S. (1980). Effects and costs of day-care services for the chronically ill: A randomized experiment. *Medical Care, 18,* 567–584.

White, J.W., Russell, W.L., Greer, M.S., & Whittle, M.T. (1994). Efficacy of screening MR angiography and Doppler ultrasonography in the evaluation of carotid artery stenosis. *American Surgeon, 60,* 340–348.

Williams, S.J., & Torrens, P.R. (1980). *Introduction to health services.* New York: John Wiley & Sons, Inc.

Wortman, P.M., & Yeaton, W.H. (1985). Cumulating quality of life results in controlled trials of coronary artery bypass graft surgery. *Controlled Clinical Trials, 6,* 289–305.

Zuckerman, H.S., Huntley, J.A., & Waterbrook, K.J. (1980). Effectiveness of patient care in a primary care clinic. *Medical Care, 18,* 1001–1012.

9

Evaluation Designs and Analysis

Every cause produces more than one effect.
Herbert Spencer, *On Progress: Its Law and Cause*

Program evaluations deal with two major questions: 1) To what extent are the program results really due to the program rather than other explanatory factors? and 2) To what extent can the results be generalized to other situations? The answer to the first question evaluates internal validity, which is the extent to which results are accurate in assessing each independent variable's power to explain the variations in each performance measure. The answer to the second question assesses external validity—that is, whether or not the evaluation results can be generalized to other situations.

IDENTIFYING THREATS TO VALIDITY

In evaluating program outcomes, investigators must identify possible threats to the validity of the evaluation findings.

Threats to Internal Validity

History   In addition to X (the variable being evaluated, or the independent variable), some other event occurring either in or out of the experimental setting may affect the dependent variable. For example, a study of the variables affecting high turnover rate in a hospital may look at change in leadership, a poor incentive system, and the like. However, another type of factor altogether—the length of time between observations—also may have an effect. The longer the time between observations, the more plausible is this hypothesized history effect.

Maturation   Biological or psychological processes can occur with the passage of time independently of any external events. Such changes in experimental subjects may affect study observations or the dependent variable. As with history, maturation variables become more important as the time between observations increases.

Testing Effect   Significant changes between the pretest and posttest results can be caused by exposure to the pretest. For instance, the conduct of a family planning survey on knowledge, attitude, and practice about birth control may affect the responses of the same subjects when the survey is given a second time.

Instrumentation   Change in the observational technique or the measurement instrument can affect study results. The difference between observations at time 1 and at time 2, for example, might be the result of the fact that, at time 2, the raters 1) were more experienced, 2) were more fatigued, 3) had learned about the purposes of the experiment, 4) had undergone maturation, or 5) had either more relaxed or more stringent standards. Differences between observations also may result if different raters administer the pretest and the posttest.

167

Regression Artifacts   The subjects selected for a study may have had extreme score distributions, and thus, after the program intervention, their posttest scores may tend to regress toward the mean.

Selectivity Bias   There may be differences in composition between the experimental and the control group.

Attrition   Dropouts or mortality cases may affect the conclusions of a study if the subjects who drop out of an experiment are not similar to those who remain. In other words, the mean posttest score could differ from the mean pretest score because some subjects are not measured at time 2. If attrition occurs, the comparison between control and treatment groups should be made in two ways: 1) the analysis of outcomes when mortality or dropout cases are included, and 2) the analysis of outcomes when those cases are excluded.

Selection–Maturation Interaction   This interaction is confounded with the effect of the experimental variable. For example, an assessment of the effectiveness of a continuing education program for nurses indicates that the intervention had little effect on their performance; however, the nurses selected for the program had little motivation for, or interest in, the program.

Threats to External Validity

First, it must be noted that, whenever threats to internal validity are present, external validity is threatened as well. Even with internal validity established, however, several threats to external validity still may appear.

Selection–Treatment Interaction   The results of a study may apply only to the population from which the experimental and control groups were taken, and may not be generalizable, because of differences in population characteristics. To increase the generalizability of a study, one should sample a number of different populations.

Testing–Treatment Interaction   The results of a study that administered a pretest are not generalizable to other populations unless a pretest also is given to those populations. The testing–treatment interaction is most likely to occur when the study population is very sensitive to the pretest, which adds to the effect of the study intervention. The testing–treatment interaction may be removed by eliminating the pretest or by adding more control groups.

Situational Effects   Multiple factors that characterize the study itself can affect the results. These factors include the personnel who work on the study, the extent to which the participants of a study realize that they are part of a study ("Hawthorne effect"), the newness of the intervention, and the particular period when the experiment is conducted. For example, an intervention program may be implemented by a charismatic leader; in another setting, without a charismatic leader, the study results might differ. Also, when the study participants are aware that they are being observed, they put forth more effort and get higher scores than they would if they did not know they were subjects of a study. Still another situational effect occurs when an intervention program is relatively new; the newness produces results that do not hold up over time. A further example is a study made at a time of increased interest in that subject, a situation that causes the study's results to differ from those obtained at a different time.

Multiple Treatment Effects   Multiple treatment effects occur when the subjects of a study participate in a number of programs either just before the study or at the same time as the study. When both experimental and control groups have been in another program before being in the study, the study results may not be generalizable to other settings where the experimental and control groups have not participated in such programs. When multiple treatments occur simultaneously, it is difficult to generalize the study program's results to settings where such multiple treatments are not occurring.

EVALUATION DESIGN

It is important to understand that a program evaluation depends on how the program intervention was designed. The initial and most crucial decision in the design of an intervention is to define the condition or problem it will address; epidemiological surveys for needs assessment are particularly useful in defining the problem, after which an intervention can be designed. Then evaluation methods appropriate to that intervention design and measures for quantifying the criteria can be selected.

In assessing a program, a researcher makes three basic assumptions. First, the intervention has been designed effectively and the integrity of the treatment has been maintained. Second, the outcome (performance) measures, which may be single or multiple, are predetermined by the goals set when the program was planned; the measurement of specific outcome(s), using either an aggregate, single index or multiple indicators, should be formulated logically and then validated empirically by the analysis. Third, measurements of these outcome indicators should be repeated. Valid and reliable indicators, measured at multiple time points, are essential for program evaluation.

The above assumptions guide the selection of measures; the structural, process, and outcome criteria previously described also apply. An intervention can be measured by a discrete variable (presence or absence of an intervention) or a continuous variable (the amount/magnitude of intervention). When evaluating populations, these measures are usually rates and odds ratios (the likelihood of events in relation to exposure to an intervention).

A researcher uses either an experiment with a single intervention variable or a complex factorial design with multiple interventions; similarly, program performance is measured by a single (or aggregate) outcome indicator or a set of correlated outcome indicators. Following the specification of intervention and outcome measures, appropriate statistical methods are used to analyze program performance, as listed in Table 9.1.

The following sections describe the types of evaluation design and analysis.

NONEVALUATIVE STUDY DESIGNS

Case Studies

The evaluation consists of a follow-up measurement after the intervention. The design can be shown diagrammatically as X O, where X refers to the program and O refers to measures of program activities that can be compared with a set of expectations.

Table 9.1. Statistical methods for analyzing program performance, by intervention design and outcome

Intervention design	Program performance	
	Single outcome	Multiple outcomes
Single intervention (Classical experiment or quasi-experimental design)	Ordinary least squares regression analysis Logistic regression model Proportional hazards analysis	Linear structural relations analysis
Multiple interventions (Factorial design or quasi-experimental design)	Analysis of variance Single or multiple time series analysis Survival analysis	Covariance structure model Meta-analysis with latent variables

Before-and-After Studies

Measurements are taken before and after a program intervention. If the differences between the before and the after measures are large, the program is assumed to be effective or successful. The design can be shown diagrammatically as O_1 X O_2, where O_1 refers to the measurement taken before intervention, X is the intervention, and O_2 refers to the measurement taken after the intervention. For example, an assessment of a risk management program documented that the percentage of insured hospitals receiving 2-year Joint Commission on Accreditation of Healthcare Organizations (JCAHO) accreditation has nearly doubled since the risk management program began:

	Before (1988)	After (1989)
Hospitals receiving 2-year accreditation	9/20	17/20

Ad Hoc Comparison Groups

When the evaluator realizes the need for a control group but is unwilling or unable to establish one, he or she can assess another conveniently available group, which is not part of a study, along with the group receiving the intervention. In selecting this reference group, there is little consideration of the similarities between the environments or the participants, and so the study results may be inaccurate; if the intervention group performs better than the reference group, the intervention is simply considered a success.

EVALUATIVE STUDY DESIGNS: SINGLE OUTCOME

Classical Experiment (Single Intervention) Design

This design uses randomization. A random process assigns people, organizations, departments, and the like to treatment or control (nontreatment) categories. This study design commonly is called a pretest–posttest control group design. The design is shown diagrammatically as R O_1 X O_2, where R refers to the random assignment, O_1 refers to the pretest results, and O_2 refers to the posttest results; X is the intervention program (treatment).

   The Solomon four-group program evaluation design is used to analyze the performance of an intervention in a pretest–posttest study design. Its purpose is to delete the effects of the pretest on program results. Four groups are randomly selected in the evaluation. The study design can be shown diagrammatically as:

	Group assignment	Pretest	Intervention	Posttest
Treatment group	R	O_1	X	O_2
Control group	R	O_3		O_4
	R		X	O_5
	R			O_6

A treatment and a control group are selected, as well as two groups designated as O_5 and O_6; neither of these groups is given a pretest, but group O_5 receives intervention while group O_6 does not. Results then are compared.

If $O_2 - O_1$ is greater than $O_4 - O_3$, we conclude that the program has had a beneficial impact. However, this does not tell us whether there is a treatment–testing interaction effect. If O_5 is greater than O_6, we are confident that there is no treatment–testing interaction effect. We compare the difference between O_4 and O_6, which gives the effect of pretesting for those who do not receive the program, and the difference between O_2 and O_5, which gives the effect of pretesting for those who receive the program; if $O_4 - O_6$ is equal to $O_2 - O_5$, we can conclude that no treatment–testing interaction effect exists.

Factorial (Multiple Intervention) Design

Because evaluation looks for effects that can be attributed directly to the program interventions, evaluations frequently include "control" areas in which changes caused by exogenous factors can be measured; then the net program effects in treatment areas can be calculated. Unfortunately, however, strictly comparable control areas are hard to find. An alternative method is to gather baseline data so that project areas can serve as their own controls. That approach, however, does not satisfy the need to measure and separate exogenous influences; one is left with the problem of balancing control and baseline information appropriately. Use of control areas multiplies the requirements for data, yet they may be essential; accordingly, the control–baseline balance must be judged case by case.

Factorial intervention design can handle many of the confounding effects of exogenous factors on the program outcome(s) or performance(s). In addition, it can analyze the joint, or interaction, effects of multiple causal variables on the outcomes. In program evaluation, investigators examine the effects of several different types of variables on the outcome variable(s). Factorial designs examine these variables simultaneously in the same experiment. This approach is economical and provides sound data. The statistical model is as follows:

$$Y = f(X_1, X_2, X_{12}) + \text{errors}$$

where Y (total effect) $= X_1$ (mean effect) $+ X_2$ (main effects [linear effects]) $+ X_{12}$ (interaction effects) $+$ errors. Analysis of variance is used to assess intervention efforts in factorial designs.

There are several types of factorial designs, including:

Randomized block design: The units are grouped into blocks, and each unit in the same block may be selected randomly and subjected to treatment.

Crossover design: Each unit receives all the treatments in succession but in differing order. For example, a third of the subjects, selected at random, get treatments A, B, and C in the order ABC, a third get treatments in the order BCA, and a third get treatments in the order CAB.

Latin square design: Each treatment variable is classified into two levels, with the high level coded as 1 and the low level coded as -1. For three treatment variables, there are eight combinations: Each of the three variables has a high level and a low level that are being investigated in the randomized experiment. This refers to a two-level, three-variable experiment (Diamond, 1981). Two performance observations are made for each of the study groups, and the main and interaction effects are calculated. Latin square design is used in the following example.

Example of Factorial Design: Incentive Reimbursement Project   An evaluation project is designed to assess the impacts of three types of incentive packages on the quality of care in nursing homes. It was hypothesized that the three incentive packages had different effects on the patient mix (measured by the proportion of low level care patients) in the study facilities. The incentive experiment includes three independent (treatment) variables (A, B, and

Table 9.2.   Classification of independent variables by level

Treatment	Incentive A	Incentive B	Incentive C
Description	Admission bonus	Quality bonus	Discharge bonus
Levels	High (+1) Low (−1)	High (+1) Low (−1)	High (+1) Low (−1)

C). Each is classified into two levels, high (+1) and low (−1) (Table 9.2). The two levels of A may be denoted by a_1 and a_2, and similarly for B and C. The treatments consist of all possible combinations of these three variables:

(1) $a_1b_1c_1$ (5) $a_1b_1c_2$
(2) $a_2b_1c_1$ (6) $a_2b_1c_2$
(3) $a_1b_2c_1$ (7) $a_1b_2c_2$
(4) $a_2b_2c_1$ (8) $a_2b_2c_2$

Comparison of treatments (2) and (1) shows that (2) − (1) is an estimate of the difference in response $a_2 - a_1$, because factors B and C are fixed at the same level. Similarly:

Treatment comparison	Difference estimate
(4) − (3)	$a_2 - a_1$
(6) − (5)	$a_2 - a_1$
(8) − (7)	$a_2 - a_1$

The average of these four differences provides a comparison of a_2 with a_1 based on two samples of size four; this is called the main effect of A. The same procedures can be carried out for B and for C, to determine their main effects.

The interaction effects are either low or high order: Low-order interactions refer to AB, BC, and CA, and high-order interaction refers to ABC. For instance, the AB interaction may be explained as the difference between the response to A when B is at its higher level and the response to A when B is at its lower level. This quantity might be called the effect of B on the response to A.

In Table 9.3, a Latin square design is used to evaluate the impacts of the three incentive packages on the performance measure (Y, quality of care). Two observations of quality of care (Y_1 and Y_2) are made for each nursing home, and the scores are used to calculate the main and interaction effects of the incentive packages. Then an analysis of variance (ANOVA) is used to evaluate the effects of the incentives on performance.

Computations of Main Effects and Interaction Effects   The treatment differences for incentive package A in the various treatment combinations is determined by subtracting the average scores for each set of combinations:

Yates order	Differences between observation averages
(2 − 1)	44 − 44 = 0
(4 − 3)	42 − 39 = 3
(6 − 5)	49 − 40 = 9
(8 − 7)	44 − 39 = 5
Sum:	17

Table 9.3. Latin square design for program evaluation

Yates order	Incentive packages			Interactions				Observations (Y)			Difference between observations
	$A(X_1)$	$B(X_2)$	$C(X_3)$	X_{12}	X_{23}	X_{13}	X_{123}	First (Y_1)	Second (Y_2)	Average $d(Y_2 - Y_1)$	
1	−1	−1	−1	1	1	1	−1	42	46	44	4
2	1	−1	−1	−1	1	−1	1	46	42	44	−4
3	−1	1	−1	−1	−1	1	1	35	43	39	8
4	1	1	−1	1	−1	−1	−1	38	46	42	8
5	−1	−1	1	1	−1	−1	1	39	41	40	2
6	1	−1	1	−1	−1	1	−1	50	48	49	−2
7	−1	1	1	−1	1	−1	−1	41	37	39	−4
8	1	1	1	1	1	1	1	47	41	44	−6

The main effect of X_1 on $Y = 17/4 = 4.25$. Similar procedures are applied to obtain the main effects of X_2 (-3.25) and X_3 (.75).

The interaction effects are calculated as follows:

$$X_{12} = \tfrac{1}{4}[(1 + 4 + 5 + 8) - (2 + 3 + 6 + 7)]$$
$$= \tfrac{1}{4}[(44 + 42 + 40 + 44) - (44 + 39 + 49 + 39)]$$
$$= -0.25$$

$$X_{23} = \tfrac{1}{4}[(1 + 2 + 7 + 8) - (3 + 4 + 5 + 6)]$$
$$= \tfrac{1}{4}[(44 + 44 + 39 + 44) - (39 + 42 + 40 + 49)]$$
$$= 0.25$$

$$X_{13} = \tfrac{1}{4}[(1 + 3 + 6 + 8) - (2 + 4 + 5 + 7)]$$
$$= \tfrac{1}{4}[(44 + 39 + 49 + 44) - (44 + 42 + 40 + 39)]$$
$$= 2.75$$

$$X_{123} = \tfrac{1}{4}[(2 + 3 + 5 + 8) - (1 + 4 + 6 + 7)]$$
$$= \tfrac{1}{4}[(44 + 39 + 40 + 44) - (44 + 42 + 49 + 39)]$$
$$= -1.75$$

Computations of Sum of Squares for ANOVA Table The sum of squares (SS) $= \tfrac{1}{4}nE^2$, where n = the number of observations ($= 16$) and E = the main effect or interaction effect. The error sum of squares (SS_E) = the residual SS

$$= \frac{\sum d_i^2}{2}$$

where d refers to the difference between Y_1 and Y_2. Thus,

$SS_1 = $ SS for $X_1 = 16/4 \times (4.25)^2 = 72.25$
$SS_2 = $ SS for $X_2 = (16/4) \times (-3.25)^2 = 42.25$
$SS_3 = $ SS for $X_3 = 2.25$
$SS_{12} = $ SS for $X_{12} = 0.25$
$SS_{23} = $ SS for $X_{23} = 0.25$
$SS_{13} = $ SS for $X_{13} = 30.25$
$SS_{123} = 12.25$

The total sum of squares (SS_T) is the sum of SS for main effects and for interaction effects ($= 269.75$). Thus,

$$SS_E = \frac{\sum d_i^2}{2} = 110$$

$$R^2 = \frac{(SS_T - SS_E)}{SS_T} = \frac{(269.75 - 110)}{269.75} = 0.592$$

The data array format for the ANOVA is presented in Table 9.4.

Conclusion From information in the ANOVA table, we conclude that the incentive packages (quality and discharge bonus) had no statistically significant effects on the performance.

Quasi-experimental Intervention Design

Although many planned interventions in the field of health care have been carried out by classical experimental designs, others, both single and multiple, have been conducted using procedures in which complete experimental control or randomization of treatment is not possible. Quasi-experimental intervention designs apply an experimental model of analysis and interpre-

Table 9.4.   ANOVA data array format for Latin square analysis

Source of variation	SS	df	MS	F statistic
X_1 (admission bonus)	SS_1 = 72.25	1	72.25	5.25 (p = .048)
X_2 (quality bonus)	SS_2 = 42.25	1	42.25	3.07 (ns)
X_3 (discharge bonus)	SS_3 = 2.25	1	2.25	0.16 (ns)
X_{12}	SS_{12} = 0.25	1	.25	0.02 (ns)
X_{23}	SS_{23} = 0.25	1	.25	0.02 (ns)
X_{13}	SS_{13} = 30.25	1	30.25	2.20 (ns)
X_{123}	SS_{123} = 12.25	1	12.25	(ns)
Residual (error)	SS_E = 110	8	13.75	
Total	SS_T = 269.75	15		

Note: $F = \dfrac{MS_{in\ question}}{MS_{error}}$.

tation to bodies of data not meeting the full requirements of experimental control. Evaluation de-signs for quasi-experimental interventions include time-series design, matched groups design, and regression-discontinuity design.

Time Series Evaluation Design

Single-Time Series   A time series is a sequence of numerical data in which each datum is associated with a particular instant in time (Ostrom, 1978). A series of measurements provides multiple pretests and posttests before and after an intervention (X)—for example:

$$0_1 \qquad 0_2 \qquad 0_3 \qquad 0_4 \qquad X \qquad 0_5 \qquad 0_6 \qquad 0_7 \qquad 0_8$$

If, in this series, $0_5 - 0_4$ shows a significant change (difference), then maturation, testing, and regression effects are shown not to be plausible, because they would predict equal or greater changes (e.g., $0_2 - 0_1$).

Multiple-Time Series   The multiple-time series design operates on the same principles de-scribed for the single-time series, except that a comparison group is matched with the treatment group to the extent possible, as follows:

$$\text{Experimental Group:}\quad 0_1 \; 0_2 \; 0_3 \quad X \quad 0_4 \; 0_5 \; 0_6$$
$$\text{Comparison Group:}\quad 0_7 \; 0_8 \; 0_9 \qquad\quad 0_{10} \; 0_{11} \; 0_{12}$$

In this design, multiple observations (O) are collected on both experimental and comparison groups, both before and after the introduction of the intervention (X). This design is most useful when no cyclical or seasonal shifts are observed in the investigation. For example, Figure 9.1 shows the average length of hospital stay in the United States and in another hypothetical coun-try during the period from 1964 to 1991. An intervention program—here, the Medicare Prospec-tive Payment System (MPPS)—is assumed to have had a significant influence on average length of stay (ALOS) if there was a substantial reduction in ALOS after the program was instituted. Data in Figure 9.1 show a steady reduction of ALOS in both the United States and the hypothet-ical country. (It should be noted, however, that the MPPS is not the only factor to account for the declining trend, because many other factors, such as changes in morbidity patterns, competition in hospital use, increased efficiency of hospital operations, increased utilization of alternative delivery systems, and the implementation of stringent utilization reviews by third-party payers, also may affect the decline in ALOS.) However, the MPPS may have an indirect impact on ALOS through other changes.

A t-test can be performed for the time-series data to determine if there is a statistical differ-ence between the experimental group and the comparison group in the preintervention period. If there is no statistical difference between the two groups in the preintervention period, then one

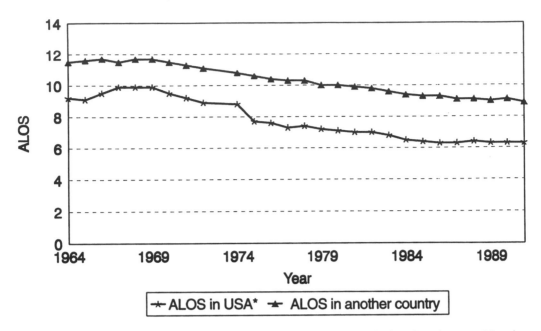

Figure 9.1.　Average length of hospital stay (ALOS) in the United States and in another hypothetical country. (*Data from National Center for Health Statistics. [1994]. *Health, United States, 1993*. Hyattsville, MD: National Center for Health Statistics.)

may apply a paired *t*-test to determine if there are any statistical differences between the two groups in the postintervention period. If the two groups are found to be statistically different in the preintervention period, a paired *t*-test still may be used to determine if there is a statistical difference between the two groups in the postintervention period. However, if in this case there is a difference between the groups in the postintervention period, one cannot know if the difference is solely attributable to the intervention or to some other factor because the groups were different to begin with. In this case, the conclusion regarding the effect of the intervention is not as strong as it is if the experimental and comparison groups are not statistically different in the preintervention period.

The paired *t*-test to be applied in the postintervention period is as follows:

$$s^2 = \left(\sum d_i^2 - n\overline{d}^2\right)/(n - 1)$$

where d = the difference in observations between the comparison and experimental groups and $\overline{d}$ = the average difference. Then

$$t = \frac{\overline{d} - 0}{s/\sqrt{n}}$$

If the *t* value is greater than the *t* statistic at the .05 level and with the appropriate degrees of freedom, it may be concluded that there is a statistically significant difference between the two groups in the postintervention period. If the two groups were not statistically different in the preintervention period, it may be concluded with some degree of certainty that the difference in the groups in the postintervention period is due to the intervention itself and no other factor.

Another example of multiple-time series design is seen in Figure 9.2, which analyzes the impact of an intervention program. In estimating the effect of an intervention program, time-series data can be plotted on a graph so that direct comparisons can be made of two or more ob-

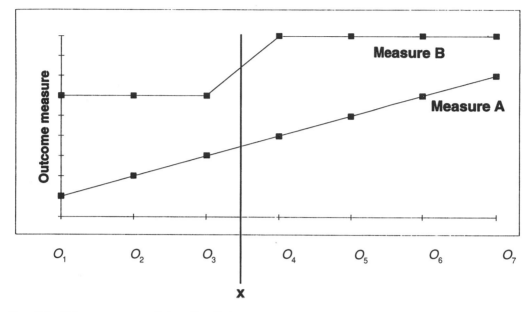

Figure 9.2.   Outcome measures and intervention effect.

servations. For example, X is the time when an intervention is made and O is the observation of a given outcome measure. In Figure 9.2, the plotted data for outcome measure A indicate a strong linear trend, but it is invalid to conclude that the increase is attributable to X. The plotted data for outcome measure B, however, show a substantial difference in the outcome measure between O_3 and O_4, which is the point when the intervention occurred. After the program intervention (O_5, O_6, etc.), however, the outcome measure stays relatively stable level. This pattern indicates an apparent intervention effect on the outcome measure (B).

Matched Groups Evaluation Design   In a matched groups design, the compared groups have members with similar characteristics. For example, suppose you wish to study the effects of management style (whether contracted or not contracted) and decision-making centralization (whether centralized or decentralized) on hospital performance as measured by worker productivity and employee satisfaction. You first would select a study group; the next step would be to select additional groups with members whose characteristics matched those of the study group. Subjects then would be selected randomly from each group and multiple observations of performance would be made. Paired t-tests would examine the differences between multiple groups:

| | Performance measures | |
Group	at T_1	at T_2
1 (contracted-centralized)	O_1	O_5
2 (contracted-decentralized)	O_2	O_6
3 (not contracted-centralized)	O_3	O_7
4 (not contracted-decentralized)	O_4	O_8

Regression-Discontinuity Evaluation Design   This design does not select the subjects randomly for experimentation. Rather, it uses a set of criteria determined by the evaluator to give an intervention (e.g., awards) to one group (experimental) and not give an intervention to another group (comparison group). The performance of each group then is assessed by the evaluator. Two regression analyses are performed to determine the intercepts. The difference in the intercepts between the two groups can be used as a measure of the intervention effect on productivity (Figure 9.3). This approach can serve as an alternative outcomes research method because it can improve the ability to assess the impact of program intervention (Luft, 1990; Trochim, 1990).

Binary Dependent-Variable Analysis

This type of performance evaluation is used to assess a single outcome measure in a single intervention design when the outcome variable is dichotomized. For instance, a surgical outcome of patients with abdominal aortic aneurysm may be coded as a binary dependent variable (death = 1; alive = 0), and analyzed by selected predictor variables such as preoperative risk factors and complications associated with the condition.

Logistic Regression Model   The logistic regression model is used when the dependent variable is binary or discrete and the independent variables (risk factors or interventions) are continuous and discrete. Because the dependent variable is discrete (e.g., the probability of being hospitalized in a specified period), the predicted probability should lie within the unity boundary. Logistic regression is preferable to ordinary least squares (OLS), because OLS estimates are biased and yield predicted values that are not between 0 and 1. If p is the probability, we assume that

$$\text{logit}\,(p) = \frac{p}{(1 - p)}$$

is a linear function of the predictor variables, or, in other terms, that

$$p(x) = \frac{1}{(1 + e^{-bx})}$$

When the probability is relatively small, $p(x)$ is roughly equivalent to e^{bx}.

The logistic model is expressed either in terms of the log-odds (the ratio of two individual odds) for a given outcome (e.g., improved population health) or in terms of the probability of

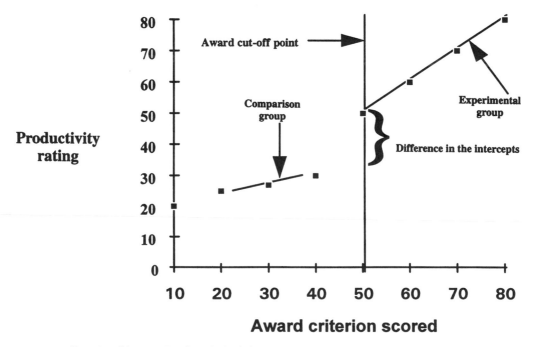

Figure 9.3.   Illustration of the regression-discontinuity design.

that outcome (e.g., the probability of improved health of the population). The log-odds is assumed to be a linear function of the magnitude of intervention instituted by a program, or log-odds $= 1_x = a + bx$, where $1_x =$ the logarithm of the odds of improved health for a specific continuous value x of the intervention/treatment variable. The coefficient b measures the change (multiplicative) in the likelihood of having improved health that is associated with a one-unit change in the intervention variable on the log-odds scale; e^b measures the change in population health associated with a one-unit change in the intervention variable on the odds scale.

The following is an example of using multiple logistic regression analysis to predict the mortality risk for abdominal aortic aneurysm in a hospital. Two models were developed to identify the mortality risk; model 1 includes only demographic factors and admission status, and model 2 includes demographic factors, admission status, and a number of complications. Table 9.5 reports estimated coefficient (B), estimated standard error (SE), and odds ratio (relative risk) for each model. The odds ratio, which refers to the relative risk of dying from abdominal aortic aneurysm, is computed by exponentiating the estimated coefficient for a given predictor. For example, patients 70 years and older were 4.29 times more likely to die than those younger than 70. A comparative statistic for the difference between two log-likelihood ratios for the two models is 24.06 (96.68 − 72.62) with 4 degrees of freedom. Evidently, model 2 is a better model in accounting for the mortality differentials.

The reader who desires to learn more about the application of multiple logistic regression is referred to the texts by Hosmer and Lemeshow (1989) and Maddala (1983).

Cox Proportional Hazards Analysis   This type of evaluation can be illustrated by the example of an investigation of how multiple factors affect the likelihood and timing of hospitalization or institutionalization episodes. These effects can be examined in two ways. First, using the nonparametric Kaplan-Meier estimator, the likelihood of an episode can be shown graphically for each characteristic as a function of time. Because we examine only one characteristic at a time, capturing the effect of that characteristic and everything correlated with it, an estimation of the gross effect of the characteristic is obtained. Second, using a Weibull regression model, one can estimate the joint effect of all independent variables (characteristics) on the likelihood over time of experiencing an event. This approach can detect the incremental or partial effect of each characteristic. For both the individual and the joint estimates, one can examine the relationship between each characteristic and the likelihood of having experienced an event both over the course of a year (a within-1-year approach) and over the course of the study period (a within-the-study approach). Finally, it is possible to extend the proportional hazards model to allow for time-varying explanatory variables. For example, the analysis of nursing home use can include a set of constant independent variables (e.g., gender, educational attainment) and a set of time-varying independent variables (e.g., caregiver burden, informal care use, and health functional status).

EVALUATIVE STUDY DESIGNS: MULTIPLE OUTCOMES

Single Intervention Design Evaluation: Linear Structural Relationships Model

For a program evaluation on hospital performance, researchers often need to analyze multiple outcomes (e.g., the complication rate, repeated hospitalization rate, hospital mortality rate, etc.). Sometimes these outcome variables are correlated with each other. In that case, use of a multivariate statistical technique is imperative to examine the effect of an intervention on multiple outcome variables, with or without correlated errors or residuals. The outcome variables are treated as endogenous variables, and the intervention variable is treated as an exogenous variable.

Table 9.5. Multiple logistic regression analysis of mortality risk for abdominal aortic aneurysm ($N = 174$ patients treated): two models

Variable	Model 1				Model 2			
	B	SE	B/SE	Odds ratio	B	SE	B/SE	Odds ratio
Age (70+ = 1; <70 = 0)	1.46	0.62	2.35*	4.29	1.58	0.81	1.95	4.84
Gender (female = 1; male = 0)	1.24	0.56	2.21*	3.47	1.65	0.68	2.43*	5.19
Admission status (elective = 0; nonelective = 1)	2.32	0.59	3.93*	10.16	2.24	0.70	3.20*	9.36
Ventricular tachycardia (yes = 1; no = 0)					2.24	1.05	2.13*	7.98
Perioperative myocardial infarction (yes = 1; no = 0)					2.52	1.07	2.36*	12.37
Acute renal failure with dialysis (yes = 1; no = 0)					2.17	0.98	2.21*	8.73
Pneumonia (yes = 1; no = 0)					1.71	0.80	2.14*	5.53
Constant (intercept)	−4.04	0.64			−5.25	0.93		
Log-likelihood (degrees of freedom)	−96.68 (3)				−72.62 (7)			

*Significant at .05 or lower.

The analysis of linear structural relationships (LISREL) among quantitative outcome variables is useful in data analysis and theory construction. The LISREL model contains two parts. One is the measurement model, which specifies how the latent variables (e.g., adverse health care outcomes) or hypothetical constructs are measured by observable indicators (e.g., hospital mortality rate, complication rate). The other is the structural equation model that represents the causal relationships among the exogenous and endogenous variables. The structural equation model is like the path-analytical model in three aspects: 1) model construction, 2) parameter estimation of the model, and 3) testing the fit of the model to the data by comparing observed correlations with predicted correlations among the study variables. However, the LISREL model is less restrictive than the path-analytical model. For instance, it allows the investigator to ask direct questions about the data, in the form of different restrictions on the coefficients. LISREL easily can handle errors in measurement, correlated errors and residuals, and reciprocal causation. Thus, LISREL's advanced procedures can specify, compare, and evaluate the impact of an intervention on a set of correlated outcome variables (Bollen, 1989; Joreskog & Sorbom, 1989).

The following example illustrates how a measurement model of adverse patient care outcomes is developed and validated. Then, this latent variable regresses on a set of exogenous variables to show how hospital performance (i.e., adverse patient outcomes) is influenced by a variety of exogenous variables. "Adverse patient outcomes" (patients with specific unfavorable results of hospitalization) is an unobserved, or latent, construct.

To develop a measurement model, Wan (1992) selected five indicators of adverse outcomes, using the hospital as the unit of analysis (see also Chapter 10). The indicators included in-hospital trauma rate (TRAUMA RATE), rate of discharges with unstable medical conditions (MEDPROB RATE), rate of treatment problems (TXPROB RATE), postoperative complication rate (COMP RATE), and rate of unexpected deaths (DEDPRO RATE). The measurement model (Figure 9.4) specifies the relationship between the five observed indicators and the unobserved theoretical construct (i.e., adverse patient outcomes).

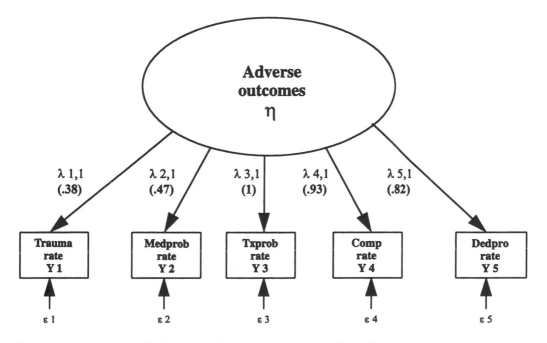

Figure 9.4.   Measurement model of adverse health care outcomes in acute care hospitals.

Each indicator is considered a linear function of the common factor, adverse patient outcomes. The common factor (η) may affect more than one observed indicator directly. A measurement error term (unique factor, or ε) is associated with each specific outcome indicator (Y). The common factor is not correlated with the unique residual factors. However, the measurement errors ($\varepsilon1$, $\varepsilon2$, etc.) may be correlated with each other. Therefore, the relationship between the observed indicators and the common factor can be expressed as $Y = \lambda_y\eta + \varepsilon$, where Y is a vector of observed outcome variables, λ_y is a matrix of factor loadings relating the observed Y's to the common factor (η), and measurement errors (ε) are the residual or unique factors. Change in η will result in a direct change in Y. It is also assumed that the number of observed variables in Y is greater than the number of common factors.

After a model has been specified, the next step is identification of the model, which means deciding whether there is a unique solution for the parameters of the model. If the number of unknowns is greater than the number of known parameters, the parameters cannot be estimated. In that case, respecification of the measurement model is necessary.

Guided by the original theoretical model, three steps can improve the goodness of fit. The first step is to eliminate observed variables (indicators) that do not make a statistically significant contribution to the latent variable. The second step is to add other related indicators that are appropriate measures of the latent variable. The third step is to free the parameter (λ or ε) with the largest modification index generated by the LISREL program, within constraints imposed by the theoretical model.

Multiple Intervention Design Evaluation

Covariance Structure Model   By using validated measures of a latent variable such as adverse patient outcomes, we can examine further the effect of such interventions as total quality improvement programs and incentive programs on adverse outcomes. The specification of this structural equation model is: adverse outcomes = f(interventions) + residual term. If researchers deal with confounding or extraneous variables in the causal analysis, these variables must be included as control variables in the structural equation in order to find the net effect of an intervention on outcomes. This model can be validated through covariance structure analysis, which provides parameter estimates simultaneously for the measurement model and the structural equation model.

The covariance structure model consists of the simultaneous specification of a measurement model—in our example, adverse patient outcomes in hospitals—and a structural equation model (Wan, 1992). In our example, the explanatory variables included hospital bed size, number of high-technology services offered, case mix, severity of patients treated, ownership, cost, technical efficiency, average length of stay, market share, net profit, and metropolitan size. Adverse outcomes, the latent construct, was regressed on 13 predictor variables. Parameter estimates were derived using maximum likelihood methods for both measurement and structural equation models.

The results for this example are shown in Table 9.6. The explanatory variables account for 39.8% of the total variance in hospitals' adverse patient outcomes. The average length of stay is related positively to adverse outcomes when other explanatory variables are controlled simultaneously. Technical efficiency is associated negatively with adverse outcomes; the higher the degree of technical efficiency, the lower the level of adverse outcomes (see Table 9.6). The analysis shows that hospitals' problems with quality of care can be explained by hospital operational factors. (For a more detailed discussion of this example, see Chapter 10.)

Program evaluations must consider the relationship among different outcomes. Failure to do so can lead to inappropriate conclusions about program effects. The use of structural equation modeling techniques not only allows assessment of the effect of each intervention on multiple

Table 9.6. Net effects of predictors on adverse patient outcomes

	Predictor variables[a]												
Dependent variable	1	2	3	4	5	6	7	8	9	10	11	12	13
Outcomes	−0.170	−0.038	−0.070	0.071	0.083	−0.002	−0.110	−0.072	−0.128	0.230	−0.447	−0.120	−0.043
T value	−0.767	−0.222	−0.437	0.758	0.631	−0.015	−0.835	−0.687	−1.103	1.986*	−4.611*	−1.061	−0.412

Note: $R^2 = 0.398$. Goodness-of-fit (GOF) statistics: $\chi^2 = 78.330$ with 57 degrees of freedom ($P = 0.049$); GOF index = 0.918; adjusted GOF index = 0.755; root mean squares residual = 0.058.

[a]Variables are: 1, hospital bed size; 2, number of high-technology services offered; 3, case mix; 4, severity of patients treated; 5, metropolitan size; 6, multisystem participation; 7, affiliated medical school; 8, ownership (for profit); 9, cost; 10, average length of stay; 11, technical efficiency; 12, percent market share; and 13, net profit.

*Significant at .05 or lower level.

outcome (endogenous) variables, but also allows assessment of the net effect of each intervention variable when the effects of other factors are controlled simultaneously.

A variety of epidemiological statistical techniques are appropriate in longitudinal program evaluations. Structural equation modeling techniques, applied to the panel data described earlier, are a useful method of panel analysis. Because this technique analyzes the relationship between endogenous (outcome) variables, one can examine the relationship between those variables across time as well. For example, structural equation modeling can control for other factors when assessing how the use of various types of community-based long-term care service are related to later use of nursing home services.

Meta-analysis   This is a popular analytical strategy for assessing program outcomes. For program evaluation, meta-analysis may be used to estimate the effect size, or intervention effect, of specific program outcomes. If it is used properly, meta-analysis can strengthen causal interpretations of nonexperimental data (Chalmers, 1993; Corday, 1990; Hunink & Wong, 1994; Petitti, 1994). Furthermore, evaluation researchers can develop a covariance structure model for multiple, comparable studies and then empirically test the model's goodness of the fit by using meta-analysis. For example, the impact of case-managed services on such geriatric patient outcomes as quality of life (a latent construct) can be evaluated for different study samples if comparable outcome measures are used. In that case, the measurement model of quality of life is evaluated first; then the equality constraints for observed indicators are assumed for the multiple samples. The net effect of case-managed services on patient outcomes in the study groups thus is measured while the effect of other extraneous factors is controlled simultaneously.

CONCLUSION

Health outcomes research has become a central theme in evaluation studies. Epidemiologists and evaluation researchers play an important role in designing, monitoring, and evaluating changes in health services and their outcomes. This chapter has summarized a variety of scientific research designs that can be applied to outcomes research.

It is important to note that scientific evaluation research designs must investigate not only intervention (treatment) effects but also confounding effects of extraneous factors on health care outcomes. The strategy of risk adjustment is essential to the detection of effects of any intervention (Iezzoni, 1994). If the effects of extraneous factors such as the severity of condition/patient acuity level, symptomatology, age, gender, race, and other demographic variables are controlled simultaneously, the net influence of health service intervention on single or multiple outcomes can be ascertained.

REFERENCES

Bollen, K. (1989). *Structural equations with latent variables*. New York: John Wiley & Sons.

Chalmers, T.C. (1993). Meta-analytic stimulus for changes in clinical trials. *Statistical Methods in Medical Research, 2*, 161–172.

Corday, D.S. (1990). Strengthening causal interpretations of nonexperimental data: The role of meta analysis. In L. Sechrest, E. Perrin, & J. Bunker (Eds.), *Research methodology: Strengthening causal interpretations of nonexperimental data* (pp. 151–172). Rockville, MD: Agency for Health Care Policy and Research.

Diamond, W.J. (1981). *Practical experiment designs*. Belmont, CA: Lifetime Learning Publications.

Hosmer, D.W., & Lemeshow, S. (1989). *Applied logistic regression*. New York: John Wiley & Sons.

Hunink, M.G., & Wong, J.B. (1994). Meta-analysis of failure-time data with adjustment for covariates. *Medical Decision Making, 14*(1), 59–70.

Iezzoni, L.I. (1994). *Risk adjustment strategies for measuring health care outcomes*. Ann Arbor, MI: Health Administration Press.

Joreskog, K.G., & Sorbom, D. (1989). *Lisrel 7: A guide to the program and applications.* Chicago: SPSS, Inc.

Luft, H.S. (1990). The applicability of the regression-discontinuity design in health services research. In L. Sechrest, E. Perrin, & J. Bunker (Eds.), *Research methodology: Strengthening causal interpretations of nonexperimental data* (pp. 141–143). (DHHS publication no. [PHS] 90-3454). Rockville, MD: Agency for Health Care Policy and Research.

Maddala, G.S. (1983). *Limited dependent and qualitative variables in econometrics.* New York: Cambridge University Press.

Ostrom, C.W. (1978). *Time series analysis: Regression technique.* Beverly Hills, CA: Sage Publications.

Petitti, D.B. (1994). *Meta-analysis, decision analysis, and cost-effectiveness analysis.* New York: Oxford University Press.

Trochim, W.M.K. (1990). The regression-discontinuity design. In L. Sechrest, E. Perrin, & J. Bunker (Eds.), *Research methodology: Strengthening causal interpretations of nonexperimental data* (pp. 119–139). (DHHS publication no. [PHS] 90-3454). Rockville, MD: Agency for Health Care Policy and Research.

Wan, T.T.H. (1992). Hospital variations in adverse patient outcomes. *Quality Assurance and Utilization Review, 7*(2), 50–53.

10

Assessing Effectiveness and Efficiency of Hospital Performance

A Multivariate Analytical Approach

It requires a very unusual mind
to undertake the analysis of the obvious.

A.N. Whitehead, *Science and the Modern World*

Hospitals are complex organizations; they perform multiple activities simultaneously and employ a wide variety of resources to generate distinctive outcomes: utilization of services, attainment of therapeutic goals, and sound financial condition. Hence, the assessment of hospitals' organizational performance may require the use of multiple indicators. Varying conceptualizations of organizational performance have produced several different analytical methods for assessing performance: 1) the goal attainment model (Daft, 1989) to assess whether the organization has achieved its intended level of outputs; 2) the strategic orientation model (Friedman & Shortell, 1988) to investigate how strategic orientation affects financial performance; 3) the internal process model (Daft, 1989) to evaluate internal well-being and efficiency; and 4) the system resource model (Cameron, 1984) to ascertain whether the organization effectively has obtained the resources needed for high performance. All these conceptual perspectives investigate effectiveness and efficiency as interrelated domains.

A hospital's overall effectiveness is demonstrated by the quality of care rendered (Ruchlin, 1977), by the level of productivity (Ruchlin, 1977; Zaretsky, 1977), and by the degree of financial soundness (Cleverley, 1987; Ehreth, 1994). A criterion closely related to productivity is hospital efficiency, which evaluates the cost of the inputs used in production of outputs. When a procedure minimizes the cost for producing a specific output, efficiency is achieved. Organizational researchers assume that efficiency and effectiveness are interrelated constructs (Kanter &

This chapter was prepared by Thomas T. H. Wan and Dolores G. Clement, with the assistance of Marilyn F. Spotswood.

Brinkerhoff, 1981; Scott & Shortell, 1988), yet little empirical evidence to support this relationship exists in the health care literature.

Because it is possible that some cost/quality trade-offs undermine patient outcomes, it is imperative to examine the structural relationships among the many dimensions of hospital performance. In particular, empirical analysis should investigate how hospital efficiency and other characteristics affect not only financial viability but also quality of care. The following sections provide an example of conducting a thorough organizational analysis of hospital performance. The first step in such an analysis is a survey of the literature on relevant previous research.

RELATED RESEARCH

This review of the research literature discusses factors found to influence hospitals' organizational performance in each of three domains: quality of care, efficiency and service intensity.

Hospital Studies on Quality of Care

Previous investigators have examined how organizational effectiveness affects the quality of care as indicated by various measures: hospital incidents (Elnicki & Schmitt, 1989; Wan & Shukla, 1987), postsurgical infection rates (Flood, Scott, Ewy, & Forrest, 1987), repeated hospitalization (Riley et al., 1993; Wan & Ozcan, 1991), and mortality rates (Ballard et al., 1994; Blumberg, 1986; Chassin, Park, Lohr, Keesey, & Brook, 1989; Dubois, Brook, & Rogers, 1987; Hartz, Sigmann, Guse, & Hagen, 1989; Iezzoni, 1994; Shortell & Hughes, 1988). The use of crude hospital mortality rate as a quality problem indicator has been criticized for its lack of adjustment for risk or confounding factors such as the severity of illness and other patient characteristics (Ballard et al., 1994; Horn et al., 1991; Iezzoni, 1993).

These studies used the hospital as the unit of analysis. Although several studies (Luft, Bunker, & Enthoven, 1979; Luft, Hunt, & Maerki, 1987; Payne & Lyons, 1972; Rhee, 1983) found bed size to be related to quality of care, that relationship is complicated by other variables, such as medical school affiliation and having the volume of a particular procedure or type of patient that is sufficient to support specialized services; low volume may reduce the quality of care, although high volume in itself does not ensure high quality. In other studies, no significant association was found between type of ownership and quality of care (Shortell & Hughes, 1988; Sloan, Perrin, & Valvona, 1986).

An important goal for research on quality of care as measured by hospital mortality rates is to identify factors that affect those rates. Scott, Forrest, and Brown (1976) examined how structural features (differentiation, coordination, the power of members or subunits to influence organizational decisions, and staff qualifications) affect medical outcomes of selected types of surgical patients. They found that increased coordination and differentiation may improve the quality of care in the operating room, but not overall, by the hospital. The power of the surgical staff, as measured by membership criteria, was found to be related positively to the quality of surgical care. The registered nurse (RN) ratio of the nursing staff was related positively to outcomes for surgical patients. In contrast, the relationship between the proportion of board-certified staff surgeons and surgical patients' outcomes was not statistically significant.

Shortell, Becker, and Neuhauser (1976) studied how management and organizational variables affect the quality of care as measured by postsurgical complication rate and medical–surgical death rate, after controlling for differences in hospital case mix. They found that regular meetings among nursing, laboratory, and radiology staff, as well as department heads' participation in hospital decisions, all were related to better quality of care; greater perceived medical staff autonomy was related to diminished quality of care. Higher cost per case was associated with a higher medical–surgical death rate, suggesting that some cost-control mechanisms also may improve the quality of care.

Shortell and LoGerfo (1981) examined care factors affecting outcomes for acute myocardial infarction and for appendicitis, using the standardized mortality ratio and the standardized percentage of normal tissue removed as outcome measures. They found quality of care to be affected less by hospital or physician characteristics than by medical staff organization: how involved its president is with the hospital governing board, how much physicians participate in hospital decisions, how often medical staff committees meet, and the percentage of active staff physicians on contract. Wan and Shukla (1987) studied the quality of nursing care in 45 community acute-care hospitals. They used incident rates of errors in medication or in intravenous line administration, inappropriate diagnostic and therapeutic interventions, patient falls, and patient injuries as outcome measures. The authors found strong correlations among the first three quality-of-care measures, as well as a strong correlation between patient falls and patient injuries. When contextual and organizational variables were examined, neither the nursing staff's mix, model or resource use, the hospital's physical design, nor patient characteristics accounted for much of the variation in incident rates. Interestingly, the community's hospital bed supply was related directly to a hospital's quality of care. Age and education of the population also influenced outcomes.

Ideally, a study of hospital performance would incorporate both patient and community attributes, along with hospitals' structural and functional characteristics—an integrated perspective. For example, Flood et al. (1987) assessed surgical care by measuring morbidity 7 days after surgery, or death within 40 days, while adjusting for the patients' physical status, stage of disease, age, and sex. They found that quality of care was associated less strongly with differences among surgeons than with characteristics of the hospital organization and with the component structure of the professional group. In another integrated-perspective study of 351 hospitals, Goldfarb and Coffey (1987) examined the differences in case mix between teaching and nonteaching hospitals. The authors found no significant differences between non–medical-school-based teaching hospitals and nonteaching hospitals in inpatient death rates.

Dubois et al. (1987), in a study of discharge data from 93 American Medical International hospitals, examined adjusted hospital mortality rates. They used multiple regression to predict each hospital's death rate, by treating mortality as a function of age, origin of patient from the emergency department or nursing home, and hospital case-mix index. An adjusted death rate was obtained by dividing the actual hospital death rate by predicted hospital death rate. The authors concluded that such adjusted death rates could identify hospitals likely to deliver poor care.

In examining the influence of regulation, competition, and ownership on hospital mortality, Shortell et al. (1988) used multiple regression to analyze the mortality rate for Medicare beneficiaries in 981 hospitals. The analysis used 21 variables, including patient-based measures, environmental factors, and organizational factors. The total variance accounted for by these variables was relatively small. The study found a statistically significant association between mortality rates and the stringency of the state certificate-of-need review and rate review programs. Neither ownership nor hospital competition in the marketplace influenced mortality rates.

Hartz et al. (1989) examined the association of particular structural characteristics of hospitals with mortality rates adjusted for indicators of severity of illness. The predictor variables included occupancy rate, ownership, medical training, technological sophistication, and bed size. The regression results showed that the hospitals with lower adjusted mortality rates were teaching hospitals and those with higher percentages of board-certified specialists, with higher RN–nurse ratios, with higher levels of technological sophistication, and with higher occupancy rates. In addition, for-profit hospitals had higher adjusted mortality rates than did not-for-profit hospitals. Unfortunately, however, this study did not examine the effect of hospital location. Because for-profit hospitals are disproportionately rural, the effect of hospital ownership on mortality may be confounded with the effect of geographic area. Thus, without control for rural/urban location, the relationship between ownership and mortality may be spurious.

After analyzing data obtained from the 34,252 Medicare discharge records of 13 hospitals, Green, Sharkey, and Passman (1990) reported that the predictive power of the Health Care Financing Administration (HCFA) mortality model could be improved greatly by including a severity-of-illness measure (Disease Stage Subscale). This finding substantiates the utility of severity measures such as the Acute Physiology and Chronic Health Evaluation's disease-severity scoring system (Daley et al., 1988), MedisGroups (Iezzoni, 1988), the Severity of Disease Classification System (Knaus, Draper, Wagner, & Zimmerman, 1985), and Risk-Adjusted Mortality Indexes (DesHarnais, Chesney, Wroblewski, Fleming, & McMahon, 1988; DesHarnais, McMahon, & Wroblewski, 1991; DesHarnais, McMahon, Wroblewski, & Hogan, 1990).

Chassin et al. (1989) analyzed the variation in hospital mortality rates of Medicare patients in all acute-care hospitals. They found large differences in hospital mortality rates for 22 of 48 specific conditions studied, and for all conditions combined. Medical conditions, rather than surgical conditions, contributed more to the variation in hospitals' mortality rates. The authors suggested examination of the effect on variability in mortality rates of such factors as the hospital's geographic location, patient condition mix, length of stay, and severity of illness. Silber, Williams, Krakauer, and Schwartz (1992) stated that understanding the reasons behind variation in mortality rates across hospitals should improve the ability to use mortality statistics to help hospitals upgrade the quality of care. In their study, Hartz, Gottlieb, Kuhn, and Rimm (1993) suggested that the HCFA adjusted mortality rate and the peer review organization's confirmed problem rate are related measures to compare hospitals on the basis of quality of care. Both measurement approaches compare quality the best if used within a group of homogeneous hospitals.

In a study of the relationship between hospital outcomes and resource expenditures adjusted for the severity of illness and other patient attributes, Bradbury, Golec, and Steen (1994) found that the length of stay was associated positively with mortality. Little of the variation in adjusted mortality was explained by hospital characteristics such as size, staffing, teaching status, and urban/rural residence. The study finding implies that hospital inefficiency is associated with poor quality of hospital care.

In order to interpret and understand outcomes data, such as mortality and longevity, acute physiological stability, chronic disease and morbidity, complications, physical functioning, psychosocial functioning, quality-of-life, and resource utilization, most successfully, it is important to adjust for patients' risks for various adverse outcomes. The goal of risk adjustment is to account for patient and organizational characteristics before making inferences about the effectiveness of care. The risk factors that must be controlled for when collecting and interpreting outcomes data are many. First, there are certain clinical risk factors that must be accounted for. These factors include demographic factors such as the age and gender of patients; severity-of-illness factors such as the principle diagnosis of patients, the physical functioning of patients, and acute clinical stability as well as the severity of the principle diagnosis; and comorbid factors such as the extent and severity of comorbidities of patients. The administrative data set should be supplemented by clinical review data sets so that the validity of risk-adjusted factors for mortality rate can be solidified (Hartz et al., 1994; Romano, 1993). Second, there are certain nonclinical risk factors that must be controlled for when collecting and analyzing outcomes data. These factors include patient attitudes and preferences; health status and quality of life; cultural, ethnic, and socioeconomic attributes and behaviors; and psychological, cognitive, and psychosocial functioning (Iezzoni, 1994). Thomas, Holloway, and Guire (1993) purported that risk-adjusted mortality rates are perhaps the most commonly used outcome indicator for assessment of hospital quality today. They conclude, however, that, before inferences can be drawn about hospital quality using a risk-adjusted mortality indicator, the validity of the quality–outcome relationship must be established for that measure.

In summary, examination of the literature suggests that the conceptual problem in analyzing hospitals' quality of care is the difficulty of identifying domains of performance. Methodological problems are the lack of large representative and longitudinal study samples and inadequate causal analysis of the relationships between hospital attributes and the quality of care. Blumberg (1986) pointed out that, when using such an aggregate outcome as hospital mortality rate, it is essential to consider multiple confounding factors in hospital performance. Future studies should provide information on the sensitivity and specificity of mortality data as quality-of-care measures (Fink, Yano, & Brook, 1989; Iezzoni et al., 1994; Phelps, 1993; Romano, 1993). Another useful step would be development and evaluation of an appropriate measurement model using multiple indicators of hospital quality of care.

Hospital Studies on Efficiency as an Aspect of Productivity

In an increasingly competitive industry, hospitals must control costs by pursuing efficiency—that is, achieving the same end at less cost. In the literature on hospital care, three types of efficiency are studied: cost, process, and technical.

Cost efficiency typically is measured by costs per admission or per patient day. Zaretsky (1977) emphasized the importance of controlling for both service mix and case mix when analyzing cost efficiency. He used 176 hospitals to test a cost model in which costs per admission are a function of admissions, case flow, services, case mix, and location. Service and case mix were predictors of higher costs, while case flow (admissions per bed) was a predictor of lower costs. There were also strong correlations between case mix, service mix, size, and costs; however, controlling for case mix and service mix negated the relationship between size and cost. Flood and Scott (1987), in a study of 17 hospitals, examined hospital structures, processes, outputs, and costs. Structural variables such as size, specialization, intensity of staffing, teaching status, staff qualifications, and slack resources served as latent indicators of service capacity. Other structural variables, such as administrative and surgical staff influence, served as latent indicators of hospital control. The researchers ran zero-order correlations and found staff size, specialization, teaching status, and board certification to be related positively to higher costs. Labor intensity (ratio of direct-care nurses to average daily census) was correlated negatively with costs. Greater surgical staff influence and a higher proportion of contract physicians (hospital control) both were associated with higher costs. In a linear regression of average expenditures per patient episode on selected measures of hospital capacity and control, only administrative influence was significant. Results are limited by a small sample size and a cost measure not standardized for patient mix.

Productivity, or process efficiency, measures the work expended to produce a unit of output, or the ratio of outputs to inputs (Scott & Shortell, 1988). Unfortunately, hospital outputs or products are not easily defined or measured. Proxy measures of hospital productivity include: 1) patient days per full-time employee (FTE), 2) admissions per FTE, and 3) physician visits per full-time physician. Levitz and Brooke (1985) analyzed the effects of system affiliation on both costs and productivity. Indicators of cost were cost per case, cost per day, pay per day, and pay per admission. Indicators of productivity were: number of FTEs per average daily census, fixed assets per average daily census, admissions per bed, and case mix–adjusted average length of stay (ALOS). The study found system-affiliated hospitals to have higher case mix–adjusted costs per case and higher labor productivity (number of FTEs per average daily census) but lower plant and total assets productivity. Coyne (1982) studied how system affiliation and ownership affect cost and productivity of hospital care. Efficiency was measured as cost per case and pay per day, and productivity by admissions per bed and number of FTEs per 100 occupied beds. Coyne controlled for several variables affecting costs: case mix, demographics, competition, and regulation. The results indicate that system-affiliated hospitals of all ownership types (except county) have greater costs per case as well as more admissions per bed.

Technical efficiency, calculated through data envelopment analysis (DEA), is an improvement over typical ratio measures of productive efficiency. This technique incorporates multiple outputs and inputs, accounting for the multidimensional character of hospital production. DEA examines how resources (supplies, labor, and capital) produce different outputs (patient care, teaching, and research). DEA incorporates case-mix differences into efficiency scores, and it measures variables in their natural units rather than trying to convert resources to dollar amounts (Nunamaker, 1983). Several researchers have applied DEA to assess the technical efficiency of hospitals and then compared results to other indicators of efficiency (Ozcan, 1992–1993; Ozcan, Luke, & Haksever, 1992; Rosko, 1990). Nunamaker (1983) analyzed technical efficiency scores and total cost savings (cost/patient day) of inpatient routine nursing services in a sample of 17 nonprofit hospitals over a 2-year period. For those hospitals with a similar mix of outputs, high efficiency scores were paired with low costs per patient day. A particular strength of this study is its demonstration of the sensitivity of efficiency scores to variation in input, output, or sample size. For example, disaggregating output variables or reducing the sample size resulted in higher efficiency scores.

Sherman (1984) studied the technical efficiency of medical–surgical services in a set of 17 teaching hospitals. Inputs included the number of non-MD FTEs, the dollar value of supplies and purchased services, and the number of bed days available. Outputs included patient days for those over 65, patient days for those under 65, number of RN students, and number of interns and residents. In Sherman's comparison of technical efficiency scores to costs per patient day, the hospitals identified as inefficient differed depending on the specific technique employed. In a sensitivity analysis, Sherman re-ran DEA using different inputs and found that efficiency scores increased. Grosskopf and Valdmanis (1987) looked at the effect of ownership on the performance of public and of nonprofit, private hospitals. Inputs included the number of MDs, number of non-MD FTEs, number of admissions, and net plant assets. Outputs were acute-care inpatient days, intensive-care inpatient days, number of inpatient and outpatient surgeries, and number of ambulatory and emergency care visits. Public hospitals were found to have higher average efficiency ratings than did nonprofit, private hospitals. Valdmanis (1990) not only confirmed those results, but also showed correlations between technical efficiency and lower costs. This finding was confirmed further by a recent study conducted by Ehreth (1994) in the evaluation of hospital performance measures for policy analysis.

In summary, efficiency is a complex concept, incorporating the cost, process, and technical aspects of production. Weighted indices of technical efficiency, using DEA techniques, offer potential for refining the crude measures of hospital efficiency.

Hospital Studies on Service Intensity

No set of guidelines can establish definitive measures of whether a hospital is financially sound or not. However, various measures of hospital service intensity may indicate the ability of a hospital to survive in a competitive market. Previous studies of service intensity have focused on health services to inpatients, and used unidimensional measures such as cost per discharge (Cleverley, 1987), case mix (Goldfarb & Coffey, 1987), market share (Wan & Cooper, 1987), occupancy rate (Gianfrancesco, 1990), and average length of stay (Chassin et al., 1989). Empirical research has focused on developing an aggregate index of service consumption, reflecting the number and variety of inpatient services. For example, Scott, Flood, and Ewy (1987), in their study of 17 acute-care hospitals, reported that the weighted index of service intensity was not associated with ALOS. However, a higher than expected level of services within a hospital was associated significantly with a lower than expected mortality rate. Furthermore, ALOS also was associated positively with the mortality rate.

Treating hospital performance as a joint function of patient, organizational, and community/environmental attributes can illuminate better the determinants of hospital performance. If the relative importance of each of these factors can be assessed, then analyzing differences in hospital performance can lead to insights on how to formulate quality improvement and other managerial intervention programs. This rationale suggests a research question: What are the relationships among hospital performance indicators when hospital size, technical specialization, service complexity, and facility location are being considered simultaneously?

The next sections of this chapter present an account of such a study of hospital performance, to demonstrate the uses of multivariate analysis in a complex assessment.

STUDY DESIGN AND METHODS

Design

There are numerous possibilities for the design of an organizational analysis of health care outcomes. However, an investigator always is constrained by the availability of hospital data. In this study, hospital performance was assumed to be a function of hospital characteristics—size, specialization, and location—in 85 acute-care hospitals. Five sources of data were available for this study:

1. The American Hospital Association's 1986 and 1987 files describing hospital activities and attributes provided such aggregate hospital-based variables as bed size, total FTEs, and ALOS.
2. The 1987 HCFA's case-mix index for the study hospitals was compiled from the *Federal Register*.
3. Hospital-based outcome data for 1988 were obtained from the peer review organization.
4. Data on medical market areas were derived from a small area analysis of 1987 Medicare beneficiary utilization files (Codman Research Group, 1989).
5. Financial data for 1987 were compiled from the annual report of the Health Services Cost Review Council.

Efficiency, market share, hospital financial viability, and adverse hospitalization outcomes are four endogenous latent variables. Efficiency—a neutral term denoting levels of either efficiency or inefficiency—refers to cost, process, and technical efficiency, measured respectively by average cost per patient discharge (COST), average length of stay (ALOS), and technical efficiency (TEFF). The technical efficiency score, calculated through DEA, refers to the relative ratio of outputs (patient care) to inputs (labor). Labor inputs were disaggregated to different skill levels to reflect staff mix differences. The levels include the number of full-time administrative staff, RNs, licensed practical nurses, ancillary nursing personnel, support staff, and active and associate physicians. Patient care outputs include the total number of discharges, surgical operations, outpatient visits, inpatient days, and intensive care unit days. Note that the technical efficiency score was recoded so that a higher score reflects reduced efficiency.

Market share (%SHARE) is reflected by the percentage of Medicare patients served by a hospital in a given medical market area. The indicator of financial viability is hospital net profit (NET PROFIT). Adverse hospitalization outcomes refer to patients with specific negative results caused by hospitalization; five indicators are used: in-hospital trauma rate (TRAUMAR), rate of discharges with unstable medical conditions (MEDPROBR), rate of treatment problems

(TXPROBR), postoperative complication rate (COMPRATE), and rate of unexpected deaths (DEDPROR).

The exogenous (predictor) variables include hospital size (BEDSIZE), number of high-technology services offered (HITECH), case-mix index (CASEMIX), percentage of patients treated in the special care units (SEVERITY), metropolitan size (METROSIZE), participation in a multihospital system (MULTI), affiliation with a medical school (MEDSCHOOL), and private-for-profit hospital (FOR PROFIT). A detailed list of the study variables with operational definitions appears in the appendix at the end of this chapter. The distribution of each study variable was analyzed to determine its normality.

Analytical Methods

To demonstrate the structural relationship among multiple indicators of hospital performance, multivariate statistical techniques are essential. Because many of the independent variables are highly correlated, the problem of multicollinearity among them may produce biased regression estimates. Because conventional regression methods have very restrictive statistical assumptions, this study used a linear structural relations (LISREL) approach. The specific reasons for doing so are as follows. First, with LISREL, several key organizational performance factors (i.e., efficiency, market share, financial viability, and adverse hospitalization outcomes), rather than a single factor, can be considered as underlying constructs (latent variables) measured by related indicators. Second, the measurement model of hospital performance specifies the relations between those observed indicators and the latent variables (theoretical constructs) while correlated measurement errors are considered. Third, LISREL can validate the measurement model's goodness of fit for the underlying constructs before they are incorporated in the structural equation. Fourth, the study of multiple causal factors often encounters correlated errors; LISREL modeling should be used to detect them (Bollen, 1989; Joreskog & Sorbom, 1979). A brief description of the LISREL approach to this study follows.

Proposed Measurement Model of Hospital Performance   The measurement model specifies the relationship between the observed variables and the unobserved theoretical constructs (latent variables). In other words, the purpose of the measurement model is to describe how well the observed indicators work as a measurement instrument for the latent variables. In this study, four organizational (latent) concepts were used as endogenous variables of hospital performance: efficiency, market share, financial viability, and adverse outcomes of hospitalization. Indicators of adverse hospitalization outcomes include incidents of patient trauma, unstable patients discharged, treatment problems, postoperative complications, and unexpected deaths. (Adverse hospitalization outcomes as measured by these indicators can reflect the quality of care.) Measurement errors associated with the observed indicators for the latent variables also are indicated, because such errors occur from imperfections in the measurement and may cause serious biases in the estimation if not taken into account.

Structural Equation Model of Hospital Performance   The second component of the LISREL analysis is the structural equation model. It defines the causal links among the exogenous latent variables factored from observed variables in the measurement model, as well as the effects of the exogenous variables. In this instance, we need to determine the causal linkages 1) among the hospital performance indicators themselves, and also 2) between measurable hospital characteristics and hospital performance. As suggested by previous studies (Al-Haider & Wan, 1991; Hartz et al., 1989; Scott et al., 1987), a variable such as the size of the hospital's metropolitan area was included in the analysis so that possible spurious relationships between organizational factors and hospital performance could be detected.

The LISREL model was used to test these alternative statistical hypotheses:

1. Hospital efficiency is influenced directly by hospital characteristics.
2. Hospital financial viability is affected positively by efficiency and market share when the effects of selected hospital characteristics are controlled.
3. Lower market share is associated with hospital inefficiency, large metropolitan size, affiliation with a multihospital system, and for-profit status.
4. Hospital efficiency, market share, and financial viability positively affect patient care outcomes when the effect of teaching status is controlled simultaneously.

These hypotheses were examined empirically in a one-tailed test for statistical significance at .05 or lower level. Because multivariate analysis was used to test the hypotheses, each conclusion drawn from the results can be stated as the net effect of a given predictor on an endogenous variable while other variables are being controlled simultaneously.

ANALYSIS

There were a total of 101 short-term acute care hospitals in the study areas (Table 10.1). This investigation focused on the adverse patient care outcomes reported by hospitals that participate in Medicare, so only 85 hospitals were studied. The studied hospitals had on average 220 beds and 63% occupancy. A majority of their physicians (70%) were board certified. More than 71% of their nurses were RNs. The hospitals had an ALOS in 1987 of 8.6 days. Only 6% of the inpatients were treated in special care units such as intensive care units and coronary care units. Twenty-one percent of the hospitals had an affiliation with a medical school. Fourteen percent were identified as for-profit hospitals, and almost half of the study hospitals were located in nonmetropolitan areas.

The measurement model of hospital performance shows the relationships of the underlying constructs to their respective indicators. Table 10.2 shows that efficiency is indicated more strongly by process efficiency (i.e., ALOS) and cost efficiency than by technical efficiency. Financial viability and market share are treated as perfect indicators that are measured, respectively, by the amount of hospital net profit (NET PROFIT) and by the percentage of patients drawn from a medical market area served by a hospital (%SHARE). For the underlying con-

Table 10.1. Percentage and mean distribution of major characteristics of hospitals in the total and study samples

Characteristics of hospital	Total (N 4 101)	Study sample[a] (N 4 85)	Difference between total and sampled hospitals
Average bed size	233.00	220.00	13.00
Average occupancy rate	62.67	62.66	0.01
% Board-certified doctors	68.35	69.74	− 1.39
% RNs on staff	71.86	71.40	0.46
HCFA case-mix index	1.11	1.13	− 0.02
ALOS	8.71	8.64	0.07
% Patients treated in special units (ICU, CCU, PCU)	6.23	6.12	0.11
% Affiliated with a medical school	22.77	21.18	1.59
% Private, for-profit hospitals	14.55	14.12	0.43
% Hospitals located in a nonmetropolitan area	44.6	49.4	14.80

[a]A subset (N = 85) of the total number of hospitals participating in Medicare in the study area.

Table 10.2.　Measurement model of hospital performance indicators

Parameter	(λ_y)	Indicator	Construct
1,1	.930[a]	Cost efficiency (COST)	Efficiency
2,1	.435[a]	Technical efficiency (TEFF)	Efficiency
3,1	1.000	Product efficiency (ALOS)	Efficiency
4,2	1.000	Market share (%SHARE)	Market share
5,3	1.000	Net profit (NET PROFIT)	Financial viability
6,4	.272[a]	Trauma rate (TRAUMAR)	Adverse outcome
7,4	.298[a]	Rate of discharges w/unstable condition (MEDPROBR)	Adverse outcome
8,4	.983[a]	Treatment problems rate (TXPROBR)	Adverse outcome
9,4	.729[a]	Postoperative complication rate (COMPRATE)	Adverse outcome
10,4	.807[a]	Unexpected death rate (DEDPROR)	Adverse outcome

[a]Significant at .05 or lower level.

struct of adverse outcomes of hospitalization, the treatment problems rate is the strongest of five outcome indicators; the postoperative complication rate and unexpected death rate are moderately related, and the trauma rate and the discharge rate for patients with unstable medical conditions are weakly related to adverse hospitalization outcomes.

The structural equation model shows casual linkages between eight exogenous (organizational structure/context) variables and the endogenous variable "efficiency." Table 10.3 reveals that eight exogenous variables account for 46% of the total variation in hospital efficiency. However, only three exogenous variables (BEDSIZE, SEVERITY, and METROSIZE) have a statistically significant relationship to hospital efficiency: Hospitals with a large bed size, that have treated more severe patients in special units, and that are located in a large metropolitan area all tend to be less efficient. Market share is related inversely to metropolitan size and hospital inefficiency: The larger the metropolitan area where a hospital is located or the lower the level of its efficiency, the smaller its share of its medical market area. This is because of the strong competition in a large metropolitan area. Hospital financial viability is associated positively with more high-technology services, higher case-mix index, and for-profit status; it is related negatively to metropolitan size and to membership in a multihospital system. It is interesting to note that hospital efficiency and market share have no significant influence on financial viability.

It appears that none of the hospital characteristics (exogenous variables) are related directly to adverse outcomes of hospitalization. However, in order to tease out the confounding effect of teaching status on patient care outcomes, a proxy indicator of teaching status (affiliation with a medical school) was introduced as a control variable in the analysis of the effects of the other endogenous variables—hospital efficiency, market share, and financial viability—on adverse outcomes of hospitalization. The LISREL results suggest that the effects of hospital efficiency, market share, and financial viability on adverse hospital outcomes are in the expected direction: The higher the level of hospital efficiency, market share, and financial viability, the lower the rates of adverse hospitalization outcomes. Careful inspection of the data reveals that almost 3% of the total variation in adverse hospitalization outcomes can be accounted for by the four predictor variables (efficiency, market share, financial viability, and teaching status); the effect of financial viability, however, is not statistically significant.

The goodness-of-fit (GOF) statistics presented in Table 10.3 suggest that the model of hospital performance is reasonably well fitted to the data, having a chi-square value of 78.33 with 85 degrees of freedom ($p = .892$). The overall GOF index is .913, and the adjusted GOF index is .843.

Table 10.3. Structural equation model of hospital performance: parameter estimates

| Endogenous variable | Exogenous variables[a] | | | | | | | | η_1 | η_2 | η_3 | R^2 |
	1	2	3	4	5	6	7	8				
Efficiency (η_1)	.314*	.016	.165	.130*	.357*	.044	-.119	.000	—	—	—	.464
Market share (η_2)	—	—	—	—	-.626*	-.180	—	-.073	-.065	—	—	.428
Financial viability (η_3)	—	.340*	.406*	—	-.227*	-.239*	—	.307*	-.011	.096	—	.323
Adverse outcomes (η_4)	—	—	—	—	—	—	-.189*	—	.222*	-.163*	-.138	.128

Note: Goodness of fit (GOF) statistics: X^2 (with 85 degrees of freedom) = 78.330 (p = .892; GOF index = .913; adjusted GOF index = .843; root mean squares residual = .065).

[a]Variables are: 1, BEDSIZE; 2, HITECH; 3, CASEMIX; 4, SEVERITY; 5, METROSIZE; 6, MULTI; 7, MEDSCHOOL; 8, FOR PROFIT.

*Significant at .05 or lower level; —, the variable is not included in the equation.

CONCLUSION

This chapter has illustrated the uses of a multivariate analytical approach for the complex problem of assessing hospital performance. First, the structural relationship between hospital efficiency and effectiveness is portrayed by using multiple indicators. The analysis shows that reduced efficiency is associated with a higher level of adverse hospitalization outcomes. However, hospital efficiency does not influence market share or financial viability when the effects of other hospital characteristics are controlled simultaneously. These findings suggest that, if a hospital operates efficiently, it helps reduce the risk of adverse patient outcomes, yet without detriment to either market share or net profit. Furthermore, reduced efficiency is associated positively with hospital size, severity of patients treated, and metropolitan size. In order to improve hospital performance, we need to learn more about economies of scale related to the number of hospital beds operated, the type of patients admitted, and the size of the metropolitan area where the hospital should be located.

Second, this chapter demonstrated a new strategy for identifying organizational factors that affect variation in hospital performance—namely, a structural equation model that helps capture underlying theoretical constructs. For example, in contrast to previous research, which invariably has used mortality rate alone, the study presented here used multiple indicators of adverse hospitalization outcomes. That approach offers a more sophisticated and reliable measure of quality of care.

Third, metropolitan size, as an organization's contextual variable, is shown to exert a negative influence on hospital market share and financial viability. This indicates that, to understand hospitals' financial performance, it is important to understand market forces in geographic locations with different population sizes.

Fourth, hospitals affiliated with medical schools are shown to have lower rates of adverse outcomes than do hospitals without such affiliations. This finding confirms the beneficial effect of establishing an affiliation with a medical school.

There are a few limitations to the analysis in this example. The availability of adverse outcome data for only a select group of hospitals may restrict the study's achievement of a comprehensive examination of variation in hospital performance. One of the outcome variables, unexpected mortality rate, was not adjusted for the severity of illness and other patient characteristics. It would be desirable to analyze outcome data from the Uniform Clinical Data Set system (Hartz et al., 1994) from a randomly selected sample of hospitals in the United States, so that the findings can be generalized better. Another limitation of the study is that the stability over time of the measurement model has not been tested, because that requires a set of panel data. Finally, this study is a macro-level organizational study. Because process indicators of the quality of hospital care are not readily available for investigation, this analysis is restricted further in identifying critical process factors that may affect the variation in adverse hospitalization outcomes. Research efforts should try to develop a more comprehensive model that incorporates patient population, organizational, environmental, and technology indicators, as well as a multi-wave study design to ascertain more precisely the stability of the measurements and causal structure. Research also should identify: 1) a set of provider-based outcome measures, such as number of inappropriate admissions, number of omissions, physician sanctions, and other generic, screened data collected by peer review organizations; and 2) measures of patient satisfaction with hospital care, which could serve as process indicators for the quality of care. Multiple measures of adverse outcomes of hospitalization adjusted for the differences in patient risk factors can be used to monitor hospital outcomes.

APPENDIX LIST OF VARIABLES AND THEIR DEFINITIONS

Variable code		Definition
Exogenous Variables		
X1	BEDSIZE[a]	Hospital bed size
X2	HITECH[a]	Number of critical care specialty services offered, including open heart surgery, organ transplant, etc.
X3	CASEMIX[a]	HCFA diagnosis-related group–based hospital case-mix index
X4	SEVERITY[a]	% Patients treated in the special care units
X5	METROSIZE[a]	Metropolitan area size
X6	MULTI[a]	Participated in a multihospital system (yes = 1; no = 0)
X7	MEDSCHOOL[a]	Affiliated with a medical school (yes = 1; no = 0)
X8	FOR PROFIT[a]	Private-for-profit hospital (yes = 1; no = 0)
Endogenous Variables (Underlying Constructs)		
Y1	COST[a]	Cost efficiency = average charges per patient discharged
Y2	TEFF[a]	Technical efficiency rate measured by a composite index generated from the DEA
Y3	ALOS[a]	Product efficiency measured by average length of stays
Y4	%SHARE[a]	% Medicare patients served by a hospital in a given medical market area
Y5	NET PROFIT[a]	Amount of net hospital income earned per patient discharge
Y6	TRAUMAR[b]	In-hospital trauma rate measured by the number of in-hospital traumas (falls, injuries) divided by the total number of cases reviewed
Y7	MEDPROBR[b]	Rate of discharges with unstable medical conditions, calculated as the number of patients reviewed who were medically unstable at the time of discharge divided by the total number of patients reviewed
Y8	TXPROBR[b]	Rate of treatment problems, measured by the number of treatment or medication problems divided by the total number of cases reviewed
Y9	COMPRATE[b]	Postoperative complication rate, measured by the number of patients with unexpected return to the operating room divided by the total number of cases reviewed
Y10	DEDPROR[b]	Rate of unexpected deaths, calculated as the number of unexpected deaths divided by the total number of cases reviewed

[a] Indicators measured in 1987.

[b] Indicators measured in 1988.

REFERENCES

Al-Haider, A.S., & Wan, T.T.H. (1991). Modeling organizational determinants of hospital mortality. *Health Services Research, 26*, 303–323.

Ballard, D.J., Bryant, S.C., O'Brien, P.C., Smith, D.W., Pine, M.B., & Cortese, D.A. (1994). Referral selection bias in the Medicare hospital mortality prediction model: Are centers of referral for Medicare beneficiaries necessarily centers of excellence. *Health Services Research, 28*, 771–784.

Blumberg, S.M. (1986). Risk adjusted health care outcomes: A methodological review. *Medical Care Review, 43*, 352–393.

Blumberg, S.M. (1987). Comments on HCFA hospital death rate statistical outlier. *Health Services Research, 21*, 715–739.

Bollen, K.A. (1989). *Structural equations with latent variables.* New York: John Wiley & Sons.

Bradbury, R.C., Golec, J.H., & Steen, P.M. (1994). Relating hospital health outcomes and resource expenditures. *Inquiry, 31*, 56–65.

Cameron, K.S. (1984). The effectiveness of ineffectiveness. In B. Staw & L.L. Cummings (Eds.), *Research in organizational behavior* (pp. 225–285). New York. JAI Press.

Chassin, M.R., Park, R.E., Lohr, K.N., Keesey, J., & Brook, R.H. (1989). Differences among hospitals in Medicare patient mortality. *Health Services Research, 24*, 1–31.

Cleverley, W.O. (1987). *SOI-PLUS user's guide: Strategic operating indicator service.* Chicago: Healthcare Financial Management Association.

Codman Research Group, Inc. (1989). *Small area analysis of variation in utilization and outcomes for hospital care among Medicare beneficiaries: Vol. II. Zip code composition of hospital market areas.* (Project supported by the Health Standard and Quality Bureau, Health Care Financing Administration.) Lyme, New Hampshire.

Coyne, J.S. (1982). Hospital performance in multihospital systems: A comparative study of system and independent hospitals. *Health Services Research, 17,* 303–327.

Daft, R.L. (1989). *Organizational theory and design.* New York: West Publishing Company.

Daley, J., Jencks, S., Draper, D., Lenhart, G., Thomas, N., & Walker, J. (1988). Predicting hospital-associated mortality for Medicare patients. *Journal of the American Medical Association, 260,* 3617–3624.

DesHarnais, S.I., Chesney, R.T., Wroblewski, R.T., Fleming, S.T., & McMahon, L.F., Jr. (1988). The risk-adjusted mortality index: A new measure of hospital performance. *Medical Care, 26,* 1129–1148.

DesHarnais, S.I., McMahon, L.F., Jr., & Wroblewski, R.T. (1991). Measuring outcomes of hospital care using multiple risk-adjusted indexes. *Health Services Research, 26,* 425–445.

DesHarnais, S.I., McMahon, L.F., Jr., Wroblewski, R.T., & Hogan, A.J. (1990). Measuring hospital performance: The development and validation of risk-adjusted indexes of mortality, readmissions, and complications. *Medical Care, 28,* 1127–1141.

Dubois, W.R., Brook, R.H., & Rogers, W.H. (1987). Adjusted hospital death rates: A potential screen for quality of medical care. *American Journal of Public Health, 77,* 1162–1166.

Ehreth, J.L. (1994). The development and evaluation of hospital performance measures for policy analysis. *Medical Care, 32,* 568–587.

Elnicki, R.A., & Schmitt, J.P. (1989). Contribution of patient and hospital characteristics to adverse patient incidents. In G.H. DeFriese, T.C. Ricketts III, & J.S. Stein (Eds.), *Methodological advances in health services research* (pp. 167–189). Ann Arbor, MI: Health Administration Press.

Fink, A., Yano, E.M., & Brook, R.H. (1989). The condition of the literature on differences in hospital mortality. *Medical Care, 27,* 315–336.

Flood, A.B., & Scott, W.R. (Eds.). (1987). *Hospital structure and performance.* Baltimore: Johns Hopkins University Press.

Flood, A.B., Scott, W.R., Ewy, W., & Forrest, W. (1987). Effectiveness in professional organizations: The impact of surgeons and surgical staff organization on the quality of care in hospitals. *Health Services Research, 17,* 341–365.

Friedman, B., & Shortell, S.M. (1988). The financial performance of selected investor-owned and not-for-profit system hospitals before and after Medicare prospective payment. *Health Services Research, 23,* 237–267.

Gianfrancesco, F.D. (1990). The fairness of the PPS reimbursement methodology. *Health Services Research, 25,* 1–24.

Green, J., Sharkey, P., & Passman, L.J. (1990). The importance of severity of illness in assessing hospital mortality. *Journal of the American Medical Association, 263,* 241–246.

Goldfarb, M.G., & Coffey, R.M. (1987). Case-mix differences between teaching and non-teaching hospitals. *Inquiry, 24,* 68–84.

Grosskopf, S., & Valdmanis, V. (1987). Measuring hospital performance. A non-parametric approach. *Journal of Health Economics, 6,* 89–107.

Hartz, A.J., Gottlieb, M.S., Kuhn, E.M., & Rimm, A.A. (1993). The relationship between adjusted hospital mortality and the results of peer review. *Health Services Research, 27,* 765–777.

Hartz, A.J., Krakauer, H., Kuhn, E.M., Young, M., Jacobsen, S.J., Gay, G., Muenz, L., Katzoff, M., Bailey, R.C., & Rimm, A. (1989). Hospital characteristics and mortality rates. *New England Journal of Medicine, 321,* 1720–1725.

Hartz, A.J., Sigmann, P., Guse, C., & Hagen, T.C. (1994). The value of the Uniform Clinical Data Set System (UCDSS) in a hospital setting. *Journal on Quality Improvement, 20,* 140–151.

Horn, S.D., Sharkey, P.D., Buckle, J.M., Backofen, J.E., Averill, R.F., & Horn, R.A. (1991). The relationship between severity of illness and hospital length of stay and mortality. *Medical Care, 29,* 305–317.

Iezzoni, L.I. (1988). *The ability of MEDISGROUPS and clinical variables to predict cost and in-hospital deaths.* Boston: University of Boston Medical Center.

Iezzoni, L.I. (1993). Monitoring quality of care: What do we need to know? *Inquiry, 30,* 112–114.

Iezzoni, L.I. (Ed.). (1994). *Risk adjustment strategies for measuring health care outcomes.* Ann Arbor, MI: Health Administration Press.

Iezzoni, L.I., Daley, J., Heeren, T., Foley, S.M., Hughes, J.S., Fisher, E.S., Duncan, C.C., & Coffman, G.A. (1994). Using administrative data to screen hospitals for high complication rates. *Inquiry, 31,* 40–55.

Joreskog, K., & Sorbom, D. (1979). *Advances in factor analysis and structural equation models.* Cambridge, MA: Abt Books.

Kanter, R., & Brinkerhoff, D. (1981). Organizational performance. *Annual Review of Sociology, 7,* 321–349.

Knaus, W., Draper, E.A., Wagner, D.P., & Zimmerman, J.A. (1985). APACHE II: A severity of disease classification system. *Critical Care Medicine, 13,* 818–829.

Levitz, G., & Brooke, P. (1985). Independent versus system-affiliated hospitals: A comparative analysis of financial performance, cost and productivity. *Health Services Research, 20,* 313–339.

Luft, H.S., Bunker, J.P., & Enthoven, A.C. (1979). Should operations be regionalized? The empirical relation between surgical volume and mortality. *New England Journal of Medicine, 301,* 1364–1369

Luft, H.S., Hunt, S.S., & Maerki, S.C. (1987). The volume-outcome relationship: Practice makes perfect or selective-referral pattern? *Health Services Research, 22,* 157–182.

Nunamaker, T. (1983). Measuring routine nursing service efficiency: A comparison of cost per patient day and data envelopment analysis models. *Health Services Research, 18,* 183–205.

Ozcan, Y.A. (1992–1993). Sensitivity analysis of hospital efficiency under alternative output/input and peer groups: A review. *Knowledge and Policy, 5*(4), 1–29.

Ozcan, Y.A., Luke, R.D., & Haksever, C. (1992). Ownership and organizational performance: A comparison of technical efficiency across hospital types. *Medical Care, 30,* 781–794.

Payne, B.C., & Lyons, T.F. (1972). *Method of evaluating and improving personal medical care quality: Episode of illness study and office care study.* Ann Arbor: The University of Michigan School of Medicine.

Phelps, C.E. (1993). The methodologic foundations of studies of the appropriateness of medical care. *New England Journal of Medicine, 329,* 1241–1245.

Rhee, S. (1983). Organizational determinants of medical care quality: A review of the literature. In R. Luke, J. Krueger, & R. Modrow (Eds.), *Organization and change in health care quality assurance* (pp. 127–146). Rockville, MD: Aspen Systems Corporation.

Riley, G., Lubitz, J., Gornick, M., Mentnech, R., Eggers, P., & McBean, M. (1993). Medicare beneficiaries: Adverse outcomes after hospitalization to eight procedures. *Medical Care, 31,* 921–949.

Romano, P.S. (1993). Can administrative data be used to compare the quality of health care? *Medical Care Review, 50,* 451–477.

Rosko, M.D. (1990). Measuring technical efficiency in health care organizations. *Journal of Medical Systems, 14,* 307–322.

Ruchlin, H.S. (1977). Problems in measuring hospital institutional productivity. *Topics in Health Care Financing, 4,* 13–27.

Scott, W.R., Flood, A.B., & Ewy, W. (1987). Organizational determinants of services, quality, and the cost of care in hospitals. In A.B. Flood & W.R. Scott (Eds.), *Hospital structure and performance* (pp. 263–277). Baltimore: Johns Hopkins University Press.

Scott, W.R., Forrest, W., & Brown, B. (1976). Hospital structure and post-operative mortality and morbidity. In S.M. Shortell & M. Brown (Eds.), *Organizational research in hospitals* (pp. 72–89). Chicago: Blue Cross Association.

Scott, W.R., & Shortell, S.M. (1988). Organizational performance: Managing efficiency and effectiveness. In S.M. Shortell & A.D. Kaluzny (Eds.), *Health care management* (pp. 418–455). New York: John Wiley & Sons.

Sherman, H.D. (1984). Hospital efficiency measurement and evaluation: Empirical test of a new technique. *Medical Care, 22,* 922–938.

Shortell, S.M., Becker, S., & Neuhauser, D. (1976). The effect of management practices on hospital efficiency. In S.M. Shortell & M. Brown (Eds.), *Organizational research in hospitals* (pp. 90–107). Chicago: Blue Cross Association.

Shortell, S.M., & Hughes, E.F. (1988). The effects of regulation, competition, and ownership on mortality rates among hospital inpatients. *New England Journal of Medicine, 318,* 1100–1107.

Shortell, S.M., & LoGerfo, J. (1981). Hospital medical staff organization and quality of care: Results for myocardial infarction and appendectomy. *Medical Care, 19,* 1041–1055.

Silber, J.H., Williams, S.V., Krakauer, H., & Schwartz, J.S. (1992). Hospital and patient characteristics associated with death after surgery. *Medical Care, 30,* 615–629.

Sloan, F.A., Perrin, J.M., & Valvona, J. (1986). In-hospital mortality of surgical patients: Is there an empirical basis for standard setting? *Surgery, 99,* 446–453.

Thomas, J.W., Holloway, J.J., & Guire, K.E. (1993). Validating risk-adjusted mortality as an indicator for quality of care. *Inquiry, 30,* 6–22.

Valdmanis, V.G. (1990). Ownership and technical efficiency of hospitals. *Medical Care, 28,* 552–560.

Wan, T.T.H., & Cooper, P. (1987). A structural equation model of physician productivity. *Journal of Health Care Marketing, 8,* 37–45.

Wan, T.T.H., & Ozcan, Y. (1991). Determinants of psychiatric rehospitalization: A social area analysis. *Community Mental Health Journal, 27,* 3–16.

Wan, T.T.H., & Shukla, R. (1987). Contextual and organizational correlates of the quality of hospital nursing care. *Quality Review Bulletin, 13,* 61–65.

Zaretsky, H.W. (1977). The effects of patient mix and service mix on hospital costs and productivity. *Topics in Health Care Financing, 4,* 63–82.

Appendix A

Selected Indicators Measuring Personal and Community Health

Personal Health

Instrument or scale	Number of items	Indicators or dimensions
Index of Well-Being (Kaplan, Bush, & Berry, 1976)	116	Mobility, physical activity, and social activity scales
The General Well-Being Index (Wan & Livieratos, 1978)	18	General health and psychological well-being
The Center for Epidemiologic Studies–Depression Scale (Radloff, 1977)	20	Depression
Duke-UNC Health Profile (Parkerson, Gehlbach, & Wagner, 1981)	63	Symptom status; physical, emotional, and social functioning
Sickness Impact Profile (Bergner, Bobbitt, & Carter, 1981)	136	Physical, psychological, and other dysfunctions
Short-Form 36 Health Survey (Ware, 1993)	36	Physical functioning, role functioning, body pain, general perception, vitality, social functioning, mental health, and reported health transition

COMMUNITY HEALTH

Healthy People 2000 Measurable Goals

Goal	Indicators
Physical activity and fitness	• Increase moderate daily physical activity to at least 30% of people (a 36% increase) • Reduce sedentary lifestyles to no more than 15% of people (a 38% decrease)
Nutrition	• Reduce overweight to a prevalence of no more than 20% of people (a 23% decrease) • Reduce dietary fat intake to an average of 30% of calories (a 17% decrease)
Tobacco	• Reduce cigarette smoking prevalence to no more than 15% of adults (a 48% decrease) • Reduce initiation of smoking to no more than 15% by age 20 (a 50% decrease)
Alcohol and other drugs	• Reduce alcohol-related motor vehicle crash deaths to no more than 8.5 per 100,000 people (a 12% decrease) • Reduce alcohol use by school children ages 12–17 to less than 13%; marijuana use by youth ages 18–25 to less than 8%; and cocaine use by youth ages 18–25 to less than 3% (50% decreases)
Family planning	• Reduce teenage pregnancies to no more than 50 per 1,000 girls 17 and younger (a 30% decrease) • Reduce unintended pregnancies to no more than 30% of pregnancies (a 46% decrease)
Mental health and mental disorders	• Reduce suicides to no more than 10.5 per 100,000 people (a 10% decrease) • Reduce adverse effects of stress to less than 35% of people (an 18% decrease)
Violent and abusive behavior	• Reduce homicides to no more than 7.2 per 100,000 people (a 15% decrease) • Reduce assault injuries to no more than 10 per 100,000 people (a 10% decrease)
Educational and community-based programs	• Provide quality K–12 school health education in at least 75% of schools • Provide employee health promotion activities in at least 85% of workplaces with 50 or more employees (a 31% increase)

Adapted from U.S. Department of Health and Human Services. (1990).

Eighteen Indicators of Community Health Status

---

1. Race/ethnicity-specific infant mortality as measured by the rate (per 1,000 live births) of deaths among infants under 1 year of age.
2. Total deaths per 100,000 population.
3. Motor vehicle crash deaths per 100,000 population.
4. Work-related injury deaths per 100,000 population.
5. Suicides per 100,000 population.
6. Homicides per 100,000 population.
7. Lung cancer deaths per 100,000 population.
8. Female breast cancer deaths per 100,000 women.
9. Cardiovascular disease deaths per 100,000 population
10. Reported incidence (per 100,000 population) of acquired immunodeficiency syndrome.
11. Reported incidence (per 100,000 population) of measles.
12. Reported incidence (per 100,000 population) of tuberculosis.
13. Reported incidence (per 100,000 population) of primary and secondary syphilis.
14. Prevalence of low birth weight as measured by the percentage of live-born infants weighing under 2,500 grams at birth.
15. Births to adolescents (ages 10–17 years) as a percentage of total live births.
16. Prenatal care as measured by the percentage of mothers delivering live infants who did not receive care during the first trimester of pregnancy.
17. Childhood poverty, as measured by the proportion of children under 15 years of age living in families at or below the poverty level.
18. Proportion of persons living in counties exceeding U.S. Environmental Protection Agency standards for air quality during the previous year.

Adapted from Klein & Hawk (1992).

REFERENCES

Bergner, M., Bobbitt, R.A., & Carter, W. (1981). The Sickness Impact Profile: Development and final revision of a health status measure. *Medical Care, 19,* 787–805.

Kaplan, R.M., Bush, J.W., & Berry, C.C. (1976). Health status: Types of validity and the Index of Well-Being. *Health Services Research, 11,* 478–507.

Klein, R.J., & Hawk, S.A. (1992). Health status indicators: Definitions and national data. *Healthy People 2000 Statistical Notes, 1*(3), 1–8. Hyattsville, MD: National Center for Health Statistics.

Parkerson, G.R., Gehlbach, S.H., & Wagner, E.H. (1981). The Duke-UNC Health Profile: An adult health status instrument for primary care. *Medical Care, 19,* 806–828.

Radloff, L.S. (1977). CES-D Scale: A self report depression scale for research in the general population. *Applied Psychological Measurements, 1,* 385–401.

U.S. Department of Health and Human Services. (1990). *Healthy people 2000: National health promotion and disease prevention objectives, conference edition.* Washington, DC: U.S. Government Printing Office.

Wan, T.T.H., & Livieratos, B. (1978). Interpreting a general index of subjective well-being. *Milbank Memorial Fund Quarterly, 56,* 531–555.

Ware, J. (1993). *SF-36 Health Survey: Manual and interpretation guide.* Boston: New England Medical Center, The Health Institute.

Appendix B

Medicare Diagnosis-Related Groups

Appendix B

DRG no.	DRG description	Average national payment ($)[a]	Average length of stay (days)
1	Craniotomy, age > 17 except for trauma	9,782.36	19.4
2	Craniotomy for trauma, age > 17	9,728.11	15.8
3	Craniotomy, age 0–17	9,354.56	12.7
4	Spinal procedures	7,392.57	16.0
5	Extracranial vascular procedures	4,761.91	9.8
6	Carpal tunnel release	1,944.01	2.6
7	Peripheral and cranial nerve and other nervous system procedures with CC[b]	7,805.80	5.3
8	Peripheral and cranial nerve and other nervous system procedures without CC	2,658.56	4.1
9	Spinal disorders and injuries	4,153.07	9.1
10	Nervous system neoplasms with CC	3,973.89	9.6
11	Nervous system neoplasms without CC	2,384.21	8.5
12	Degenerative nervous system disorders	2,929.19	9.4
13	Multiple sclerosis and cerebellar ataxia	2,513.48	8.9
14	Specific cerebrovascular disorders except transient ischemic attack	3,737.36	9.9
15	Transient ischemic attack and precerebral occlusions	2,097.46	5.6
16	Nonspecific cerebrovascular disorders with CC	3,453.71	7.4
17	Nonspecific cerebrovascular disorders without CC	2,060.88	7.2
18	Cranial and peripheral nerve disorders with CC	2,852.62	6.6
19	Cranial and peripheral nerve disorders without CC	1,837.37	5.7
20	Nervous system infection except viral meningitis	6,390.03	7.6
21	Viral meningitis	4,434.24	4.5
22	Hypertensive encephalopathy	2,258.66	6.4
23	Nontraumatic stupor and coma	2,606.17	5.9
24	Seizure and headache, age > 17 with CC	3,025.29	5.6
25	Seizure and headache, age > 17 without CC	1,682.06	4.9
26	Seizure and headache, age 0–17	3,062.18	3.3
27	Traumatic stupor and coma, coma greater than one hour	4,126.41	4.1
28	Traumatic stupor and coma, coma less than one hour, age > 17 with CC	3,744.18	5.9
29	Traumatic stupor and coma, coma less than one hour, age > 17 without CC	1,841.71	3.8
30	Traumatic stupor and coma, coma less than one hour, age 0–17	1,134.60	2.0
31	Concussion, age > 17 with CC	2,273.85	4.6
32	Concussion, age > 17 without CC	1,393.14	3.3
33	Concussion, age 0–17	787.40	1.6
34	Other disorders of nervous system with CC	3,441.93	7.1
35	Other disorders of nervous system without CC	1,753.36	6.2
36	Retinal procedures	1,886.97	5.0
37	Orbital procedures	2,431.33	3.4
38	Primary iris procedures	1,151.96	3.0
39	Lens procedures with or without vitrectomy	1,464.13	2.8
40	Extraocular procedures except orbit, age > 17	1,731.66	2.4
41	Extraocular procedures except orbit, age 0–17	1,172.42	1.6

(continued)

DRG no.	DRG description	Average national payment ($)[a]	Average length of stay (days)
42	Intraocular procedures except retina, iris, and lens	1,790.87	3.8
43	Hyphema	1,182.34	4.2
44	Acute major eye infections	1,844.19	6.5
45	Neurological eye disorders	1,874.57	4.3
46	Other disorders of the eye, age > 17 with CC	2,259.28	4.1
47	Other disorders of the eye, age > 17, without CC	1,254.57	3.0
48	Other disorders of the eye, age 0–17	1,288.05	2.9
49	Major head and neck procedures	5,560.47	13.6
50	Sialoadenectomy	2,086.92	4.6
51	Salivary gland procedures except sialoadenectomy	2,019.65	4.2
52	Cleft lip and palate repair	2,386.07	3.8
53	Sinus and mastoid procedures, age > 17	2,369.95	3.5
54	Sinus and mastoid procedures, age 0–17	2,208.44	3.2
55	Miscellaneous ear, nose, mouth, and throat procedures	1,785.91	2.5
56	Rhinoplasty	1,987.72	2.8
57	T and A procedures except tonsillectomy and/or adenoidectomy only, age > 17	2,825.96	2.7
58	T and A procedures except tonsillectomy and/or adenoidectomy only, age 0–17	992.93	1.5
59	Tonsillectomy and/or adenoidectomy only, age > 17	1,288.98	2.0
60	Tonsillectomy and/or adenoidectomy only, age 0–17	838.24	1.5
61	Myringotomy with tube insertion, age > 17	3,195.17	2.1
62	Myringotomy with tube insertion, age 0–17	990.14	1.3
63	Other ear, nose, mouth, and throat OR procedures[c]	3,261.20	5.8
64	Ear, nose, mouth, and throat malignancy	3,587.01	5.7
65	Dysequilibrium	1,535.12	4.6
66	Epistaxis	1,521.79	3.7
67	Epiglottitis	2,629.11	4.3
68	Otitis media and URI, age > 17 with CC[d]	2,218.98	6.0
69	Otitis media and URI, age > 17 without CC	1,589.06	4.8
70	Otitis media and URI, age 0–17	1,233.18	3.1
71	Laryngotracheitis	2,119.78	2.9
72	Nasal trauma and deformity	1,884.49	3.8
73	Other ear, nose, mouth, and throat diagnoses, age > 17	2,353.21	3.5
74	Other ear, nose, mouth, and throat diagnoses, age 0–17	1,098.95	2.1
75	Major chest procedures	9,423.07	14.4
76	Other respiratory system OR procedures with CC	7,678.70	10.6
77	Other respiratory system OR procedures without CC	3,237.33	9.5
78	Pulmonary embolism	4,430.52	10.4
79	Respiratory infections and inflammations, age > 17, with CC	5,372.92	11.2
80	Respiratory infections and inflammations, age > 17, without CC	2,876.18	10.9

(continued)

DRG no.	DRG description	Average national payment ($)[a]	Average length of stay (days)
81	Respiratory infections and inflammations, age 0–17	3,536.48	6.1
82	Respiratory neoplasms	4,062.55	7.4
83	Major chest trauma with CC	2,914.93	8.1
84	Major chest trauma without CC	1,545.66	5.3
85	Pleural effusion with CC	3,686.21	8.4
86	Pleural effusion without CC	2,074.21	7.6
87	Pulmonary edema and respiratory failure	4,183.45	7.7
88	Chronic obstructive pulmonary disease	3,120.77	7.5
89	Simple pneumonia and pleurisy, age > 17 with CC	3,548.57	8.5
90	Simple pneumonia and pleurisy, age > 17 without CC	2,166.90	7.6
91	Simple pneumonia and pleurisy, age 0–17	2,407.77	4.6
92	Interstitial lung disease with CC	3,732.09	7.8
93	Interstitial lung disease without CC	2,340.50	6.9
94	Pneumothorax with CC	3,854.23	9.2
95	Pneumothorax without CC	1,880.77	7.7
96	Bronchitis and asthma, age > 17 with CC	2,720.56	6.9
97	Bronchitis and asthma, age > 17 without CC	1,880.77	6.2
98	Bronchitis and asthma, age 0–17	2,120.40	3.7
99	Respiratory signs and symptoms with CC	2,216.19	5.5
100	Respiratory signs and symptoms without CC	1,551.24	5.1
101	Other respiratory system diagnoses with CC	2,800.85	6.8
102	Other respiratory system diagnoses without CC	1,637.42	6.1
103	Heart transplant	43,466.65	0.0
104	Cardiac valve procedures with cardiac catheterization	23,733.29	20.9
105	Cardiac valve procedures without cardiac catheterization	17,976.90	16.2
106	Coronary bypass with cardiac catheterization	17,605.21	20.4
107	Coronary bypass without cardiac catheterization	13,021.55	13.5
108	Other cardiothoracic procedures	18,193.90	13.3
109	No longer valid	0.00	12.1
110	Major cardiovascular procedures with CC	12,553.14	14.3
111	Major cardiovascular procedures without CC	7,196.34	13.2
112	Percutaneous cardiovascular procedures	6,118.16	11.2
113	Amputation for circulatory system disorders except upper limb and toe	8,658.61	21.6
114	Upper limb and toe amputation for circulatory system disorders	4,845.61	16.1
115	Permanent cardiac pacemaker implant with acute myocardial infarction, heart failure or shock	11,124.66	15.8
116	Other permanent cardiac pacemaker implant or AICD lead or generator procedure[e]	7,516.88	9.3
117	Cardiac pacemaker revision except device replacement	3,511.68	6.4
118	Cardiac pacemaker device replacement	4,779.89	4.2
119	Vein ligation and stripping	3,048.54	7.2
120	Other circulatory system OR procedures	6,084.06	15.0

(continued)

DRG no.	DRG description	Average national payment ($)[a]	Average length of stay (days)
121	Circulatory disorders with acute myocardial infarction and cardiovascular complication, discharged alive	4,965.27	11.9
122	Circulatory disorders without acute myocardial infarction and cardiovascular complication, discharged alive	3,510.75	9.8
123	Circulatory disorders with acute myocardial infarction, expired	4,375.96	3.1
124	Circulatory disorders except acute myocardial infarction with cardiac catheterization and complex diagnosis	3,815.17	8.4
125	Circulatory disorders except acute myocardial infarction with cardiac catheterization without complex diagnosis	2,467.60	5.0
126	Acute and subacute endocarditis	8,462.69	18.4
127	Heart failure and shock	3,172.54	7.8
128	Deep vein thrombophlebitis	2,425.75	9.6
129	Cardiac arrest, unexplained	3,707.29	4.6
130	Peripheral vascular disorders with CC	2,803.02	7.1
131	Peripheral vascular disorders without CC	1,807.61	6.4
132	Atherosclerosis with CC	2,354.14	6.7
133	Atherosclerosis without CC	1,629.67	5.2
134	Hypertension	1,740.34	6.1
135	Cardiac congenital and valvular disorders, age > 17 with CC	2,668.79	6.1
136	Cardiac congenital and valvular disorders, age > 17 without CC	1,701.59	4.9
137	Cardiac congenital and valvular disorders, age 0–17	2,024.30	3.3
138	Cardiac arrhythmia and conduction disorders with CC	2,491.78	5.7
139	Cardiac arrhythmia and conduction disorders without CC	1,553.26	4.8
140	Angina pectoris	1,934.71	5.5
141	Syncope and collapse with CC	2,186.43	5.0
142	Syncope and collapse without CC	1,596.50	4.3
143	Chest pain	1,608.59	4.4
144	Other circulatory system diagnoses with CC	3,304.29	7.0
145	Other circulatory system diagnoses without CC	1,897.82	6.4
146	Rectal resection with CC	7,736.05	19.1
147	Rectal resection without CC	4,751.68	17.9
148	Major small and large bowel procedures with CC	9,832.89	17.0
149	Major small and large bowel procedures without CC	4,689.37	15.2
150	Peritoneal adhesiolysis with CC	7,906.55	15.3
151	Peritoneal adhesiolysis without CC	3,638.78	13.4
152	Minor small and large bowel procedures with CC	5,566.05	10.6
153	Minor small and large bowel procedures without CC	3,354.51	9.3
154	Stomach, esophageal and duodenal procedures, age > 17 with CC	12,814.78	14.

(*continued*)

DRG no.	DRG description	Average national payment ($)[a]	Average length of stay (days)
155	Stomach, esophageal and duodenal procedures, age > 17 without CC	4,281.41	13.0
156	Stomach, esophageal and duodenal procedures, age 0–17	2,687.08	6.0
157	Anal and stomal procedures with CC	3,114.88	6.0
158	Anal and stomal procedures without CC	1,581.00	5.2
159	Hernia procedures except inguinal and femoral, age > 17 with CC	3,379.31	7.1
160	Hernia procedures except inguinal and femoral, age > 17 without CC	1,977.18	6.0
161	Inguinal and femoral hernia procedures, age > 17 with CC	2,560.60	5.7
162	Inguinal and femoral hernia procedures, age > 17 without CC	1,495.13	4.8
163	Hernia procedures, age 0–17	2,106.45	2.1
164	Appendectomy with complicated principal diagnosis with CC	6,720.49	11.9
165	Appendectomy with complicated principal diagnosis without CC	3,737.05	11.3
166	Appendectomy without complicated principal diagnosis with CC	4,158.03	9.4
167	Appendectomy without complicated principal diagnosis without CC	2,418.03	7.4
168	Mouth procedures with CC	3,199.51	4.3
169	Mouth procedures without CC	1,805.44	4.2
170	Other digestive system OR procedures with CC	8,532.44	14.6
171	Other digestive system OR procedures without CC	3,377.14	13.3
172	Digestive malignancy with CC	4,049.53	8.2
173	Digestive malignancy without CC	1,958.58	6.7
174	GI hemorrhage with CC[f]	2,993.67	6.7
175	GI hemorrhage without CC	1,659.74	5.8
176	Complicated peptic ulcer	3,240.43	8.1
177	Uncomplicated peptic ulcer with CC	2,475.66	6.6
178	Uncomplicated peptic ulcer without CC	1,799.24	5.5
179	Inflammatory bowel disease	3,432.32	8.0
180	GI obstruction with CC	2,845.80	6.2
181	GI obstruction without CC	1,540.39	5.9
182	Esophagitis, gastroenteritis, and miscellaneous digestive disorders, age > 17 with CC	2,361.27	5.4
183	Esophagitis, gastroenteritis, and miscellaneous digestive disorders, age > 17 without CC	1,640.21	4.8
184	Esophagitis, gastroenteritis, and miscellaneous digestive disorders, age 0–17	1,467.85	3.3
185	Dental and oral diseases except extractions and restorations, age > 17	2,556.88	4.2
186	Dental and oral diseases except extractions and restorations, age 0–17	1,317.81	2.9
187	Dental extractions and restorations	1,814.12	2.7
188	Other digestive system diagnoses, age > 17 with CC	3,115.50	5.1

(continued)

DRG no.	DRG description	Average national payment ($)[a]	Average length of stay (days)
189	Other digestive system diagnoses, age > 17 without CC	1,480.25	4.5
190	Other digestive system diagnoses, age 0–17	2,348.87	2.1
191	Pancreas, liver, and shunt procedures with CC	13,428.87	20.8
192	Pancreas, liver, and shunt procedures without CC	5,102.60	20.1
193	Biliary tract procedures except only cholecystectomy with or without common duct exploration with CC	9,591.40	17.3
194	Biliary tract procedures except only cholecystectomy with or without common duct exploration without CC	4,957.21	13.9
195	Cholecystectomy with common duct exploration with CC	7,460.46	16.0
196	Cholecystectomy with common duct exploration without CC	4,672.63	15.8
197	Cholecystectomy except by laparoscope without common duct exploration with CC	6,225.42	11.5
198	Cholecystectomy except by laparoscope without common duct exploration without CC	3,233.92	10.1
199	Hepatobiliary diagnostic procedure for malignancy	7,302.67	17.9
200	Hepatobiliary diagnostic procedure for nonmalignancy	8,696.74	15.1
201	Other hepatobiliary or pancreas OR procedures	9,773.06	16.9
202	Cirrhosis and alcoholic hepatitis	4,084.56	9.3
203	Malignancy of hepatobiliary system or pancreas	3,775.80	8.0
204	Disorders of pancreas except malignancy	3,503.62	7.5
205	Disorders of liver except malignancy, cirrhosis and alcoholic hepatitis with CC	3,865.70	7.9
206	Disorders of liver except malignancy, cirrhosis and alcoholic hepatitis without CC	1,916.11	6.8
207	Disorders of the biliary tract with CC	3,067.76	6.6
208	Disorders of the biliary tract without CC	1,711.51	5.5
209	Major joint and limb reattachment procedures of lower extremity	7,282.21	17.1
210	Hip and femur procedures except major joint procedures, age > 17 with CC	5,797.62	17.8
211	Hip and femur procedures except major joint procedures, age > 17 without CC	4,039.61	15.9
212	Hip and femur procedures except major joint procedures, age 0–17	4,490.66	11.1
213	Amputation for musculoskeletal system and connective tissue disorders	5,420.35	14.3
214	Back and neck procedures with CC	5,845.67	15.6
215	Back and neck procedures without CC	3,387.06	13.0
216	Biopsies of musculoskeletal system and connective tissue	6,376.70	11.3
217	Wound débridement and skin graft except hand for musculoskeletal and connective tissue disorders	9,474.53	13.1
218	Lower extremity and humerus procedures except hip, foot and femur, age > 17 with CC	4,400.45	10.9

(continued)

DRG no.	DRG description	Average national payment ($)[a]	Average length of stay (days)
219	Lower extremity and humerus procedures except hip, foot and femur, age > 17 without CC	2,794.65	8.3
220	Lower extremity and humerus procedures except hip, foot and femur, age 0–17	2,962.36	5.3
221	Knee procedures with CC	5,577.52	8.3
222	Knee procedures without CC	3,052.52	6.4
223	Major shoulder/elbow procedures or other upper extremity procedures with CC	2,519.06	6.9
224	Shoulder, elbow, and forearm procedures except major joint procedures without CC	2,076.38	5.6
225	Foot procedures	2,656.08	4.8
226	Soft tissue procedures with CC	4,059.76	5.1
227	Soft tissue procedures without CC	2,128.46	4.2
228	Major thumb or joint procedures or other hand or wrist procedures with CC	2,549.75	2.2
229	Hand or wrist procedures except major joint procedures without CC	1,760.49	3.4
230	Local excision and removal of internal fixation devices of hip and femur	2,899.43	8.9
231	Local excision and removal of internal fixation devices except hip and femur	3,459.29	5.3
232	Arthroscopy	3,435.42	3.6
233	Other musculoskeletal system and connective tissue OR procedures with CC	5,720.74	13.1
234	Other musculoskeletal system and connective tissue OR procedures without CC	2,889.51	8.2
235	Fractures of femur	3,016.30	13.6
236	Fractures of hip and pelvis	2,455.82	11.9
237	Sprains, strains, and dislocations of hip, pelvis, and thigh	1,716.16	6.4
238	Osteomyelitis	4,675.42	12.3
239	Pathological fractures and musculoskeletal and connective tissue malignancy	3,220.28	9.2
240	Connective tissue disorders with CC	3,561.28	8.6
241	Connective tissue disorders without CC	1,761.42	8.0
242	Septic arthritis	3,520.36	11.2
243	Medical back problems	2,173.41	7.5
244	Bone diseases and specific arthropathies with CC	2,305.47	7.5
245	Bone diseases and specific arthropathies without CC	1,487.38	6.3
246	Nonspecific arthropathies	1,848.22	6.8
247	Signs and symptoms of musculoskeletal system and connective tissue	1,719.57	5.8
248	Tendonitis, myositis, and bursitis	2,151.09	5.4
249	Aftercare, musculoskeletal system and connective tissue	2,057.78	7.6
250	Fractures, sprains, strains and dislocations of forearm, hand and foot, age >17 with CC	2,223.94	6.0
251	Fractures, sprains, strains and dislocations of forearm, hand and foot, age > 17 without CC	1,379.19	4.2

(*continued*)

DRG no.	DRG description	Average national payment ($)[a]	Average length of stay (days)
252	Fractures, sprains, strains and dislocations of forearm, hand and foot, age 0–17	1,120.65	1.8
253	Fractures, sprains, strains and dislocations of upper arm and lower leg except foot, age >17 with CC	2,388.86	6.6
254	Fractures, sprains, strains and dislocations of upper arm and lower leg except foot, age > 17 without CC	1,324.32	5.3
255	Fractures, sprains, strains and dislocations of upper arm and lower leg except foot, age 0–17	1,486.76	2.9
256	Other musculoskeletal system and connective tissue diagnoses	1,973.46	6.5
257	Total mastectomy for malignancy with CC	2,741.95	9.3
258	Total mastectomy for malignancy without CC	2,157.29	8.9
259	Subtotal mastectomy for malignancy with CC	2,595.32	7.4
260	Subtotal mastectomy for malignancy without CC	1,780.33	6.4
261	Breast procedure for nonmalignancy except biopsy and local excision	2,254.32	4.8
262	Breast biopsy and local excision for nonmalignancy	1,882.01	3.0
263	Skin grafts and/or débridement for skin ulcer or cellulitis with CC	7,582.60	21.3
264	Skin grafts and/or débridement for skin ulcer or cellulitis without CC	3,827.26	18.2
265	Skin grafts and/or débridement except for skin ulcer or cellulitis with CC	4,360.15	8.6
266	Skin grafts and/or débridement except for skin ulcer or cellulitis without CC	2,203.48	5.9
267	Perianal and pilonidal procedures	2,043.52	5.0
268	Skin, subcutaneous tissue and breast plastic procedures	2,541.38	3.0
269	Other skin, subcutaneous tissue and breast procedures with CC	5,321.46	5.7
270	Other skin, subcutaneous tissue and breast procedures without CC	2,001.36	4.5
271	Skin ulcers	3,652.73	12.1
272	Major skin disorders with CC	3,163.86	7.8
273	Major skin disorders without CC	2,019.34	7.3
274	Malignant breast disorders with CC	3,466.73	7.5
275	Malignant breast disorders without CC	1,565.50	6.4
276	Nonmalignant breast disorders	1,968.81	4.2
277	Cellulitis, age > 17 with CC	2,764.27	8.3
278	Cellulitis, age > 17 without CC	1,806.68	7.2
279	Cellulitis, age 0–17	2,361.58	4.2
280	Trauma to skin, subcutaneous tissue and breast, age > 17 with CC	2,094.05	5.4
281	Trauma to skin, subcutaneous tissue and breast, age > 17 without CC	1,300.45	4.2
282	Trauma to skin, subcutaneous tissue and breast, age 0–17	1,097.40	2.2
283	Minor skin disorders with CC	2,248.43	5.3
284	Minor skin disorders without CC	1,385.39	4.4

(continued)

DRG no.	DRG description	Average national payment ($)[a]	Average length of stay (days)
285	Amputation of lower limb for endocrine, nutritional and metabolic disorders	7,947.47	24.0
286	Adrenal and pituitary procedures	7,074.51	16.1
287	Skin grafts and wound débridement for endocrine, nutritional and metabolic disorders	6,797.37	22.8
288	OR procedures for obesity	6,424.75	10.0
289	Parathyroid procedures	3,075.20	8.3
290	Thyroid procedures	2,367.47	6.0
291	Thyroglossal procedures	1,572.94	2.9
292	Other endocrine, nutritional and metabolic OR procedures with CC	8,573.98	10.8
293	Other endocrine, nutritional and metabolic OR procedures without CC	3,413.10	8.0
294	Diabetes, age > 35	2,314.46	7.7
295	Diabetes, age 0–35	2,344.22	5.6
296	Nutritional and miscellaneous metabolic disorders, age > 17 with CC	2,887.03	7.5
297	Nutritional and miscellaneous metabolic disorders, age > 17 without CC	1,625.64	6.0
298	Nutritional and miscellaneous metabolic disorders, age 0–17	1,744.37	5.4
299	Inborn errors of metabolism	2,564.01	6.8
300	Endocrine disorders with CC	3,404.42	7.8
301	Endocrine disorders without CC	1,790.87	6.4
302	Kidney transplant	12,050.01	24.1
303	Kidney, ureter and major bladder procedures for neoplasm	8,037.99	16.2
304	Kidney, ureter and major bladder procedures for nonneoplasms with CC	7,408.07	12.8
305	Kidney, ureter and major bladder procedures for nonneoplasms without CC	3,449.37	11.9
306	Prostatectomy with CC	3,866.94	8.6
307	Prostatectomy without CC	2,052.20	7.2
308	Minor bladder procedures with CC	4,480.12	7.1
309	Minor bladder procedures without CC	2,349.80	5.7
310	Transurethral procedures with CC	2,791.86	4.9
311	Transurethral procedures without CC	1,613.86	4.1
312	Urethral procedures, age > 17 with CC	2,583.54	5.2
313	Urethral procedures, age > 17 without CC	1,410.81	5.1
314	Urethral procedures, age 0–17	1,385.70	2.3
315	Other kidney and urinary tract OR procedures	6,305.71	9.8
316	Renal failure	3,999.93	6.7
317	Admission for renal dialysis	1,610.14	1.2
318	Kidney and urinary tract neoplasms with CC	3,476.65	5.5
319	Kidney and urinary tract neoplasms without CC	1,642.38	4.2
320	Kidney and urinary tract infections, age > 17 with CC	2,999.87	7.0
321	Kidney and urinary tract infections, age > 17 without CC	1,894.72	5.6

(continued)

DRG no.	DRG description	Average national payment ($)[a]	Average length of stay (days)
322	Kidney and urinary tract infections, age 0–17	1,535.12	3.7
323	Urinary stones with CC and/or ESW lithotripsy[g]	2,259.90	4.9
324	Urinary stones without CC	1,197.84	3.9
325	Kidney and urinary tract signs and symptoms, age > 17 with CC	2,048.17	5.4
326	Kidney and urinary tract signs and symptoms, age > 17 without CC	1,247.44	4.3
327	Kidney and urinary tract signs and symptoms, age 0–17	2,222.39	3.1
328	Urethral stricture, age > 17 with CC	2,045.07	4.8
329	Urethral stricture, age > 17 without CC	1,203.11	3.9
330	Urethral stricture, age 0–17	893.42	1.6
331	Other kidney and urinary tract diagnoses, age > 17 with CC	3,046.99	6.3
332	Other kidney and urinary tract diagnoses, age >17 without CC	1,683.30	5.0
333	Other kidney and urinary tract diagnoses, age 0–17	2,988.71	3.2
334	Major male pelvic procedures with CC	5,435.85	12.7
335	Major male pelvic procedures without CC	4,225.30	11.8
336	Transurethral prostatectomy with CC	2,647.40	8.4
337	Transurethral prostatectomy without CC	1,875.50	7.2
338	Testes procedures for malignancy	2,912.46	6.3
339	Testes procedures for nonmalignancy, age > 17	2,508.83	4.5
340	Testes procedures for nonmalignancy, age 0–17	1,389.73	2.4
341	Penis procedures	2,990.26	6.0
342	Circumcision, age > 17	1,812.88	2.8
343	Circumcision, age 0–17	1,213.96	1.7
344	Other male reproductive system OR procedures for malignancy	3,156.73	7.4
345	Other male reproductive system OR procedures except for malignancy	2,276.64	5.6
346	Malignancy of male reproductive system with CC	2,894.78	6.9
347	Malignancy of male reproductive system without CC	1,527.68	5.7
348	Benign prostatic hypertrophy with CC	2,125.36	6.2
349	Benign prostatic hypertrophy without CC	1,210.24	4.9
350	Inflammation of the male reproductive system	2,067.08	5.2
351	Sterilization, male	1,068.57	1.3
352	Other male reproductive system diagnoses	1,651.06	4.4
353	Pelvic evisceration, radical hysterectomy and radical vulvectomy	6,083.44	12.4
354	Uterine and adnexa procedures for nonovarian/adnexal malignancy with CC	4,276.14	9.6
355	Uterine and adnexa procedures for nonovarian/adnexal malignancy without CC	2,702.27	8.8
356	Female reproductive system reconstructive procedures	2,199.76	8.1
357	Uterine and adnexa procedures for ovarian or adnexal malignancy	7,177.43	13.9

(*continued*)

DRG no.	DRG description	Average national payment ($)[a]	Average length of stay (days)
358	Uterine and adnexa procedures for nonmalignancy with CC	3,423.02	8.0
359	Uterine and adnexa procedures for nonmalignancy without CC	2,428.54	2.3
360	Vagina, cervix and vulva procedures	2,519.06	4.2
361	Laparoscopy and incisional tubal interruption	3,111.47	2.6
362	Endoscopic tubal interruption	1,596.81	1.4
363	D and C, conization and radioimplant for malignancy[h]	1,965.40	4.3
364	D and C, conization except for malignancy	1,838.30	2.6
365	Other female reproductive system OR procedures	5,280.54	12.7
366	Malignancy of female reproductive system with CC	3,703.88	5.2
367	Malignancy of female reproductive system without CC	1,478.39	3.5
368	Infections of female reproductive system	2,941.59	6.7
369	Menstrual and other female reproductive system disorders	1,612.31	5.1
370	Cesarean section with CC	2,696.69	7.6
371	Cesarean section without CC	1,949.59	6.1
372	Vaginal delivery with complicating diagnoses	1,603.94	3.8
373	Vaginal delivery without complicating diagnoses	1,006.57	3.2
374	Vaginal delivery with sterilization and/or D and C	1,816.29	3.6
375	Vaginal delivery with OR procedure except sterilization and/or D and C	2,185.19	4.4
376	Postpartum and postabortion diagnoses without OR procedure	1,207.14	2.9
377	Postpartum and postabortion diagnoses with OR procedure	2,666.00	2.2
378	Ectopic pregnancy	2,349.80	5.5
379	Threatened abortion	1,037.26	2.2
380	Abortion without D and C	916.98	1.5
381	Abortion with D and C, aspiration curettage and hysterotomy	1,222.33	1.4
382	False labor	384.40	1.2
383	Other antepartum diagnoses with medical complications	1,258.29	3.4
384	Other antepartum diagnoses without medical complications	812.20	2.2
385	Neonate, died or transferred to another acute care facility	3,920.88	1.8
386	Extreme immaturity or respiratory distress syndrome of neonate	11,693.82	17.9
387	Prematurity with major problems	5,855.59	13.3
388	Prematurity without major problems	3,709.15	8.6
389	Full term neonate with major problems	4,741.45	4.7
390	Neonate with other significant problems	2,841.15	3.4
391	Normal newborn	711.14	3.1
392	Splenectomy, age > 17	10,243.33	16.4
393	Splenectomy, age 0–17	4,874.13	9.1

(continued)

DRG no.	DRG description	Average national payment ($)[a]	Average length of stay (days)
394	Other OR procedures of the blood and blood-forming organs	5,202.11	6.1
395	Red blood cell disorders, age > 17	2,497.67	6.1
396	Red blood cell disorders, age 0–17	954.49	4.1
397	Coagulation disorders	3,810.52	6.7
398	Reticuloendothelial and immunity disorders with CC	3,853.61	6.1
399	Reticuloendothelial and immunity disorders without CC	2,114.82	5.6
400	Lymphoma and leukemia with major OR procedures	7,845.79	16.9
401	Lymphoma and nonacute leukemia with other OR procedure with CC	7,371.18	8.9
402	Lymphoma and nonacute leukemia with other OR procedure without CC	2,743.50	7.1
403	Lymphoma and nonacute leukemia with CC	5,194.67	7.1
404	Lymphoma and nonacute leukemia without CC	2,286.87	6.4
405	Acute leukemia without major OR procedure, age 0–17	3,335.91	4.9
406	Myeloproliferative disorders or poorly differentiated neoplasms with major OR procedures with CC	8,101.23	15.0
407	Myeloproliferative disorders or poorly differentiated neoplasms with major OR procedures without CC	3,473.24	13.3
408	Myeloproliferative disorders or poorly differentiated neoplasms with other OR procedures	4,414.71	7.1
409	Radiotherapy	3,075.82	5.7
410	Chemotherapy without acute leukemia as secondary diagnosis	2,070.49	2.6
411	History of malignancy without endoscopy	1,287.12	4.7
412	History of malignancy with endoscopy	1,474.98	2.0
413	Other myeloproliferative disorders or poorly differentiated neoplasm diagnoses with CC	4,293.19	7.3
414	Other myeloproliferative disorders or poorly differentiated neoplasm diagnoses without CC	2,198.21	6.4
415	OR procedures for infectious and parasitic diseases	11,074.13	15.1
416	Septicemia, age > 17	4,693.71	9.2
417	Septicemia, age 0–17	2,170.62	5.2
418	Postoperative and posttraumatic infections	2,996.15	8.4
419	Fever of unknown origin, age > 17 with CC	2,948.41	6.9
420	Fever of unknown origin, age > 17 without CC	1,973.15	6.2
421	Viral illness, age > 17	2,094.98	5.4
422	Viral illness and fever of unknown origin, age 0–17	1,825.28	3.2
423	Other infectious and parasitic diseases diagnoses	5,036.26	8.8
424	OR procedures with principle diagnosis of mental illness	7,652.04	14.2
425	Acute adjustment reactions and disturbances of psychosocial dysfunction	2,209.37	5.8
426	Depressive neuroses	1,899.68	9.4
427	Neuroses except depressive	1,917.04	6.9
428	Disorders of personality and impulse control	2,196.04	8.3

(continued)

DRG no.	DRG description	Average national payment ($)[a]	Average length of stay (days)
429	Organic disturbances and mental retardation	2,907.49	8.8
430	Psychoses	2,837.43	10.8
431	Childhood mental disorders	2,163.80	15.4
432	Other mental disorder diagnoses	2,280.67	7.2
433	Alcohol/drug abuse or dependence, left against medical advice	1,088.72	2.5
434	Alcohol/drug abuse or dependence, detoxification or other symptomatic treatment with CC	2,269.51	9.1
435	Alcohol/drug abuse or dependence, detoxification or other symptomatic treatment without CC	1,403.99	8.0
436	Alcohol/drug dependence with rehabilitation therapy	3,004.21	8.1
437	Alcohol/drug dependence with combined rehabilitation and detoxification therapy	3,090.70	3.5
438	No longer valid	0.00	6.9
439	Skin grafts for injuries	4,294.43	8.9
440	Wound débridements for injuries	5,308.75	7.2
441	Hand procedures for injuries	2,207.82	3.0
442	Other OR procedures for injuries with CC	5,980.52	9.1
443	Other OR procedures for injuries without CC	2,293.38	6.6
444	Traumatic injury, age > 17 with CC	2,303.61	6.7
445	Traumatic injury, age > 17 without CC	1,436.85	5.2
446	Traumatic injury, age 0–17	1,537.29	2.4
447	Allergic reactions, age > 17	1,509.39	3.7
448	Allergic reactions, age 0–17	1,112.28	2.9
449	Poisoning and toxic effects of drugs, age > 17 with CC	2,457.99	5.6
450	Poisoning and toxic effects of drugs, age > 17 without CC	1,309.44	3.9
451	Poisoning and toxic effects of drugs, age 0–17	3,182.46	2.1
452	Complications of treatment with CC	2,551.92	5.5
453	Complications of treatment without CC	1,294.87	5.1
454	Other injury, poisoning and toxic effect diagnoses with CC	2,823.17	5.3
455	Other injury, poisoning and toxic effect diagnoses without CC	1,291.46	3.5
456	Burns, transferred to another acute care facility	6,723.28	11.6
457	Extensive burns without OR procedure	5,056.72	12.6
458	Nonextensive burns with skin graft	11,612.29	18.3
459	Nonextensive burns with wound débridement or other OR procedure	6,523.02	12.7
460	Nonextensive burns without OR procedures	3,527.48	9.0
461	OR procedures with diagnoses of other contact with health services	2,683.36	8.0
462	Rehabilitation	5,333.55	13.5
463	Signs and symptoms with CC	2,247.19	6.3
464	Signs and symptoms without CC	1,423.21	6.0
465	Aftercare with history of malignancy as secondary diagnosis	1,159.40	1.5

(continued)

DRG no.	DRG description	Average national payment ($)[a]	Average length of stay (days)
466	Aftercare without history of malignancy as secondary diagnosis	1,709.96	3.7
467	Other factors influencing health status	1,292.08	6.1
468	Extensive OR procedure unrelated to principle diagnosis	10,801.02	11.2
469	Principal diagnosis invalid as discharge diagnosis	0.00	0.0
470	Ungroupable	0.00	0.0
471	Bilateral or multiple major joint procedures of lower extremity	11,981.81	
472	Extensive burns with OR procedure	36,249.23	
473	Acute leukemia without major OR procedure, age > 17	11,067.62	
474	No longer valid	0.00	
475	Respiratory system diagnosis with ventilator support	11,524.25	
476	Prostatic OR procedure unrelated to principal diagnosis	6,931.91	
477	Nonextensive OR procedure unrelated to principal diagnosis	4,534.68	
478	Other vascular procedures with CC	6,788.07	
479	Other vascular procedures without CC	4,038.37	
480	Liver transplant	60,350.49	
481	Bone marrow transplant	44,549.79	
482	Tracheostomy for face, mouth and neck diagnoses	11,084.36	
483	Tracheostomy except for face, mouth and neck diagnoses	52,655.98	
484	Craniotomy for multiple significant trauma	17,549.72	
485	Limb reattachment, hip and femur procedures for multiple significant trauma	10,031.91	
486	Other OR procedures for multiple significant trauma	14,494.36	
487	Other multiple significant trauma	6,007.49	
488	HIV with extensive OR procedure	13,596.29	
489	HIV with major related condition	5,725.08	
490	HIV with or without other related conditions	3,463.94	
491	Major joint and limb reattachment procedures of upper extremity	4,988.52	
492	Chemotherapy with acute leukemia as secondary diagnosis	11,116.91	
493	Laparoscopic cholecystectomy without common duct exploration with CC	4,733.08	
494	Laparoscopic cholecystectomy without common duct exploration without CC	2,552.23	

[a]National averages for Medicare payments in 1993.

[b]CC, complications and comorbidities.

[c]OR, operating room.

[d]URI, upper respiratory infection.

[e]AICD, automatic implantable cardioverter/defibrillator.

[f]GI, gastrointestinal.

[g]ESW, extracorporeal shock wave.

[h]D and C, dilation and curettage.

Index

Page numbers followed by "*t*" or "*f*" indicate tables or figures, respectively.